Phenomenal Properties and the Intuition of Distinctness

Phenomenal Properties and the Intuition of Distinctness

The View from the Inside

ANDREW MELNYK

Great Clarendon Street, Oxford, OX2 6DP,
United Kingdom

Oxford University Press is a department of the University of Oxford.
It furthers the University's objective of excellence in research, scholarship,
and education by publishing worldwide. Oxford is a registered trade mark of
Oxford University Press in the UK and in certain other countries

© Andrew Melnyk 2025

The moral rights of the author have been asserted

All rights reserved. No part of this publication may be reproduced, stored in a retrieval system, transmitted, used for text and data mining, or used for training artificial intelligence, in any form or by any means, without the prior permission in writing of Oxford University Press, or as expressly permitted by law, by licence or under terms agreed with the appropriate reprographics rights organization. Enquiries concerning reproduction outside the scope of the above should be sent to the Rights Department, Oxford University Press, at the address above.

You must not circulate this work in any other form
and you must impose this same condition on any acquirer

Published in the United States of America by Oxford University Press
198 Madison Avenue, New York, NY 10016, United States of America

British Library Cataloguing in Publication Data

Data available

Library of Congress Control Number: 2024945193

ISBN 9780198942320

DOI: 10.1093/9780198942351.001.0001

Printed and bound by
CPI Group (UK) Ltd, Croydon, CR0 4YY

The manufacturer's authorised representative in the EU for product safety
is Oxford University Press España S.A. of el Parque Empresarial San
Fernando de Henares, Avenida de Castilla,
2 – 28830 Madrid (www.oup.es/en).

In loving memory of Julie Ann Melnyk (1964–2017)

Acknowledgments

I hereby thank Joe Levine and an anonymous reader for the Press for their valuable comments both large and small on earlier drafts of this book. I am immensely grateful to David Papineau both for the work of his that inspired the book and for his encouragement to develop my own ideas.

I would also like to record my gratitude to some philosophers of the generation before mine whose writings eventually persuaded me, against strong resistance, that physicalism can accommodate phenomenal properties: Christopher Hill, Terry Horgan, and Bill Lycan. And I take this opportunity to express a more general philosophical debt to the writings of Michael Tye and Ruth Millikan, whose very different influences permeate the book.

Finally, I owe more than I can say, and no doubt more than I know, to my late wife, who endured the pain and many indignities of her final year with extraordinary courage and not even the tiniest trace of self-pity; to her the book is dedicated.

Contents

1. Introduction ... 1
   1.1 The Main Question ... 1
   1.2 Preview of the Book ... 6
2. The Intuition of Distinctness and Some of Its Manifestations ... 10
   2.1 Three Puzzling Quotations ... 10
   2.2 The Intuition of Revelation ... 13
   2.3 The "Explanatory Gap" Argument ... 15
   2.4 The Knowledge Argument ... 18
   2.5 The Zombie Argument ... 24
   2.6 Conclusion ... 27
3. Why Not Take the Intuition of Distinctness at Face Value? ... 29
   3.1 The Chapter's Main Argument Outlined ... 29
   3.2 Not Seeming Physical or Functional ... 34
   3.3 Digression: A Philosophers' Argument ... 43
   3.4 Not Having a Spatial Location ... 46
   3.5 Not Seeming to Have a Spatial Location ... 48
   3.6 Phenomenal Features of Phenomenal Properties ... 51
   3.7 The Homogeneity of Phenomenal Properties ... 53
   3.8 The Directness of Phenomenal Knowledge ... 64
   3.9 Infallible Phenomenal Knowledge? ... 74
   3.10 Subjectivity ... 81
   3.11 Non-conscious Mechanisms ... 89
   3.12 Conclusion ... 94
4. Previous Accounts of the Intuition of Distinctness ... 96
   4.1 A Critical Survey ... 96
   4.2 Armstrong ... 97
   4.3 Lycan ... 101
   4.4 Papineau ... 103
   4.5 Robbins and Jack ... 108
   4.6 Fiala, Arico, and Nichols ... 113
   4.7 Elpidorou and Dove ... 116
   4.8 Molyneux ... 120
   4.9 Sundström ... 132
   4.10 Conclusion ... 135

5. What, Then, Does Account for the Intuition of Distinctness? 136
   5.1 Rehearsal of Defective Arguments? 136
   5.2 The Novel Explanation Introduced 138
   5.3 Introspection's Conceptual Encapsulation 139
   5.4 Believing an Identity Claim 148
   5.5 The Novel Explanation Elaborated 156
   5.6 Some Objections 162
      5.6.1 Churchland's Suggestion 162
      5.6.2 Deepening the Explanation 166
      5.6.3 Predicting What Isn't 173
   5.7 Conclusion 176

References 179
Index 183

1
Introduction

1.1 The Main Question

First I will work toward a formulation of the main question that this book aims to address, pausing now and again to explain certain terminological decisions, working hypotheses, and controversial assumptions that will all go undefended in the book. Then I will briefly preview the chapters to follow.

Consider our mental lives. We think that things are the case, engage in trains of thought, and so on. But our mental lives do not consist only of thinking. They consist also of feeling, and especially of *sensations*, traditionally thought to fall into two categories.[1] We have *bodily* sensations, such as pains, tingles, itches, orgasms, butterflies in the stomach, and spells of nausea or dizziness. We also have *perceptual* sensations, such as those we have when we smell gasoline, taste mustard, see blood, feel a marble countertop, or accurately sense the world in myriad other ways; we have inaccurate perceptual sensations too, including afterimages, dreams, and ringing in the ears. We naturally speak of *having* sensations, but we do not have sensations as we have fingers, hats, cars, and other *objects*. We have sensations as we have accidents, falls, fits, haircuts, surgeries, allergic reactions, and other *events*. Our sensations are *events* in which we participate, not *objects* that form parts of us (like fingers) or that we possess (like hats). Events of what kind? Sensations are naturally thought of as episodes of *someone's sensing*; a current visual sensation of yours is an episode of *your* (visually) *sensing now*.[2]

Sensations are said by philosophers to be *phenomenally conscious* or to have a *phenomenal character*.[3] The phenomenal character of a sensation is

---

[1] Moods, such as depression, restlessness, or mania, are also feelings; and emotions, such as jealousy, sorrow, or dread, are at least in part feelings too. But in this book I choose to focus on sensations; sufficient unto the day is the evil thereof.

[2] This view can explain why you cannot have my sensations, and why no sensations float free, not had by anyone at all (see Tye 1995a, ch. 3). Also, some philosophers prefer to speak not of sensations but rather of *experiences*, that is, episodes of someone's experiencing; but I suspect that in daily life we apply "experiences" only to perceptual sensations, not also to bodily sensations, though that is what I think they are (see section 3.7). Finally, to construe sensations as episodes of sensing is not yet to construe them as representations, though that is what I think they are (see section 3.7).

[3] In this common philosophical usage, "phenomenal consciousness" refers to a property of *sensations*. In a different and rarer usage, it refers to a property of *people*, namely, the property

what it is like to have the sensation, for the person having the sensation. That is, there are properties of the sensation that the person having it can become aware of "from the inside," as I will put it—from the apparently unique perspective of the person having the sensation, and without relying on any of their five external senses; and the sensation's phenomenal character is simply the totality of these properties.[4] The phenomenal character of a burning itch is the totality of properties of the itch that the person with the itch can become aware of from the inside; the phenomenal character of a wave of nausea is the totality of (very different) properties of the nausea that the person undergoing the nausea can become aware of from the inside; the phenomenal character of a visual sensation of blue produced by looking up at the clear sky on a summer's day is the totality of properties of the blue sensation that the person having the blue sensation can become aware of from the inside. In this book, I use the term "introspection" to refer to the human capacity to become aware from the inside that our sensations have certain properties. Accordingly, a sensation's phenomenal character could be said to be the totality of those properties of the sensation that the person having the sensation can become aware, through introspection, that the sensation has.

In a standard philosophical usage, I shall use "phenomenal properties" and its cognates to refer to these properties.[5] For example, what we naturally call a visual sensation of red, had either when we are really seeing a ripe tomato or when we are merely hallucinating one, seems to us introspectively to be *in some sense* red. But presumably the sensation cannot be red in the sense in which a spot of blood, or a traffic light, or anything else external to the mind is red: it doesn't reflect light of a certain frequency (or emit or transmit such light). I shall therefore say that the red sensation is *phenomenally red*, thereby meaning *red in the sense* (whatever that sense turns out to be) *in which sensations are red*, and intending with this locution to avoid premature

---

of being conscious (of things or events), but in a phenomenal way, rather than in the nonphenomenal, belief-related way in which I am conscious that I am getting older. I identify being conscious in a phenomenal way with representing in the special manner in which sensations represent according to the unorthodox representationalism of section 3.7 below.

[4] The explication of "what it is like" is necessary because in everyday English the question "What is it like?" has no special connection to mental states; it could be asked of, say, your new Volvo, and a felicitous answer might be "Boxy but safe." Admittedly, to ask what it is like to *do* something, for example, to skydive, seems to invite a description of the action's effect on one's feelings ("Thrilling!").

[5] "The properties of sensations that people having sensations can become aware, through introspection, that their sensations have" is intended merely to fix the reference, not to give the meaning, of "phenomenal properties."

commitment to an account of what exactly phenomenal redness is (though I will endorse an account in section 3.7). Phenomenal redness is an example of a phenomenal property. Similarly, what some victims of a heart attack naturally call a crushing pain seems to them introspectively to be *in some sense* crushing. But presumably the pain cannot be crushing in the same sense in which the water in the Atlantic at a depth of one mile is crushing. I shall therefore say that the pain is *phenomenally crushing*, meaning thereby *crushing in the sense* (whatever that sense turns out to be) *in which pains are crushing*, and intending with this locution to avoid premature commitment to an account of the exact nature of phenomenal crushingness. Phenomenal crushingness, if I may put it so, is another example of a phenomenal property.[6]

My use of "introspection" to refer to our capacity to become aware from the inside that our sensations have certain properties deserves further comment. As used in the philosophy of mind, "introspection" is always a term of art, but other philosophers use it more broadly than I do, to refer to our capacity to become aware from the inside that mental states of *any* kind, not just sensations, have certain properties, for example, the representational properties of our thoughts. My narrower usage is intended to leave open the possibility that our capacity to become aware from the inside that our *sensations* have certain properties differs importantly from our capacity to become aware from the inside that our *thoughts* have certain properties.[7] I should also note that the only outputs of what, in my narrower usage, I call "introspection" are beliefs, that is, states of believing; and that, when these beliefs are true, they normally constitute states of introspective awareness (or introspective knowledge) that our sensations have certain phenomenal properties.[8] (Introspective awareness is just introspective knowledge, for in everyday usage "awareness" is just a synonym for "knowledge," and nothing changes when "introspective" precedes it.) It's true that we speak of our being introspectively aware *of* phenomenal properties as well as being introspectively aware *that* our sensations have phenomenal properties.[9] But I doubt

---

[6] I avoid the word "qualia" (singular: "quale"), even though, in one usage, it is a harmless synonym for "phenomenal properties." For in other usages it refers to phenomenal properties that meet further conditions, for example, being non-representational and intrinsic, or even being non-physical and non-physically realized; and there are yet further usages.
[7] I will claim in Chapter 5 (section 5.2) that this possibility is actual.
[8] Or that phenomenal properties themselves have certain (phenomenal) features; see section 3.6.
[9] Michael Tye (2000) denies that we are ever introspectively aware *of* the phenomenal properties of our sensations, insisting instead that we are only ever introspectively aware *that* our sensations have these properties.

that there are two fundamentally different kinds of introspective awareness. So I assume that introspective awareness *of* can somehow be understood in terms of introspective awareness *that*, just as, presumably, non-introspective awareness *of* can be understood in terms of non-introspective awareness *that* (on the face of it, if I am aware of the president's dishonesty, I am aware *that* the president's dishonesty *exists*, that is, that the president is dishonest).

We have sensations, then, and our sensations have phenomenal properties.[10] Now there is, I take it, strong evidence for the physicalist view that phenomenal properties are, in some suitable sense that needs to be spelled out, nothing over and above physical properties—physical properties being understood, for the theoretical purposes of this book, to be the properties that physical sciences such as biochemistry, neurophysiology, and cell biology, as well as physics proper, attribute to things, including to us.[11] Moreover, in order for phenomenal properties to be "nothing over and above physical properties" in a way that suffices for physicalism, each phenomenal property must turn out to be identical with—to be literally the very same thing as—either a physical property or a functional property that is physically realized (an example of a physically realized functional property would be an information-processing property realized by a certain pattern of neuronal firing in a certain neural network).[12] The strong evidence for physicalism about phenomenal properties that I have in mind consists of the results of psychological experiments in which human subjects are found never to exhibit *phenomenal* variation in their sensations, as revealed by their introspective reports, without their also exhibiting simultaneous *neural* variation, as revealed by brain-scanning techniques (e.g., fMRI). And these results

---

[10] Recently, David Papineau has taken phenomenal properties, which he calls "conscious sensory properties," to be properties of the people who have sensations, rather than of the sensations themselves (2021, 1). But if, as I hold, a sensation of mine is an episode of my sensing, then a property of my sensation is a property of my sensing—which seems pretty close to being a property of me. Even if there is a difference, I expect that nearly everything I have to say in this book could also be said, mutatis mutandis, if phenomenal properties were treated as properties of people.

[11] The theoretical purposes of this book require articulating an interesting thesis of physicalism about phenomenal properties and indeed mental properties more generally. For other theoretical purposes, for example, in order to formulate a doctrine of comprehensive physicalism that also embraced, say, chemical, biological, and geological properties, we might decide to understand physical properties narrowly, by reference to physics proper (see Melnyk 2003, 11–20 and 223–37).

[12] My view that physicalism requires claims of property-identity (either mental-to-physical or mental-to-functional) is controversial, but less so than it was. For a concise elaboration and defense of the view, and in particular of the very liberal notions of *functional property* and of *realization* that it invokes, see Melnyk (2018); the longer-winded version is Melnyk (2003, chs. 1 and 2).

constitute evidence for physicalism because the physicalist explanation of the results that takes the phenomenal properties of the subjects' sensations just to *be* certain physical properties, or physically realized functional properties, of the subjects' brain-states is better, because more economical, than any dualist explanation of the results.[13]

But we got trouble.[14] Imagine that you're standing in front of Mark Rothko's *Untitled* (1970), gazing intently at it, and attending introspectively to the phenomenal redness of the visual sensation that the painting causes you to have.[15] Imagine also that, at the same time, you're reflecting on the physicalist claim that *that very property*—the phenomenal redness—of your visual sensation is *literally one and the same thing* as a certain physical or physically realized functional property of the neural activity in a certain tiny region of your brain. Under these conditions, it will seem to you, and seem to you strongly, that your visual sensation's phenomenal redness couldn't possibly be such a property—that *that very property* couldn't literally *be* a neurophysiological property of a certain pattern of firing in a neural circuit, or an information-processing property realized by such a neurophysiological property.[16] Its seeming to us, under conditions such as these, that an introspected phenomenal property of a current sensation just couldn't be a certain physical or physically realized functional property is what David Papineau calls the *intuition of distinctness* (2002, 94). He suggests that all of us, including even the self-professed physicalists in our midst, are prone to have the intuition of distinctness under the sort of conditions described. Joseph Levine is surely reporting his experience of the intuition of distinctness when he writes: "I am told that my concept of reddishness is really about a neurophysiological or functional property. I then wonder, as I ostend the reddishness of my visual experience, how could a functional or physiological state be that?" (2001, 83; see also Levine 2007, 148). John Perry writes in a similar vein: "To say that *this*, the feeling I am aware of when I, so to speak,

---

[13] Elsewhere I have elaborated and defended this empirical argument for physicalism with specific reference to the phenomenal properties of pain (Melnyk 2015).
[14] And not just right here in River City.
[15] The painting can be seen in the National Gallery of Art, Washington, DC <https://www.nga.gov/collection/art-object-page.67531.html>. I assume that you needn't be *seeing* the painting; were you merely *hallucinating* an identical painting, your visual sensation would exemplify phenomenal redness in the same way. I assume too that you are not red-green color blind.
[16] My use of the expression "that very property" is intended to communicate the idea that, when you think that phenomenal redness couldn't possibly be such a property, you are thinking of phenomenal redness in the special way (whatever that way comes to) made possible by your capacity to introspect your current sensations; much more on this special way in Chapter 5.

look inward, is *that*, the thing [the physical or functional state] I read about, just seems crazy" (2001, 4). I also have the intuition of distinctness, and so too, presumably, does the laity.[17] In my experience, once non-philosophers understand that physicalism about sensations entails that, when they're introspectively aware of a *backache*, they're actually aware of *neuronal activity*, they regard physicalism as a complete non-starter. Some of them find the physicalist view so incredible that, out of interpretative charity, they construe it as denying that sensations *exist*, the denial of sensations' existence striking them as less implausible than the *identification* of sensations with physical or physically realized events.

So we have evidence for the physicalist view that phenomenal properties are identical either with certain physical properties or with certain functional but physically realized properties.[18] But we also experience a strong inclination to disbelieve this physicalist view when we attend introspectively to the phenomenal properties of our own sensations. If the phenomenal properties of sensations really *are* physical or physically realized functional properties, why is it that, when we introspect them, they seem to us so strongly *not* to be? What explains why, if physicalism is true, we have the intuition of distinctness—even those of us who profess physicalism? These are two ways of posing the central question that the present book aims to address.[19]

1.2 Preview of the Book

Dualists will probably respond that there is no mystery here. Perhaps it would be surprising for the phenomenal properties of sensations to seem to us not to be physical or physically realized if in fact they *are* physical or physically

---

[17] We only experience the intuition of distinctness in connection with the phenomenal properties of sensations. We do not experience it in connection with, say, the representational properties of beliefs and desires. An explanation of the intuition of distinctness must account for this difference, and my proposed explanation does so (see section 5.2).

[18] This view is, of course, physicalism's solution to the so-called hard problem of consciousness, "Why and how do physical processes in the brain give rise to conscious experience?" as David Chalmers, who originated the term "hard problem," formulated it in a recent paper (2018, 6).

[19] At first glance, this question seems narrower than what Chalmers calls "the meta-problem [of consciousness] . . . the problem of explaining . . . intuitions that reflect our sense that there is some sort of special problem involving consciousness" (2018, 12); for there are many such intuitions in addition to the intuition of distinctness. However, I will argue in Chapter 2 that the intuition of distinctness underlies several of the intuitions that Chalmers has in mind. If I am right, then to explain the intuition of distinctness is at least to *approach* solving Chalmers's "meta-problem of consciousness."

realized. But surely it wouldn't be surprising for them to seem to us not to be so if in fact they aren't. For many true things seem to us (perceptually, say) to be true, and, indeed, their seeming to us to be true is most naturally regarded as giving us *reason to believe* that they are true. So, instead of assuming that the intuition of distinctness misleads us, as physicalists must do, we should take the intuition of distinctness as giving us reason to believe that the phenomenal properties we are introspecting really are distinct from the physical or physically realized properties that we are considering as candidates for identity with the phenomenal properties. On this view, the intuition of distinctness is not an embarrassment for physicalism that needs to be explained away; rather, it gives us reason to think that physicalism is false.

But Chapter 3 argues that this response can't be developed in a satisfactory way. Even if the intuition of distinctness does give us reason to believe that introspected phenomenal properties are distinct from whatever physical or physically realized properties we might be considering, there must still be some explanation of how the intuition arises in us. And the explanation of how it arises must be such as to make it the case that the intuition gives us reason to believe that introspected phenomenal properties are distinct from whatever physical or physically realized properties we might be considering. Chapter 3 surveys a wide variety of psychological mechanisms that might be hypothesized to meet this condition *and* actually to operate in us to produce the intuition of distinctness; and it argues that none of the mechanisms surveyed plausibly meet both conditions. It then takes this sub-conclusion to be inductive evidence that no mechanisms at all plausibly meet both conditions. The critical survey of possible mechanisms also supports the independently interesting conclusion that there is no good argument based on introspection for thinking that phenomenal properties are neither physical nor physically realized. The survey is constructive, too, sketching positive accounts of what phenomenal properties are, how we know about them introspectively, how we could in principle tell introspectively that an introspected property is physical, what the subjectivity of phenomenal properties could be, and so on.

Chapter 4 is propaedeutic, critically examining earlier theories intended to explain, or plausibly regarded as able to explain, consistently with physicalism, why we have the intuition of distinctness. Though it concludes that none of these theories adequately accounts for the intuition of distinctness, it leaves open the possibility that they have something to contribute to accounting for a more general aversion to physicalism about phenomenal properties. Chapter 5 then proposes and elaborates a novel explanation of why we have the intuition of distinctness. This explanation makes it very likely that the intuition of distinctness gives us no reason to think that physicalism is false but is instead (if physicalism is true) a systematic error to which we seem inevitably prone. We may not be able to make the intuition of distinctness go away, but we can at least ignore it in good conscience. The explanation proposes that our introspection of phenomenal properties is in a certain way *conceptually encapsulated*. The beliefs about our current sensations and their properties that introspection delivers are constructed out of a limited repertoire of concepts.[20] That repertoire can perhaps be expanded, but not expanded to include concepts that we acquire as a result of perception or of learning scientific vocabulary. So though introspection delivers beliefs that our sensations have phenomenal properties, it cannot deliver representations of our sensations *as* having physical or physically realized functional properties, even if phenomenal properties in fact *are* physical or physically realized functional properties. This limitation on introspection turns out to mean that we are unable to do something that we can do in the case of every other kind of identity claim that we believe or entertain. As a result, we can neither believe nor even imagine believing that a phenomenal property, conceived in the special way made possible by introspection, is the very same thing as a physical or a physically realized functional property.

Before all that, however, comes Chapter 2. The intuition of distinctness was introduced as something whose reality we can all come to know in a first-person way, by experiencing it for ourselves more or less at will. But Chapter 2 argues that we have a further reason—a third-person reason—to think that the intuition of distinctness is real. It argues that some participants in the debate on physicalism and phenomenal properties exhibit certain puzzling attitudes, but that these attitudes can be explained by the hypothesis that those who have them experience the intuition of distinctness and, whether consciously or not, take it to give them reason to believe that their introspected phenomenal properties are neither physical nor physically realized.

According to Chapter 2, the standard philosophical arguments against physicalism about sensations—the arguments that justify the claim that there is, for phenomenal properties, a genuine mind-body *problem*—owe their persistent appeal, at least in part, to the intuition of distinctness. But

---

[20] Here and throughout, I use the word "concept" psychologically, to refer to a kind of mental representation that enables anyone capable of hosting such a representation to think about some individual, or stuff, or kind, or property. There is also a non-psychological usage in which, for example, the concept of happiness is *what it is to be* happy, but I avoid this usage.

if they do, then it is plausible to construe the mind-body problem, at least as it arises for sensations, as being, at bottom, the problem of reconciling two views of sensations: the view of them that we get as outside observers of other people as they move through, talk about, and successfully interact with their environments, and the view of them that we get from the inside. And the two views need to be reconciled because the hypothesis about sensations naturally suggested by the view from the outside—that they are internal physiological or physiologically realized states of the person caused by peripheral stimulation and helping to cause other mental states and behavioral output—is contradicted by the view from the inside. If it is right to construe the mind-body problem for sensations in this way, then the intuition of distinctness is no mere footnote to the mind-body problem; it is instead one of its two essential constituents. To address the mind-body problem for sensations at all, we must investigate the intuition of distinctness.

2
The Intuition of Distinctness and Some of Its Manifestations

2.1 Three Puzzling Quotations

The intuition of distinctness might have been merely something that we experience while introspecting and reflecting on the phenomenal properties of our sensations, but without interesting effects on any other aspect of our psychology. In this chapter, however, I will argue that hypothesizing that people have the intuition of distinctness can account for certain otherwise puzzling attitudes manifested in debates both inside and outside philosophy about whether physicalism can accommodate phenomenal properties. Specifically, I will argue that intuition of distinctness can plausibly be invoked to explain why some philosophers and non-philosophers take an otherwise inexplicably dismissive or uncomprehending attitude toward physicalism, claiming to find it self-evidently false or unintelligible (the present section); why many philosophers experience a second and more widely discussed intuition about phenomenal properties, the intuition of *revelation* (section 2.2); why many philosophers feel that there is an "explanatory gap" between our physical states and our phenomenal states (section 2.3); and why some philosophers resist powerful objections to standard anti-physicalist arguments on rather obscure grounds (sections 2.4 and 2.5). If the intuition of distinctness can plausibly be invoked to explain these attitudes on the part of those who reject a physicalist view of phenomenal properties, then these attitudes count as non-introspective evidence that the intuition of distinctness is real. A further consequence is that an explanation of the intuition of distinctness itself would also contribute—at one remove—to explaining these attitudes. An explanation of the intuition of distinctness would therefore come close to solving David Chalmers's "meta-problem of consciousness," what he calls (2018, 12) "the problem of explaining ... intuitions that reflect our sense that there is some sort of special problem involving consciousness."

Let me begin with three quotations in which their respective authors express attitudes to physicalism about phenomenal properties that are initially puzzling. In each case, I will suggest that the attitude is no longer puzzling if we take the author to have been influenced in his thinking by the intuition of distinctness.

Here, first, is Michael Lockwood—and the context of the passage is clearly the phenomenal properties of sensations (1993, 272):

> For those not blinded by science, the falsity of reductionist physicalism will probably
>
> seem almost too obvious to require argument: Galen Strawson aptly describes it as "moonshine."

Lockwood's remarks are puzzling because the "reductionist physicalism" of which he wrote is a widely discussed view endorsed by internationally admired philosophers of the caliber of David Lewis and David Armstrong, and yet he said that the view's falsity "will probably seem almost too obvious to require argument." How would Lockwood have explained why the likes of Lewis and Armstrong nonetheless accepted the view? Presumably, by saying that they have been "blinded by science." But such an explanation has no substance. Talk of being "blinded by science" is a metaphor. What does it mean literally? Under what conditions is one "blinded by science"? And why exactly would being "blinded by science" make one endorse "reductionist physicalism," especially if "the falsity of reductionist physicalism" really is "almost too obvious to require argument"? Finally, how did Lockwood (and presumably Strawson too) manage to *avoid* being "blinded by science," while the likes of Armstrong and Lewis did not?[1]

It is tempting to think that Lockwood simply got carried away rhetorically. But we need not accept this uncharitable conclusion.[2] Instead, we can take his talk of obviousness ("almost too obvious to require argument") to stem from the intuition of distinctness. Surely reductionist physicalism didn't seem obviously false to him in the same way that the proposition that 2 > 1 seemed obviously false to him. Its seeming obviously false to him had something to do with his ability to *introspect* his own phenomenally conscious mental states; it wouldn't have seemed obviously false to him if he hadn't had that introspective ability. Plausibly, then, Lockwood's conviction that "the

---

[1] Not by remaining ignorant of science, as one might cattily suggest, for Lockwood was well informed scientifically.
[2] And we should not. Lockwood was a philosopher whose work I much admired for its astuteness and integrity.

falsity of reductionist physicalism will probably seem almost too obvious to require argument" stemmed from his often having had the intuition of distinctness: the falsity of reductionist physicalism was obvious, not to his intellect, but to his introspection.[3]

Consider now a second quotation, this one from the science journalist Robert Wright, writing in *Time* magazine (1996, 53):

> Some laypeople (like me, for example) have trouble seeing the difference between ... saying consciousness doesn't exist and saying it is nothing more than the brain.

Wright's remark is puzzling because there is a rather obvious difference between saying that consciousness doesn't exist and saying that it is nothing more than the brain, at least if "nothing more than the brain" means or entails being identical to the brain. Saying that consciousness doesn't exist commits you (obviously) to holding that consciousness doesn't exist. But saying that consciousness *is* the brain commits you to holding that consciousness does exist, because the brain exists, and whatever is identical to something that exists must itself exist. So why does Wright nonetheless claim that saying that consciousness is nothing more than the brain is tantamount to saying that consciousness doesn't exist? A charitable, and plausible, explanation is this: because Wright has the intuition of distinctness, he has become convinced that consciousness couldn't possibly be identical to—so couldn't possibly be nothing more than—the brain. He then concludes, not unreasonably, that intelligent people who *say* that consciousness is nothing more than the brain couldn't really mean it and must therefore be interpreted as saying instead that the brain is all there is—in which case, why not just say in the first place that consciousness doesn't exist?

Consider, finally, Sir John Eccles (1903–1997), the Nobel-Prize-winning Australian neurophysiologist who took a great interest throughout his life in the mind-body problem. Several times in his writings he professed himself baffled by the physicalist view that mental states are identical with certain brain-states, describing the identity theory as, for example, "enigmatic" (Eccles 1994, 167). Because what is enigmatic is mystifying, Eccles might seem in these passages to have been expressing an inability to *understand* the

---

[3] I am following my policy, announced in Chapter 1, of using "introspection" to refer solely to the human capacity to become aware from the inside that our sensations have certain properties (or that those properties themselves have certain features).

identity theory. But it is beyond belief that a man of Eccles's intellectual distinction couldn't *understand* a philosophical theory that is routinely taught to undergraduate philosophy students by reference to such homely examples as the identity of table salt with sodium chloride. Much more likely is that, because he experienced the intuition of distinctness, he could understand but not *believe* the identity theory's claim that phenomenally conscious mental states are identical with certain brain-states. He then inferred—practicing charity in interpretation—that proponents of the identity theory must have meant something else that, regrettably, they never expressed; and a view that never gets expressed by its proponents could quite properly be described as "enigmatic."

2.2 The Intuition of Revelation

I will now suggest that the intuition of *distinctness* plays a part in explaining why we typically have a *second* intuition when we introspect the phenomenal properties of our current sensations, the intuition of *revelation* (see, e.g., Damnjanovic 2012). The intuition of revelation is its seeming to us, when we introspect a phenomenal property, that we thereby have access to the whole essence, or complete nature, of the introspected phenomenal property—informally, its seeming to us introspectively that there is no more to the phenomenal property than *that*. To illustrate, let us return to your gazing fixedly at Rothko's *Untitled* (1970) and introspecting the phenomenal redness of the resulting visual sensation. Your experiencing the intuition of revelation in these circumstances is its seeming to you that the whole essence, or complete nature, of phenomenal redness is being revealed or exposed to you there and then, so that no aspect of its essence or nature (e.g., a physical or functional essence) is hidden to you.

The intuition of revelation seems to threaten physicalism, as I have just hinted. For if the intuition of revelation is veridical, then, in introspecting phenomenal redness, we thereby have access to the whole essence of phenomenal redness. But if phenomenal redness is a physical property or a functional but physically realized property, then its whole essence is physical or functional. So introspection of phenomenal redness ought to reveal its physical or functional essence. In fact, however, introspection of phenomenal redness doesn't reveal a physical or functional essence. So phenomenal redness can't have a physical or functional essence and can't therefore be a physical or functional property. This argument, however, fails, because it has an unsupported or question-begging premise. Introspection of phenomenal redness certainly doesn't reveal a physical or functional essence *as* physical or functional. But it doesn't follow that the essence it reveals isn't *in fact* physical or functional. We have no reason to expect that, if introspection reveals a physical or functional essence, the physical or functional character of this essence will also be manifest to introspection.[4]

If the intuition of revelation is veridical, and non-accidentally so, then it is a cognitive state analogous to knowledge. But it is puzzling how such a state could arise in us. Even if introspection does reveal to us what is *in fact* the whole essence of a phenomenal property, why would it come to seem to us—accurately and reliably—that it *is* the property's whole essence? Why would it come to seem to us—accurately and reliably—that introspection has revealed *everything* essential to the property? For it to come to seem to us—accurately and reliably—that introspection has revealed everything essential to a phenomenal property seems analogous to coming to know that one's knowledge of something is *complete*; but coming to know that one's knowledge of something is complete would seem to be a highly sophisticated cognitive achievement, requiring sustained investigation and theoretical inference, rather than a matter of intuiting. We can always take the easy way out and posit a primitive faculty of intuition by which it *just does* come to seem to us—accurately and reliably—that introspection has revealed *everything* essential to an introspected property; but if instead we try to imagine a *mechanism* underlying a veridical intuition of revelation, it is not easy to do so. A veridical intuition of revelation is puzzling.

That we have the intuition of revelation can, however, be explained, though not necessarily explained as veridical: it can be explained as a consequence of our having the intuition of distinctness.[5] The crucial link between the two intuitions is that, even if something's complete essence is not obvious to superficial consideration, its essence can still in principle always be specified explicitly by a non-trivial identity claim. For example, the complete essence of table salt, which we have found to be chemical, is not obvious to unaided vision or taste; but it can still be specified explicitly by the non-trivial identity claim that to be table salt just is to be a crystalline ionic compound

---

[4] This remark is elaborated in Chapter 3, especially in section 3.2. The anti-physicalist argument in the text is discussed more fully in section 3.3.

[5] Papineau briefly considers but then rejects the converse hypothesis that the intuition of distinctness is explained by the intuition of revelation (2011, 17). But the converse hypothesis wouldn't provide much of an explanation of the intuition of distinctness unless the rather peculiar intuition of revelation was itself explained.

of sodium and chlorine. Now suppose that we implicitly grasp this link, and also its consequence that, if the complete essence of phenomenal redness is not revealed to introspection, then there must be a non-trivial identity claim that specifies explicitly what its complete essence is, hence a non-trivial identity claim to the effect that phenomenal redness, conceived introspectively, just is so-and-so. But to have the intuition of distinctness with regard to phenomenal redness is precisely for such an identity claim to seem to us, introspectively, to be impossible. So, if we have the intuition of distinctness, it will seem to us that the complete essence of phenomenal redness is revealed to our introspection; the alternative would require something that seems impossible to us.[6] If this explanation is correct, then the intuition of revelation is another manifestation of the intuition of distinctness.

2.3 The "Explanatory Gap" Argument

In the present section, and the two sections that follow it, I will argue that certain reactions to the three most widely discussed arguments against physicalism about phenomenal properties are influenced in non-obvious ways by the intuition of distinctness. I take these three arguments to be (1) Joseph Levine's (2001) "explanatory gap" argument, (2) Frank Jackson's (1986) knowledge argument, and (3) David Chalmers's (1996 and 2010) zombie (or two-dimensional) argument. I will devote one section to each argument, beginning with Levine's "explanatory gap" argument.

By the "explanatory gap," I understand something *psychological*: a certain difference between (1) how people *react* to familiar reductive explanations of non-phenomenal properties (e.g., of water's boiling at 100°C) and (2) how people react to purported reductive explanations of phenomenal properties (e.g., of a visual sensation's phenomenal redness). People find reductive

---

[6] The suggested explanation, it might be objected, accounts for our sense that introspected phenomenal redness doesn't have a hidden physical or functional essence, but not for our sense that it has *this* phenomenal essence rather than some *other* (hidden) phenomenal essence. I suggest that we have an intuition of distinctness not only to the effect that phenomenal redness couldn't possibly be a physical or functional property but also to the effect that it couldn't be a different *phenomenal* property, say, phenomenal greenness. And perhaps the proposed explanation of the intuition of distinctness in Chapter 5 can be extended to account for this second intuition of distinctness by appeal to an idea from section 3.9. The formation of an introspective belief that a current visual sensation is phenomenally red might be physically necessary, given that the sensation *is* phenomenally red (and that our attention is not elsewhere), in which case we can't even *imagine* forming an introspective belief that a phenomenally red sensation is (say) phenomenally green.

explanations of non-phenomenal properties very satisfying, even when the explanations contain very little information. For example, people are typically delighted with the explanation that water boils at 100°C because, when heated water reaches that temperature, putting in additional energy agitates the molecules that make up water so much that the comparatively weak hydrogen bonds between them break. But people find purported reductive explanations of phenomenal properties entirely unsatisfying, no matter how detailed the explanations given. For example, a physicalist might suggest that one has a phenomenally red visual sensation because one is in a brain-state such that, when conditions are biologically normal, it is triggered if and only if light with a wavelength that falls within a certain range strikes one's retinal cells. People would treat this proposed reductive explanation of phenomenal redness as a complete non-starter. And they would still do so even if the explanation was enriched with neurophysiologically plausible detail. Indeed, people typically can't even *imagine* further details that, if added to the explanation, would make the explanation satisfying to them. Merely physical or merely functional properties of human brain-states strike people as simply incapable of reductively explaining the phenomenal properties of sensations.

The explanatory gap, when understood in this way, has often been thought to count against physicalism. But I want to ask why the explanatory gap—the psychological phenomenon—exists in the first place. Why do people have these dramatically different reactions to the different kinds of reductive explanations? That people are satisfied by familiar reductive explanations of *non*-phenomenal properties is unsurprising. What needs explaining is why, by contrast, people are so completely *dissatisfied* with proposed reductive explanations of *phenomenal* properties. The explanation that I suggest is that people are influenced by the intuition of distinctness when they assess proposed reductive explanations of phenomenal properties, whereas they are not influenced by the intuition of distinctness, or by anything comparable to it, when they assess proposed reductive explanations of non-phenomenal properties. Let me elaborate.

What makes the intuition of distinctness relevant to reductive explanations? Typically, a reductive explanation must include, or at least presuppose, an a posteriori *identity claim* about the property to be reductively explained. For example, a reductive explanation of the boiling point of water must include, or presuppose, the a posteriori identity claim that for a liquid to boil *just is* for the bonds between the molecules that make up the liquid to break; otherwise someone who has only been told that the bonds between the molecules that make up water break under certain conditions will be left wondering why this fact about water counts as an explanation of water's boiling. Similarly, a reductive explanation of why nitrogen is invisible must include, or presuppose, the a posteriori identity claim that to be invisible *just is* to have no disposition to reflect or to emit photons; otherwise someone who has only been told that nitrogen has no disposition to reflect or to emit photons will be left wondering why this fact about nitrogen constitutes an explanation of nitrogen's invisibility. And there is, of course, a reason why reductive explanations must typically include or presuppose such a posteriori identity claims. Typically, in a reductive explanation, the claim that describes the explanatory factors, on the one hand, and the claim ascribing the property to be explained, on the other, are framed in different theoretical vocabularies that are disjoint from one another in the sense that someone who understands the two vocabularies isn't thereby enabled to translate claims made in one of the vocabularies into claims made in the other. As a result, the claim that describes the explanatory factors cannot by itself *formally entail* the claim ascribing the property to be explained, just as a premise of the form "*is* so-and-so" cannot formally entail a conclusion of the form "*ought to be* so-and-so." But an a posteriori identity claim about the property to be reductively explained makes formal entailment possible.[7] For the identity claim has the form "being F = being G,"[8] where being F is the property to be reductively explained, being G is a property posited by the reductively explaining theory, and there is no a priori entailment from the predicate "is G" to the predicate "is F."[9] And such an identity claim entails that, necessarily, something is F if and only if it is G.

It is now clear how people's having the intuition of distinctness could explain why they are so completely dissatisfied with proposed reductive explanations of phenomenal properties. As has often been noted, the vocabulary that we use to ascribe phenomenal properties has no a priori definition in

---

[7] Contingent bridge laws expressing a nomic link between two properties would also make formal entailment possible, but the resulting explanation would not be reductive.

[8] I intend the symbol "=" to be understood in its logical sense, in which it expresses the relation of *being one and the same thing as*; this is a relation in which, of course, everything stands to itself.

[9] The claim that reductive explanations must typically include or presuppose non-trivial identity claims does not entail that for the mental to be reductively explained in terms of the physical, mental properties must be identical with *physical* properties (which would contradict the multiple realizability of mental properties by physical properties). For the mental to be reductively explained in terms of the physical, mental properties must be identical *either* with physical properties *or* with *functional* properties that can be physically realized. A functional property that can be physically realized is not for that reason a physical property (see Melnyk 2018).

the vocabulary of any proposed reductive explanation of phenomenal properties. So any reductive explanation of a sensation's phenomenal property must include, or presuppose, an a posteriori identity claim about the phenomenal property—for example, the claim that phenomenal redness *just is* a certain neurological property, or that phenomenal redness *just is* the (functional) property of non-conceptually representing that some external surface is red. But because people have the intuition of distinctness, it seems to them that phenomenal properties couldn't possibly *be* neurological or functional properties. People therefore find incredible precisely those identity claims that would be necessary for reductive explanations of phenomenal properties to succeed. No wonder, then, that they find all purported reductive explanations of phenomenal properties entirely unsatisfying.[10]

2.4 The Knowledge Argument

According to Frank Jackson's much-discussed knowledge argument against physicalism, Mary is an adult scientist who has been confined since birth to a purely black-and-white environment in which things are contrived so that she never has a visual experience of color; for example, she has never seen a green bean or even her own blood. Thanks to grayscale computer screens and textbooks, she has nonetheless managed to learn absolutely everything known to the completed physical sciences (physics, chemistry, biochemistry, the neurosciences) and functionalist psychology (e.g., computational psychology) about color vision, including its objects. Now if physicalism is true, then Mary has managed to learn *everything* about color vision—for she has learned all the *physical* facts about color vision (even on a very liberal construal of "physical facts"), and if physicalism is true, physical facts are all the facts there are. One day, however, she is released from her black-and-white environment into the normal world, whereupon she sees a red rose—the first time she has ever seen any (chromatically) colored object. What will happen to her? She will have a visual experience that is new to her, obviously; but it seems clear that she will also *learn* something from the new experience— that she will also gain new *knowledge*. For example, she may think to herself, "My current sensation is so-and-so," where "is so-and-so" predicates, of her current visual sensation, the property of being phenomenally red. Or

---

[10] David Papineau suggested some years ago that the intuition of distinctness underlies the explanatory gap (2002, 145), but I think I reached the same conclusion independently.

she may think to herself, "*That* [property] exists!", where "that" refers to her sensation's phenomenal redness. Either way, her belief will constitute new knowledge—knowledge that she did not previously have. But if she gains new knowledge about the visual sensation of red when she first sees a red rose, then it can't be true that she already knew *everything* about color vision. Since physicalism implies that she *did* know everything about color vision, it follows that physicalism is false (Jackson 1986).

Now there is a popular physicalist reply to the knowledge argument, sometimes called the "phenomenal concept strategy," though I will call it—more helpfully—the "new concept, old property" reply (originated, I think, in Horgan [1984]).[11] But there is also widespread dissatisfaction (of a specific kind) with this reply. What I will suggest in the present section is that this dissatisfaction is explained by the intuition of distinctness. If I am right, then this dissatisfaction is another manifestation of the intuition of distinctness.

The "new concept, old property" reply to the knowledge argument acknowledges that Mary gains new propositional knowledge when she sees something red for the first time; so her previous state of propositional knowledge must have been incomplete. But the "new concept, old property" reply construes her gaining new propositional knowledge in such a way that her gaining it does not entail that there is a real property of whose existence she had been quite unaware, and which she was unable to ascribe to sensations, *before* her release; and only if there is such a property is physicalism false. The reply claims that, when she gains the new propositional knowledge that her current sensation is so-and-so, what's new is only the *predicative concept*—that is, the *phenomenal concept*—that she employs in forming the introspective belief that her current sensation is so-and-so.[12] This predicative concept is one that she did not possess before she saw the red rose and therefore one that she has never previously employed in thinking a thought (e.g., forming a belief). But—and this is the crux—though the *predicative*

---

[11] I make no attempt to engage with the vast literature on the "new concept, old property" reply, but I say more about how I understand phenomenal concepts in Chapter 5. The best account of phenomenal concepts known to me, on which I draw below, is Michael Tye's 2003 account. He repudiates the account in later work (Tye 2009); but I think he is wrong to do so (see, e.g., McLaughlin 2012). I also recommend a splendid series of papers by Esa Díaz-León in defense of phenomenal concepts against well-known objections (2008, 2010, 2014, 2016).

[12] If I think to myself that Vienna is charming, then I use two concepts: a *subject-concept* of Vienna, and a *predicative concept* of the property of being charming. A predicative concept is a concept of a property that can be used in thought to attribute the property to a subject; it is therefore (roughly) analogous to a predicate in a sentence. A predicative concept that, in this way, *expresses* a property should not be confused with a *subject-concept* that *refers* to—that *names*—the property.

concept is new, the *property* that she now uses this predicative concept to ascribe to her current sensation is *old*: it was expressed by *some* concept, drawn from the physical sciences or functionalist psychology, that she could and did employ in thinking thoughts while she was still confined in her black-and-white environment. Mary's gaining the knowledge that her current sensation is so-and-so is therefore consistent with physicalism.

But, you might ask, why should we count Mary's belief that her current sensation is so-and-so as new *knowledge* just because she forms the belief by using a new *concept*? After all, Mary's new belief is true under exactly the same conditions as some belief that she formed, or could have formed, before her release, by using a concept drawn from the physical sciences or functionalist psychology; the two beliefs would be attributing exactly the same property to exactly the same thing at the same time.[13] To this question, the "new concept, old property" reply can give the following answer. The new concept employed by Mary when she thinks that her current sensation is so-and-so has a very different *functional role* from that of any concept drawn from the physical sciences or functionalist psychology. Very roughly speaking, a predicative concept's functional role is certain of the concept's features distinct from the fact that the concept expresses the particular property that it expresses, namely, its being triggered by certain distinctive causes, and its having certain distinctive effects on other events, for example, behaviors. A plausible suggestion is that the new concept employed by Mary when she thinks that her current sensation is so-and-so is distinctive because the concept can be activated directly by introspection of a phenomenally red sensation, and automatically tends in turn to cause the belief that something is red. By contrast, no concept drawn from the physical sciences or functionalist psychology has that functional role. Even if you use a concept drawn from the neurosciences to form the (true) belief that one of your current (or future) sensations has (or will have) such-and-such a neurophysiological property, your use of this concept is not triggered directly by introspection, and it has no automatic tendency to make you believe that something is red.

Given this difference in functional role, we should count Mary's belief that her current sensation is so-and-so as genuinely new knowledge. For we count people as having acquired genuinely new knowledge when they learn that *a* is *F*, even though (1) they already knew that *a* is *G*, and (2) their concept of being *F* expresses the same property as their concept of being *G*, just

---

[13] This is true even though the belief before her release would have the form "My *future* sensation *will* be so-and-so."

so long as the respective functional roles of the two concepts are sufficiently different. To illustrate how new states of knowledge can arise from differences between the functional roles of coreferential concepts, consider the following little story:

> Because of a blow to the head, I suffer terrible amnesia and forget who I am. But I read in a newspaper I come across that next week, for reasons that don't matter, one Andrew Melnyk is scheduled to be publicly flogged. "Very bad news for this Melnyk fellow!" I think to myself, but I soon return to my quest to find out who I am. Later, however, after carefully examining the contents of the wallet in my pocket and seeing my reflection in a mirror, I realize that *I* am Melnyk, and further realize, to my horror, that *I* am due to be publicly flogged next week.

In this story, it seems that my state of knowledge changes dramatically when I conclude (1) that I am AM, and (2) that I am due to be publicly flogged next week. I gain two items of genuinely new (and highly alarming) knowledge, the second of which might prompt such novel action as trying to hide from the authorities. But my new knowledge isn't knowledge of states of affairs of which I had been unaware before I examined the driver's license and looked in the mirror. For my belief that I am AM is true under exactly the same conditions as my earlier belief that AM = AM (and my earlier belief that I am myself); and my belief that I am due to be publicly flogged next week is true under exactly the same conditions as my earlier belief that AM is due to be publicly flogged next week. So what *is* new about my new knowledge? The natural explanation of why I gain genuinely new knowledge is that the difference between (1) the functional role of my "I" concept and (2) the functional role of my "AM" concept is large enough by the standards of everyday life to warrant the classification of my knowledge that *I* am AM as *different* knowledge from my prior knowledge that AM = AM (or that I am myself), and my knowledge that *I* am due to be flogged as *different* knowledge from my prior knowledge that AM is due to be flogged—*different* knowledge and hence (given the story) *new* knowledge.

There is a second route to the conclusion that Mary's belief that her current sensation is so-and-so amounts to new knowledge, and it is perhaps more intuitive than an overt appeal to differences in the functional roles of two concepts of the same property. No one disputes that my belief that I am AM is a different *belief* from my earlier belief that AM = AM (or my earlier belief that I am myself). After all, I can believe that AM = AM without believing that I am AM, as the little story above also shows. Similarly, my belief that I will be flogged is a different *belief* from my earlier belief that AM will be flogged. But *knowing* is constituted, at least in part, by *believing*; *knowing* that *p* requires at least *believing* that *p*. It's plausible, then, that I can enter a different (hence new) state of *knowing* just by forming a different *belief* (even if my new belief is true under exactly the same conditions as my previous belief). And that, on a physicalist view of the matter, is exactly what Mary does. Before she is released from her black-and-white environment, she can make a prediction: she can believe that because, after her release, she *will* see a red rose for the first time, certain activity in so-and-so region of her visual cortex *will* have such-and-such a neurophysiological characteristic. And that future activity in so-and-so region of her visual cortex may just *be* her future sensation of red, and such-and-such a neurophysiological characteristic of that activity may just *be* phenomenal redness. Nonetheless, when she actually sees the red rose, and forms the belief that her current visual sensation *is* phenomenally red, she will clearly have formed a new *belief* (i.e., a belief different from any belief she has previously held). And because this new belief constitutes knowledge, it's plausible to think that the knowledge it constitutes will also be new.

Now what I want to emphasize is that, when the "new concept, old property" reply to the knowledge argument is developed in this way, it gets the job done: it explains how Mary could gain new knowledge even if physicalism is true. The knowledge argument, in a nutshell, is this:

(1) Mary gains new knowledge after her release from the black-and-white environment.
(2) If physicalism is true, Mary can't gain new knowledge after her release from the black-and-white environment.
∴ Physicalism is not true.

And the "new concept, old property" reply shows that premise (2) is false: it shows that Mary *can* gain what we would classify, by everyday criteria, as new knowledge, even if physicalism is true. But precisely because the "new concept, old property" reply gets the job done in this way, it *ought* to strike people as highly plausible. However, the "new concept, old property" reply strikes some philosophers as quite *im*plausible. Surely, these philosophers protest, Mary's new knowledge when she sees a red rose for the first time couldn't just be her using a concept with a new functional role to attribute to her current sensation a physical or functional property that she *already* knew about from her study of science. Surely the knowledge she gains when she sees a red rose for the first time is more substantive—meatier—than a mere difference in the functional roles of concepts could account for (see, e.g., Schroer 2010). Surely Mary gains knowledge of a new *subject matter*. These protests may well resonate with the reader, as they have often done with my students.

It is precisely *this* kind of reaction to the "new concept, old property" reply that, I suggest, the intuition of distinctness can help to explain. Whence comes the strong conviction that Mary's new knowledge can't just be a matter of a new functional role but is instead substantive knowledge of a new subject matter? Surely no one who lacked the capacity for introspecting their sensations would have this conviction; so it must arise somehow from introspection. It arises, I suggest, from taking the intuition of distinctness at face value. Philosophers who react to the "new concept, old property" reply in the way described put themselves in Mary's shoes, as we all naturally do when presented with the story of Mary, and imagine seeing a red rose for the first time and attending to the phenomenal redness of the resulting visual sensation. But in imagining themselves in Mary's shoes, they naturally imagine their having the intuition of distinctness: they imagine its seeming to them that the property they are imagining attending to can't possibly be a physical or functional property. And because these philosophers are (I suggest) generally inclined to take their intuitions of distinctness at face value, they imagine *believing* that the property they are imagining attending to can't possibly be a physical or functional property. They conclude that Mary must therefore be acquiring knowledge of a non-physical and non-functional property, and so she cannot just be using a new concept to form a new belief about a physical or functional property familiar to her from her black-and-white environment.

This explanation of why some philosophers react to the "new concept, old property" reply in the way described has a corollary: these philosophers aren't just begging the question against physicalists, as they might appear to be. Yes, they take Mary's new knowledge to be substantive in the sense that the phenomenal redness she attributes to her visual sensation is neither physical nor functional, which entails dualism about phenomenal redness. But, according to the proposed explanation, they don't just *assume* that Mary's new knowledge is substantive in this sense; they *conclude* that it is, from their having of the intuition of distinctness.

2.5 The Zombie Argument

David Chalmers's zombie (or two-dimensional) argument belongs to a class of anti-physicalist arguments that depend on the fact that, if physicalism is true, then a certain kind of situation is *metaphysically impossible*, that is, couldn't possibly happen, no matter how different the laws of nature were. If physicalism is true, then any possible world that was exactly the same as the actual world in all *physical* respects would have all the *mental* features that the actual world has, so that there are no possible worlds that are exactly the same as the actual world in all physical respects, but that don't have all the mental features that the actual world has.

Now Chalmers's zombie argument claims that there are such possible worlds: *zombie worlds*. A zombie world is a possible world physically indistinguishable from the actual world (hence containing an atom-for-atom physical replica of everyone who in the actual world is in a phenomenally conscious mental state) in which, however, *no one* is in any phenomenally conscious mental state whatsoever. And we know that zombie worlds are metaphysically possible, according to the zombie argument, because we can *conceive* of zombie worlds. The heart of the zombie argument, therefore, is the inference from the premise that zombie worlds are *conceivable* to the conclusion that zombie worlds are (metaphysically) *possible*. Chalmers introduces an elaborate technical machinery to mediate the step from premise to conclusion in this inference, but luckily we don't need to know about this machinery for present purposes (1996 and 2010, ch. 6). It suffices to know that while Chalmers thinks that there is a logically valid way of moving from the premise to the conclusion, he doesn't think that *in general* the conceivability of something entails its metaphysical possibility. Now there is a popular physicalist objection to the zombie argument that targets, precisely, the inference from the conceivability of zombie worlds to their possibility. But there is also an attractive reply to this objection on behalf of the original argument. This reply, I will suggest, owes its attractiveness to the intuition of distinctness.

The popular physicalist objection to the zombie argument accepts the truth of the premise in the inference from conceivability to possibility, so long as the premise is understood to say that zombie worlds are conceivable in the specific sense of being *epistemically possible*. To say that zombie worlds are epistemically possible is to say that zombie worlds are logically consistent with all the truths that we can know a priori. The truths that we can know a priori fall into two classes: (1) logical and mathematical truths (e.g., that if *p* or q, and not-q, then p) and (2) certain conceptual or semantic truths (e.g., that every sister is a sibling). Zombie worlds are epistemically possible because, as most physicalists agree, no combination of truths in classes (1) and (2) allows one to rule out zombie worlds, that is, to show that possible worlds physically indistinguishable from the actual world would *have* to contain creatures in phenomenally conscious mental states. To show this would require a priori conceptual or semantic truths that could serve as bridge principles that allow the derivation of a description of someone as having, say, a phenomenally red visual sensation from a description of that person framed only in the distinctive vocabulary of, say, the neurosciences. Such truths would have to express, in physical terms, conditions that are conceptually or semantically sufficient for the instantiation of phenomenal properties, expressed in phenomenal terms. But no such truths seem to exist. So zombie worlds are conceivable in the sense of being epistemically possible. But, the physicalist objection continues, it doesn't follow that zombie worlds are metaphysically possible. For suppose that phenomenal redness just *is* a certain neurophysiological property. Then an atom-for-atom physical replica of you as you gaze at Rothko's *Untitled* would indeed have to have a phenomenally red visual sensation (given the actual world's physical laws), because it would have to have every neurophysiological property that you have while you gaze; zombie worlds would therefore *not* be metaphysically possible. But they *would* be epistemically possible, because the truth that phenomenal redness just is a certain neurophysiological property is neither a mathematical or logical nor a conceptual or semantic truth; nor does it follow a priori from any such truths; nor does it follow a priori from any such truths plus a complete physical description of zombie worlds.[14]

Now for the attractive reply to this objection on behalf of the original argument (Bogardus 2013, 456–7). The key claim is that zombie worlds are conceivable to us in a way that goes beyond their being epistemically possible for us: zombie worlds, as I shall put it, *seem genuinely possible* to us. And if zombie worlds *do* seem genuinely possible to us, then, even if their *epistemic possibility* doesn't entail that they're metaphysically possible, their *seeming genuinely possible* might still provide defeasible but undefeated evidence that they're metaphysically possible—in which case the zombie argument would be back in business. Why think that the conceivability of zombie worlds is something more than their epistemic possibility? The answer is that some

---

[14] This last claim requires further argument. It can be provided (see Melnyk 2001; Levine 2001, ch. 2), but it doesn't matter for present purposes.

things are epistemically possible for us that *don't* seem conceivable to us in the way in which zombie worlds do. For example, a beaker that contains menthol but no methanol is epistemically possible for us—it's consistent with everything we know a priori. But is a beaker containing menthol but no methanol conceivable to us in the same way in which zombie worlds are? Do we regard the possibility of a beaker that contains menthol but no methanol in the same way we regard the possibility of a zombie world? Many people will say that, unlike a zombie world, a beaker that contains menthol but no methanol doesn't *seem genuinely possible* to them. They might add that it would be *rash* to claim that a beaker that contains menthol but no methanol is really possible, because, for all they know, menthol just *is* methanol, in which case a beaker *couldn't* contain menthol but no methanol.[15] The conceivability of zombie worlds, then, cannot be reduced to the epistemic possibility of zombie worlds; it is something stronger than the epistemic possibility of zombie worlds.

I don't doubt that zombie worlds are conceivable to some people in a way in which merely epistemically possible things *aren't* conceivable to them— that zombie worlds seem genuinely possible to them. But *why* do zombie worlds seem genuinely possible to them, whereas a beaker that contains menthol but no methanol doesn't seem so? The answer, I propose, is that people to whom zombie worlds seem genuinely possible have the intuition of distinctness that phenomenal redness, say, is distinct from any physical or functional property, whereas they have no corresponding intuition that menthol is distinct from methanol. And then, because they take the intuition of distinctness at face value, they *believe* that phenomenal redness is distinct from any physical or functional property. But if it *is* distinct, then it must be metaphysically possible for a creature to be in a brain-state that has any physical or functional property you like but that does not have phenomenal redness.[16] People who take their intuitions of distinctness at face value

---

[15] My example assumes that, like me, the reader has only a hazy idea of what menthol is. If you happen to know that it is not methanol, then please devise a case that works for your particular state of incomplete chemical knowledge.

[16] Despite its great plausibility, Bogardus denies that the distinctness of property *P* and property *Q* entails the metaphysical possibility of something's having *P* but not *Q* (2013, 447). He says that triangularity and trilaterality are distinct properties but that it's not metaphysically possible for something to be triangular but not trilateral. I am more inclined to think that triangularity and trilaterality are in fact one and the same geometrical property, and that the appearance that they are distinct arises from the fact that the two *words*, "triangularity" and "trilaterality," though coreferential, are associated with two different (rigidified) definite descriptions. Perhaps "triangularity" is semantically equivalent to "the geometrical property that entails having three *angles*," while "trilaterality" is semantically equivalent to "the geometrical property that entails having three *sides*."

can be expected to feel very strongly that zombie worlds are metaphysically possible.[17]

2.6 Conclusion

In this chapter, I have argued that the intuition of distinctness manifests itself in multiple ways. We can experience it for ourselves more or less at will. But we can also be aware of it from a third-person point of view, as what explains various psychological attitudes: why some people dismiss physicalism about phenomenal properties as unintelligible or unworthy of discussion; why people have the intuition of revelation; why people have the sense of an explanatory gap; and why defenders of the knowledge argument and of the zombie argument both charge that certain physicalist objections don't do justice to their intuitions.

The intuition of distinctness is its *seeming* to us that a certain introspected phenomenal property of a current sensation just couldn't be a physical or functional property. But I haven't asked whether such a seeming gives us reason to *believe* that a certain introspected phenomenal property of a current sensation isn't a physical or functional property. In Chapter 3, I will address this question, arguing that the intuition of distinctness should not be taken at face value in this way. But if that conclusion is correct, it raises a question about the present chapter: do the explanations suggested here have the effect of *debunking* the attitudes explained, of undermining their epistemic status as justified or justifying?

If the dismissal of physicalism about phenomenal properties as unintelligible or unworthy of discussion arises from the intuition of distinctness, and the intuition gives us no reason to reject physicalism about phenomenal properties, then the dismissal of physicalism is unwarranted and can safely be disregarded. Similarly, if the intuition of revelation and the sense of an explanatory gap arise from the intuition of distinctness, then they give us reason to reject physicalism only if the intuition of distinctness gives us reason to reject physicalism, so that, if the intuition of distinctness doesn't give us reason to reject physicalism, neither does the intuition of revelation

---

[17] Though other hypotheses are possible, it may be that what David Chalmers (2010) calls the "positive conceivability" of a zombie world, something that in my view he never spells out adequately, is in fact what I have called a zombie world's seeming really possible to us, and that it therefore arises from the intuition of distinctness.

or the sense of an explanatory gap. What about the rejection, as intuitively unsatisfactory, of the "new concept, old property" reply to the knowledge argument? If this rejection is explained by the epistemically valueless intuition of distinctness, then it is unwarranted and can safely be disregarded; but the "new concept, old property" reply might still be open to other objections (e.g., that there are no phenomenal concepts) that do not rely on the intuition of distinctness. What, finally, about the zombie argument? To the extent that the conviction that zombie worlds are conceivable in some stronger sense than that of being epistemically possible arises from the intuition of distinctness, this conviction is unwarranted and can safely be disregarded. But I haven't tried to show that this conviction arises *only* from the intuition of distinctness. David Chalmers speaks of the "positive conceivability" of zombie worlds, which he contrasts with their mere "negative conceivability," that is, their epistemic possibility (2010). I have speculated that their "positive conceivability" arises from the intuition of distinctness, rather than from some independent source, but perhaps it doesn't. Moreover, Chalmers insists that their "negative conceivability" is all that the zombie argument needs, and I have not tried (here) to show that he is wrong.[18]

---

[18] I have tried to show this elsewhere (Melnyk 2001). My objection needs modifying to take account of Chalmers's later clarification that his primary intensions were intended as epistemic rather than as contextual. In 2001, I conceded that our phenomenal concepts have *contextual* primary intensions but denied that our possession of phenomenal concepts automatically endows us with knowledge, either explicit or implicit, of their contextual primary intensions. But I deny that our phenomenal concepts even have primary intensions if these are understood as epistemic—or at least I see no reason to accept that they have them.

3
Why Not Take the Intuition of Distinctness at Face Value?

3.1 The Chapter's Main Argument Outlined

The central question addressed by this book is why, if physicalism is true, we have the intuition of distinctness—why, if physicalism is true, it nonetheless seems to us, under certain conditions, that the phenomenal properties we are introspecting just couldn't be one and the same as the physical or physically realized properties we are considering as candidates for identity with the phenomenal properties. As we saw in Chapter 1, however, a possible response to this question is to reject the question's assumption of physicalism, and then to take the intuition of distinctness at face value, as giving us reason to believe that introspected phenomenal properties *are* distinct from the physical or physically realized properties that we are considering. And at least one philosopher, Tomas Bogardus, takes the intuition of distinctness at face value in just this way. In doing so, he explicitly sees himself as taking the same view of the intuition of distinctness that he, and many other philosophers, take of intuitions in general—the view that, under certain conditions, they give us reason to *believe* the thing that merely *seems* true to us as we have the intuition (Bogardus 2013, 448–9). In this chapter, I will argue that, to the contrary, the intuition of distinctness gives us no reason to believe that the phenomenal properties we are introspecting really are distinct from the physical or physically realized properties that we are considering as candidates for identity with the phenomenal properties, and hence that property dualism is true.[1]

---

[1] David Papineau argues briefly that the intuition of distinctness is no evidence for dualism: "It is arguable that dualism requires epiphenomenalism," he notes, in which case the non-physical character of phenomenal properties can't explain the intuition of distinctness, and so dualism can't make the intuition more probable than physicalism does (2011, 13–14). But the argument for holding that dualism requires epiphenomenalism needs the premise that the physical is causally closed, and the case for the causal closure of the physical is empirical. Whatever the actual strength of the empirical case, I doubt that dualists will find it so strong as to persuade them to discount the evidential value of the intuition of distinctness.

Arguing for this negative conclusion is the main business of the present chapter. But the detailed discussions that substantiate one of the two premises of my argument may be appreciated by readers whose main interest lies in the wider debate about physicalism and phenomenal properties, rather than just the intuition of distinctness. In the first place, these detailed discussions, when taken together, amount to a case for thinking that there are no good arguments against physicalism about phenomenal properties that are *introspection-based*, that is, that (i) contain a premise that ascribes some feature to phenomenal properties, which premise (ii) is claimed to be known through, or evidenced by, introspection.[2] Second, these detailed discussions sketch positive accounts of what phenomenal properties are, how we know about them introspectively, how we could tell introspectively that an introspected property is physical, what the subjectivity of phenomenal properties could be, and so on. Of these positive accounts some are minor variations on familiar themes (though better, I hope, for the variations), while others can lay claim to greater originality. Either way, they clothe in decent plausibility the shockingly stark claim that every phenomenal property just is some or other physical or physically realized property; by explaining how such a claim could be elaborated, they help it to earn a second look from those whose first reaction is disbelief.

The present chapter's main argument concludes that the intuition of distinctness gives us no reason to believe that the phenomenal properties we are introspecting really are distinct from the physical or physically realized properties that we are considering as candidates for identity with the phenomenal properties. Now the contrary supposition that the intuition of distinctness *does* give us reason to believe that the phenomenal properties we are introspecting are distinct from the physical or physically realized properties we are considering doesn't by itself explain *how* the intuition arises in us, that is, from the operation of what psychological mechanism it arises. Nor does the contrary supposition absolve us of the responsibility to provide such an explanation. The only difference that the supposition makes is that the psychological mechanism that produces the intuition of distinctness in us must be such that, if *it* produces the intuition of distinctness in us, then the resulting intuition gives us reason to believe that the phenomenal properties

---

[2] By this criterion, the standard anti-physicalist arguments discussed in Chapter 2 probably aren't introspection-based. It is certainly plausible that they wouldn't be found at all persuasive by anyone who lacked the capacity for introspection. But the capacity for introspection is necessary because it makes possible certain acts of first-person imagining or conceiving, rather than because the arguments include a premise that (i) ascribes some feature to phenomenal properties, and that (ii) is allegedly known through, or evidenced by, introspection.

we are introspecting are distinct from the physical or physically realized properties that we are considering. There seem, however, to be just two kinds of psychological mechanism that would have this effect.

I will call a psychological mechanism of the first kind a *conscious mechanism*. Such a mechanism, operating when we introspect a phenomenal property of one of our current sensations, consists of our more or less consciously *rehearsing a good argument* for the conclusion that the phenomenal property we are introspecting is not the physical or physically realized property that we are considering as a candidate for identity with the phenomenal property. Here it is the goodness of the argument, of course, that makes it the case that the intuition of distinctness gives us reason to believe that the phenomenal property we are introspecting is not the physical or physically realized property that we are considering. The premises of this argument need not be on the tips of our tongues, nor need they even be claims that we could easily reconstruct if we were questioned; but they would strike us as plausibly underlying our intuition of distinctness if they were articulated for us by someone else.

A psychological mechanism of the second kind I will call a *non-conscious mechanism*. Such a mechanism operates entirely unconsciously but is *reliable* in the sense that the (objective) probability that what seems to us to be the case, as we have the intuition, actually is the case is high, or at least higher, *given* that the intuition is the output of the mechanism, where this high, or just higher, probability is suitably non-accidental. Here the reliability of the mechanism is what makes it the case that the intuition of distinctness gives us reason to believe that the phenomenal property we are introspecting is not the physical or physically realized property that we are considering. The operation of a non-conscious mechanism may amount to entirely unconscious reasoning, but it need not.[3]

Talk of mechanisms is pervasive in the sciences, of course, including in the sciences of the mind (Craver and Tabery 2019), but an objector might worry that, in the present context, even though my talk of psychological mechanisms doesn't presuppose that *phenomenal properties* are physical or physically realized, it nonetheless presupposes a generally physicalist view of the mind, and therefore begs the question against dualism. But such a worry is unfounded. I need not assume that mechanisms must be physical or physically

---

[3] To see why, suppose that facial recognition is underwritten by an entirely unconscious psychological mechanism that seeks *matches* between inputted representations of faces and stored representations of faces. The operation of such a mechanism might well be reliable, but intuitively it doesn't seem to me to count as *reasoning*, even unconscious reasoning.

realized; for if there are entities and properties that are neither physical nor physically realized, then they can perfectly well constitute, or help to constitute, mechanisms. I needn't even assume that mechanisms, or their constituents, must be governed by laws, either universal or statistical. For nearly all of the possible mechanisms that I consider are more or less conscious trains of reasoning, and my critical discussions of them are compatible with the possibility that trains of reasoning are not, and cannot be reduced to, processes governed by laws of any kind (though perhaps a person can have a tendency to reason well).[4] There is one view, admittedly, that my appeal to mechanisms does preclude—the view that mental phenomena are, or might be, such as to elude in principle the possibility of *any* kind of systematic description. This view would permit dualists to say that our minds *just do* produce an intuition of distinctness that *just does* give us reason to believe that phenomenal properties are not physical or physically realized properties—and there's an end on it; and since no more *can* be said, the demand for a mechanism is unreasonable. But the view of the mental as beyond the reach of any systematic description is a strange and implausible one (Melnyk 2003, 302–4). Also, because it treats the property of giving reason to believe as a *fundamental* property of the intuition of distinctness, not supervening on any feature of how the intuition was produced (e.g., on its arising from the more or less conscious rehearsal of a good argument), it cannot treat the property of giving reason to believe as physically realized, and must therefore be a non-physicalist view. If, therefore, the view of the mental as beyond the reach of any systematic description is *required* in order to vindicate the claim that the intuition of distinctness gives us reason to believe that introspected phenomenal properties are not physical or physically realized, then the reason to believe dualism that the intuition of distinctness gives us presupposes an *antecedent* reason to believe a very radical form of dualism. The reason given by the intuition can therefore be no stronger than that antecedent reason, and the intuition can provide no fresh reason to believe dualism.

Let me now explain how the main argument of the present chapter is meant to go. Its form is *modus tollens*, and its conclusion, of course, is that:

> The intuition of distinctness gives us no reason to believe that the phenomenal properties we are introspecting really are distinct from the physical or physically realized properties that we are considering as candidates for identity with the phenomenal properties.

---

[4] I'm not saying that it's clear how to understand such a tendency other than by appeal to laws.

Its first premise claims that:

> *If* the intuition of distinctness gives us reason to believe that the phenomenal properties we are introspecting really are distinct from the physical or physically realized properties that we are considering as candidates for identity with the phenomenal properties, *then* the intuition of distinctness arises in us *either* from the operation of a conscious mechanism *or* from the operation of a non-conscious mechanism.

The argument's second premise is that:

> The intuition of distinctness arises in us *neither* from the operation of a conscious mechanism *nor* from the operation of a non-conscious mechanism.

I have already made my case for the first premise. I will make a case for the second by surveying a wide range of possible conscious and non-conscious psychological mechanisms whose operation in us might be thought to produce the intuition of distinctness.[5] In the case of each possible *conscious* mechanism, I will argue *either* that the argument we are hypothesized more or less consciously to rehearse is not a *good* argument (so that the hypothesized mechanism turns out not actually to be a conscious mechanism as defined above) *or* that the possible mechanism can't plausibly be thought in fact to operate in us to produce the intuition of distinctness. In the case of each possible *non-conscious* mechanism, I will argue that the mechanism, if reliable, can't plausibly be thought in fact to operate in us. If these arguments are correct, then it follows that the intuition of distinctness does not arise in us from the operation either of the possible conscious mechanisms that I survey or of the possible non-conscious mechanisms that I survey. It may well be, of course, that I have not thought of *all* the possible conscious or non-conscious mechanisms whose operation in us might produce the intuition of distinctness. Nonetheless, the failure, after extended reflection, to come up with a conscious or a non-conscious psychological mechanism that can plausibly be thought actually to operate in us provides good inductive evidence—without, of course, deductively entailing—that the intuition of distinctness does not arise in us from the operation of *any* conscious or

---

[5] "Possible conscious and non-conscious psychological mechanisms" are psychological mechanisms that *might turn out to be* conscious or non-conscious mechanisms as I have stipulatively defined them, that is, as conferring a reason-giving power on the resulting intuition.

non-conscious mechanism, so that the second premise of the chapter's main argument is true.

My critical survey of possible psychological mechanisms of the two kinds falls into two very unequal parts. In the first and much longer part, occupying sections 3.2 through 3.10, I consider possible conscious mechanisms; I consider possible non-conscious mechanisms in section 3.11.

3.2 Not Seeming Physical or Functional

Suppose we suggest to an intelligent non-philosopher that her current visual sensation of red—a sensation caused, perhaps, by her close inspection of Mark Rothko's *Untitled* (1970)—literally *is* certain simultaneous electrochemical activity in her brain—a particular pattern of neuronal firing in the V4 region of her visual cortex that we can call "*N*." According to the suggestion, her current visual sensation of red, on the one hand, and *N*, on the other, are in fact one and the same thing. The suggestion entails that, in being aware of her current visual sensation of red, she is, objectively speaking, aware of *N*—aware of what is, in fact, *N*. So far, perhaps, so good. Now suppose we make a second suggestion to her: that the *phenomenal redness* of her current visual sensation literally *is* a certain neuroscientific property of *N*—the property of having a certain functional organization and rate of firing, say.[6] A very natural reaction on her part to this second suggestion would be to think to herself, "But it certainly doesn't *seem* to be a neuroscientific property."[7] This sort of reaction to the claim that a phenomenal property just is a physical or functional property suggests a possible conscious mechanism by which the intuition of distinctness might be produced in us. If this first mechanism operates, then the intuition of distinctness arises in us because we more or less consciously rehearse the following

---

[6] "Having so-and-so functional organization and rate of firing" is intended merely to gesture at a particular physical or functional property; but any genuine scientific term for a particular physical or functional property could be substituted.

[7] This reaction mustn't be confused with her thinking to herself that phenomenal redness *does* seem *non*-physical; the latter reaction is simply the original intuition of distinctness, which we are trying to explain. The reaction is voiced, and made part of a philosophical argument, by William Robinson: "a difference in seeing colors does not seem to be remotely like a difference in sets of neural firing properties" (2007, 323) and "Use of our phenomenal concepts does not show us that the relevant properties of our experiences are highly complex" (2007, 327). Note that the complaint in the second quotation is that phenomenal properties *fail to seem* physically complex, not that they *do seem* physically *non*-complex. The latter complaint, in effect, will be addressed in section 3.7.

argument (not necessarily in English, of course) as we introspect a current visual sensation of red:

Argument A

A1. My current sensation's phenomenal redness doesn't *seem* to me to be a physical or functional property.
A2. If phenomenal redness were (i.e., were identical to) the property of having so-and-so functional organization and rate of firing, then my current sensation's phenomenal redness *would* seem to me to be a physical or functional property.
∴ Phenomenal redness is not the property of having so-and-so functional organization and rate of firing.

Argument A is formulated here in English, but obviously none of the possible conscious mechanisms that I discuss requires that we mentally rehearse an argument in English, or indeed any other natural language.

Actually, Argument A is not one argument but three, because there are three importantly different ways of understanding the key expression "seem to be a physical or functional property." The expression may be paraphrased in each of the following three inequivalent ways:

SP1. Seem to be *identical with* a certain physical or functional property (that I have in mind).
SP2. Seem to be a property correctly classifiable as physical or functional (i.e., seem to be a property with the *meta-property* of being a physical or functional property).
SP3. Have introspectible features (roughly, an introspective appearance) that you would expect it to have if it were a physical or functional property. (Compare: "That nine-banded armadillo doesn't *seem mammalian*, for it doesn't have fur, which one expects mammals to have.")

"SP" is intended to suggest "*seem physical*."

I shall argue that, whichever paraphrase we pick, either A1 or A2 is unacceptable, and so Argument A fails. So even if the intuition of distinctness is produced in us by our more or less consciously rehearsing Argument A, it gives us no reason to believe that the phenomenal properties we are introspecting really are distinct from the physical or physically realized properties that we are considering as candidates for identity with the phenomenal properties.

First, then, let me consider premise A2 when "seem to be a physical or functional property" is paraphrased as SP1. So understood, A2 says this:

A2-SP1. If phenomenal redness were the very same property as having so-and-so functional organization and rate of firing, then my current sensation's phenomenal redness would seem to me to be identical with the property of having so-and-so functional organization and rate of firing.

The claim here is that, if phenomenal redness were having so-and-so functional organization and rate of firing, then a certain non-trivial identity claim would seem to me to be true. But for the identity claim to be non-trivial, two distinct concepts of the same property—two distinct ways of thinking about the same property—would need to be activated in my mind. One of the two concepts would obviously be whatever concept of phenomenal redness I use when I think introspectively about the phenomenal redness of a current sensation. What would the other concept be? Presumably it would be a concept of the property of having so-and-so functional organization and rate of firing that, like my concept of quantum-mechanical spin, I acquired as a result not of everyday perception or even of scientific observation but of *exposure to new words*—words new to me—in the specialist vocabulary of some relevant branch of science. *How* we acquire new *concepts* as part and parcel of learning new *words* is highly controversial, but *that* we do so seems hard to deny on reflection. How else to explain our ability to think about electrons or neurotransmitters or black holes?[8]

But now that the meaning of A2-SP1 is clear, the claim can easily be seen to be false. For it to be true, there would have to be psychological mechanisms that would (were physicalism true) generate mental states in which the phenomenal properties of one's sensations *seem* to be identical with those very physical or functional properties with which in fact they *are* identical. These mechanisms would therefore have to have reliable information concerning which particular physical or functional property is identical with which particular phenomenal property. But there is no remotely plausible way in which these mechanisms could have come to have such information. The information could hardly be innate, or manifest itself automatically in the course of normal human development. So it would have to be learnt. But

---

[8] Ruth Millikan has emphasized the datum, and offered an explanation of it (see, e.g., Millikan 1984, 151–3, and Millikan 2000, 89–90). I like her explanation, but I assume the datum could also be accommodated by other theories of concept-acquisition. Section 5.3 contains more of my views regarding concepts.

learning which particular phenomenal property is identical with which particular physical or functional property would require sophisticated empirical investigation—for example, to discover that a particular phenomenal property and a particular physical or functional property invariably co-occur, or turn out to play the same causal role.[9] Patently we do not conduct such empirical investigation consciously, and it would be extravagant to think we do so unconsciously, with the results fed to the mechanisms that generate identity-seemings. So A2-SP1 is not true.

Let me now consider premise A2 when "seem to be a physical or functional property" is paraphrased as SP2. Understood in this way, A2 claims this:

A2-SP2. If phenomenal redness were the very same property as having so-and-so functional organization and rate of firing, then my current sensation's phenomenal redness would seem to me to be a property correctly classifiable as physical or functional.

The claim here is that, if phenomenal redness were the physical or functional property of having so-and-so functional organization and rate of firing, then my current sensation's phenomenal redness would wear its status *as* physical or functional on its sleeve—it would somehow appear to my introspection already *labeled* as physical or functional.

But premise A2-SP2 is as implausible as its predecessor. For it to be true, we would have to contain a psychological mechanism that brought it about that an introspected property, *if* it were correctly classifiable as physical or functional, would automatically *seem* to the subject to be correctly classifiable as physical or functional. At a minimum, this mechanism would have to be capable of recognizing, whenever an introspected property is in fact physical or functional, *that* it is physical or functional (so that it could generate the mental state of seeming in response). The mechanism would therefore have to be sensitive to an introspected physical or functional property's meta-property of *being* physical or functional. What makes A2-SP2 highly implausible is this: (1) on the understanding of what makes a property physical that is relevant to whether phenomenal properties are physical, it is highly implausible that we contain a psychological mechanism sensitive to an introspected property's meta-property of being physical; and (2) it is also

---

[9] Some philosophers think that if physicalism is true, then, if we only knew *enough* about our physical natures, we could in principle discover a priori what mental properties we have (see, e.g., Chalmers 1996). But even if this is true, which I deny, it is clear that the intuition of distinctness does not arise in us in this way. We do not *in fact* know enough about our physical natures, and we do not *in fact* go through the necessary reasoning.

highly implausible that we contain a psychological mechanism sensitive to an introspected property's meta-property of being functional.

To elaborate: as noted in Chapter 1, for the theoretical purposes of this book we are taking physical properties to be those that physical sciences such as biochemistry, neurophysiology, and cell biology, as well as physics proper, attribute to things. For a property to be physical, then, is for it to be expressed, or expressible, by a term or terms drawn from the physical sciences. Accordingly, having a mass of 2.3 kg, having a charge of −0.35 C, and being electronegative all count as physical properties, as do having a firing rate in the 40–70 Hz range, being a synaptic vesicle, or occurring in visual area V4. My imaginary property of having so-and-so functional organization and rate of firing is, of course, intended to count as physical by this standard.[10] It is, however, implausible in the extreme that we contain a psychological mechanism sensitive to whether an introspected property is expressed, or expressible, by a term or terms drawn from the physical sciences. It would be absurd to suppose that everyone who experiences the intuition of distinctness possesses concepts of all such properties relevant to (i.e., perhaps identical with) phenomenal properties. But how otherwise could such a mechanism possibly work? And what advantage could the possession of such a mechanism confer on us? For essentially the same reasons, it is also highly implausible that we contain a psychological mechanism sensitive to an introspected property's meta-property of being functional. In this book, a functional property is understood, very liberally and very abstractly, as a *higher-order* property: a property such that something has the functional property if and only if the thing has some or other property that plays a certain causal (or computational) role, or has a certain teleo-function, or, more generally, meets a certain condition. But to identify a property with a functional property in this highly abstract sense is a very sophisticated cognitive act, and it is hard to see how a psychological mechanism could do it unless, incredibly, it was in effect a whole human mind in miniature; but a

---

[10] One can also understand a physical property more liberally as a property expressed, or expressible, by a term or terms drawn from the set of theories, whatever they turn out to be, that do a certain distinctive theoretical job, for example, that completely explain all non-biological and non-psychological phenomena. But our current best guess as to what those theories are is that they largely coincide with those that make up the physical sciences in their present form, and to the extent that they diverge from the physical sciences in their present form we don't know what they're like. So it would make little difference to the subsequent discussion if we adopted this alternative understanding of what is to count as a physical property. There is also an everyday use of "physical" of which, no doubt, perfectly good sense can be made (e.g., as in "physical methods of contraception"); but I doubt that neurotransmitters or electrons count as physical in this sense, and so I set it aside as irrelevant to current purposes.

psychological mechanism that couldn't do it presumably couldn't be sensitive to whether an introspected property is a functional property.

So much, then, for A2-SP2. Let us consider the third and final option: premise A2 when "seem to be a physical or functional property" is paraphrased as SP3. When A2 is understood in this third way, it claims this:

> A2-SP3. If phenomenal redness were the very same property as having so-and-so functional organization and rate of firing, then my current sensation's phenomenal redness would have introspectible features (roughly, an introspective appearance) that you would expect it to have if it were a physical or functional property.[11]

But Argument A still fails if "seem to be a physical or functional property" is paraphrased as SP3. For the expression "seem to be a physical or functional property" appears not only in premise A2 but also in premise A1. So if Argument A is to succeed, then both premise A1 and premise A2 must be acceptable to the introspecting subject when "seem to be a physical or functional property" is paraphrased as SP3. But premise A1 is not acceptable under that condition. When "seem to be a physical or functional property" is paraphrased as SP3, premise A1 claims this:

> A1-SP3. My current sensation's phenomenal redness doesn't have introspectible features (roughly, an introspective appearance) that you would expect it to have if it were a physical or functional property.

Is A1-SP3 acceptable to the introspecting subject? The phenomenal redness of a current visual sensation does indeed have introspectible features: it seems introspectively to have such features as being a phenomenal property, being a visual-phenomenal property, and being a color-phenomenal property. But for A1-SP3 to be true, these features must *not* be features that you would expect phenomenal redness to have if it were a physical or functional property. Are they not such features? At first sight, it may seem obvious that they are not, but on reflection it should not. If it seems obvious that they are not, then that is because we implicitly reason as follows: any features that you would expect phenomenal redness to have if it were a physical or functional property would be *physical* features; but being a visual-phenomenal property, being a color-phenomenal property, and any other introspectible features of phenomenal

---

[11] Recall William Robinson's observation (2007, 323): "a difference in seeing colors does not seem to be remotely like a difference in sets of neural firing properties."

redness are obviously not physical features; so they are not features that you would expect phenomenal redness to have if it were a physical or functional property. But it is *not* obvious that the introspectible features of phenomenal redness are not physical or functional features. (And, of course, if physicalism is true, they are!) Admittedly, they don't *seem* to be physical or functional features. But whether that's a reason to think that they *aren't* physical or functional features is tantamount to the question of whether Argument A is good, for the gist of Argument A is precisely that, since phenomenal properties don't *seem* to be physical or functional, they *aren't* physical or functional. So just to assume that, since the phenomenal features of phenomenal properties don't *seem* to be physical or functional, they *aren't* physical or functional is to assume the goodness of Argument A—or, more precisely, a variant of Argument A that concerns not the phenomenal properties of sensations but rather the phenomenal features of phenomenal properties. Premise A1-SP3 is therefore not a premise to which the introspecting subject is entitled.[12]

At this stage, it is tempting to suggest a modification to A1-SP3 that acknowledges the point just made:

> A1-SP3*. My current sensation's phenomenal redness doesn't have introspectible features that (i) you would expect it to have if phenomenal redness were a physical or functional property, and that (ii) seem physical or functional to me.

This premise seems to be true, because phenomenal redness doesn't seem to us introspectively to have *any* features that seem physical or functional to us, still less any such features that also meet condition (i). But for premise A1-SP3* to support the conclusion that phenomenal redness is not the property of having so-and-so functional organization and rate of firing, it must be combined with the following modification of premise A2:

> A2-SP3*. If phenomenal redness were the very same property as having so-and-so functional organization and rate of firing, then my current

---

[12] An introspecting subject might, of course, have some completely independent reason to think that all introspectible properties are neither physical nor functional—some completely independent argument for property dualism, say. But if *that* is the subject's reason to believe A1-SP3, then the intuition of distinctness cannot give the subject any reason to think that phenomenal properties are neither physical nor functional that is *independent* of the prior reason to think that all introspectible properties are neither physical nor functional; nor can the intuition of distinctness provide a reason *stronger* than the prior reason, because the reason to believe a deductive argument's conclusion that is provided by the argument can be no stronger than the reason to believe the argument's weakest premise.

sensation's phenomenal redness would have introspectible features that (i) you would expect it to have if phenomenal redness were a physical or functional property, and that (ii) seem physical or functional to me.

Premise A2-SP3*, however, is not at all plausible.

To see why, let us first ask what it is for a property that I am thinking of to *seem* physical or functional to me as I think of it—to seem to me physical or functional, that is, in the relevant senses of "physical" and "functional" explained above. For example, as I think of the properties of having a mass of 2.3 kg and having a charge of −0.35 C (e.g., in thoughts that I would express in English by using the predicates "has a mass of 2.3 kg" and "has a charge of −0.35 C"), these properties seem physical to me. How so? There is surely no perceptual or introspective *appearance* common to all physical properties; and in any case a property that I am thinking of doesn't have a perceptual or introspective appearance simply in virtue of my thinking of it. The answer, I suggest, is that a property that I am thinking of seems physical to me because I am thinking of it *by using a particular kind of concept*, a concept that I have acquired as a result of my exposure (via reading a science textbook, say) to a particular *expression* that is antecedently thought by me to belong to the distinctive theoretical vocabulary of the physical sciences. Consider a homely illustration. Even if one has never seen table salt, one can think of it by using a concept of table salt acquired during early childhood by hearing one's parents use the word "salt" at mealtimes. If one thinks of table salt in *this* way, it *doesn't* seem physical (or rather chemical) to one. (One might, of course, be *told* that salt is a chemical; but we're talking about its seeming physical or chemical to one just in virtue of one's thinking about it.) But one can also think of table salt by using a concept of table salt acquired during a school chemistry lesson by hearing or reading the complex chemical expression "sodium chloride." If one thinks of table salt in this second way, then it *does* seem physical (or rather chemical) to one. What is going on here? Presumably, when we have acquired a concept as a result of exposure to a particular term, a psychological connection between the concept and the term remains, perhaps in the form of our retaining a *disposition* (i) to use the term to give linguistic expression to beliefs involving the concept, and (ii) to form beliefs involving the concept when we hear or see the term in sentences. If so, then it may be that, whenever we use the *concept* to think about the property it expresses, the connection with the *term* is activated, together with any information we might retain about the term (e.g., that it belongs to the distinctive theoretical vocabulary of one of the physical sciences). And likewise, I suggest, for a property's seeming *functional* to one as one thinks of it: a property that I am thinking of seems functional to me because I am thinking of it by using a concept that I have acquired as a result of my exposure to an expression antecedently thought by me—as a result, no doubt, of very sophisticated reflections—to belong to the distinctive theoretical vocabulary of a science that deals in functional properties.[13]

Now if I am right about what it is for a property about which one is thinking to seem physical or functional to one, then, in order for A2-SP3* to be true of everyone who experiences the intuition of distinctness, everyone who experiences the intuition would have to be capable of expressing the phenomenal features of phenomenal properties (should these features turn out to be physical or functional) by using concepts of these features acquired from exposure to the distinctive theoretical vocabulary of the relevant physical or functional sciences; otherwise the phenomenal features of their phenomenal properties would not *seem* physical or functional to them, even if in fact they *were*. In that case, however, A2-SP3* could not possibly be true, because the vast majority of people who experience the intuition of distinctness have never been exposed to the distinctive theoretical vocabulary of the relevant physical or functional sciences; their scientific education did not extend anything like that far.

What about people whose scientific education *did* extend that far? Might A2-SP3* be true of them, at least? Probably not. An initial doubt arises from a consideration concerning the representational repertoire of introspection. If I am right about what it is for a property about which one is thinking to seem physical or functional to one, and if the phenomenal features of the phenomenal redness of one's current sensation seem physical or functional to one, then, as we have already noted, one must be expressing these features by using concepts acquired as a result of exposure to terms belonging to the distinctive theoretical vocabulary of the relevant physical or functional sciences. But more is required: the representations that contain these concepts must be the outputs of one's capacity to introspect, for the phenomenal redness of one's current sensation seems to one *introspectively* to have the feature of being a visual-phenomenal property. But it seems doubtful that the output-representations of one's capacity to introspect contain concepts acquired as a result of exposure to the distinctive theoretical vocabulary of any science, even for people who have such concepts. More likely, the capacity to introspect would resemble other specialized representational capacities in this regard. For example, the sensory systems that inform us about

---

[13] Most properties that are in fact functional cannot, I hold, be known to be so a priori; for example, to be one kind of acid is to be a proton donor, but this truth had to be discovered empirically.

what is going on right now inside our bodies (e.g., systems that monitor our CO_2 levels, the stretching of our lungs, vasodilation in our skin, and so on) represent indisputably physical or functional features of bodily states, but they don't do so by using concepts produced by exposure to the proprietary vocabulary of the biomedical sciences, not even in scientifically educated people awash with such concepts. Neither, of course, do our external senses (e.g., vision) represent everyday objects in ways made possible by exposure to the proprietary vocabulary of chemistry. People who are fully convinced that grains of salt are large crystals of sodium chloride still do not *see* grains of salt as large crystals of sodium chloride.[14]

But even if the output-representations of one's capacity to introspect could and do contain concepts acquired as a result of exposure to scientific vocabulary, the truth of A2-SP3* is not assured. If I am right about what it is for a property about which one is thinking to seem physical or functional to one, then, in order for features of the phenomenal redness of one's current sensation to seem physical or functional to one, one's capacity for introspection would have to be able to generate *accurate* representations of the phenomenal features of phenomenal redness: one's capacity for introspection would have somehow to embody correct information concerning *which* physical or functional feature each phenomenal feature of phenomenal redness was. But there is no remotely plausible way in which it could do so. As noted already, learning which phenomenal *property* of a sensation is identical with which physical or functional property would require sophisticated empirical investigation that it would be extravagant to think we carry out unconsciously; and exactly the same goes for learning which phenomenal *feature* of a phenomenal property is identical with which physical or functional feature.

Argument A fails, I conclude, no matter how interpreted. So even if the intuition of distinctness is produced by our more or less consciously rehearsing Argument A, it gives us no reason to believe that introspected phenomenal properties really are distinct from whatever physical or physically realized properties we are considering.

3.3 Digression: A Philosophers' Argument

I introduced Argument A as articulating a commonsensically skeptical reaction to the suggestion that phenomenal redness just is a certain physical or

---

[14] Here I anticipate a major element in my proposed explanation of why we have the intuition of distinctness; see section 5.3 passim.

functional property, rather than as a philosophers' objection to the suggestion. Unsurprisingly, however, there *is* a philosophers' objection to physicalism about phenomenal properties that closely resembles Argument A (see, e.g., Nida-Rümelin 2007; Goff 2011; see also Damnjanovic 2012). Since it fails for the same reason that Argument A fails, it is worth a brief digression. The objection can be formulated as follows:

Argument P

P1. If phenomenal redness is a physical (or functional) property, then the essence of phenomenal redness is physical (or functional).
P2. Introspection reveals the essence of phenomenal redness.
P3. If introspection reveals the essence of phenomenal redness, and the essence of phenomenal redness is physical (or functional), then introspection reveals the essence of phenomenal redness *as* physical (or functional).
P4. Introspection doesn't reveal the essence of phenomenal redness *as* physical (or functional).
∴. Phenomenal redness isn't a physical (or functional) property.

Premise P1 is hard to deny, since, whatever exactly the essence of a property is meant to be, it's hard to see how the essence of phenomenal redness could fail to be physical or functional if phenomenal redness itself is a physical or functional property. Premise P2 results from taking the intuition of revelation (discussed in section 2.2) at face value. And premise P4 is clearly true. Presumably, if introspection revealed the essence of phenomenal redness *as* physical or functional, then physicalism about phenomenal redness would be uncontroversial!

The trouble with Argument P arises from premise P3, which expresses the conviction that, if phenomenal redness really had a physical or functional essence, then our introspective representation of this essence would somehow be bound, automatically, to make its physical or functional character *manifest* to us. But, as I claimed in section 3.2, the only way in which our introspective representation of this essence could automatically make the physical or functional character of the essence manifest to us would be by using explicitly physical or functional concepts to represent the essence, explicitly physical or functional concepts being those acquired as a result of exposure to expressions antecedently thought by us to belong to the proprietary vocabulary of the physical or functional sciences. And there is no reason to expect—and abundant reason not to expect—that introspection is capable of using explicitly physical or functional concepts to represent the essence. First, hardly anybody even possesses the explicitly physical or functional concepts (e.g., cognitive neuroscientific concepts) that would be needed (if the phenomenal properties of our current sensations were indeed physical or functional). Secondly, none of us—not even the best educated scientifically—seem ever to form *introspective* beliefs that contain explicitly physical or functional concepts. Finally, the vast majority (at least) of the concepts that we use in thinking introspectively about phenomenal properties can't have been acquired from exposure to linguistic expressions of *any* kind. We can, for example, think introspectively about thousands of phenomenal colors, even though (unless we are painters or interior decorators) we only know a few dozen *words* for the (non-phenomenal) colors of material objects. So it can't be that *all* the concepts we use to think introspectively about phenomenal colors have arisen from our learning of words, and it may well be that none of them have; they may be innate, or they may develop automatically when our mechanisms of introspection are activated by novel phenomenal properties. And if none of them have arisen from our learning of words, then we might simply have no ability at all to use explicitly physical or functional concepts to think introspectively about properties. It is true that by reading *Architectural Digest* we can learn a new word for a non-phenomenal color, "persimmon," say, and then generate from this English word *a* new concept expressing the property of being phenomenally persimmon; but, as is clear from our failure thereby to gain an ability to *imagine seeing* something persimmon, we don't thereby gain a *phenomenal* concept of the property of being phenomenally persimmon, a concept that we can use to think *introspectively* that a current visual sensation is phenomenally persimmon.[15]

Perhaps I am wrong, and there *is* another way in which our introspective representation of the physical or functional essence of phenomenal redness could automatically make the physical or functional character of the essence manifest to us; but if so, then someone should be able to say what it is and explain how it works. Until they do, we are not entitled, I say, to infer that phenomenal redness doesn't have a physical or functional essence from the evident fact that introspection doesn't reveal the essence of phenomenal redness to us *as* physical (or functional).

---

[15] Chapter 5 contains much more discussion of these ideas, especially section 5.3.

3.4 Not Having a Spatial Location

An initially plausible idea is that every physical (or physically realized) thing has a spatial location. The idea is most plausible for physical things that are *objects*, because everyday physical objects such as spoons, trees, and buildings have spatial locations. True, if electrons and other physical objects are point particles, then they lack spatial *extensions*; but they can still have spatial *locations*. True, too, electrons and other physical particles can be in quantum-mechanical superpositions of different spatial locations and so, on some understandings of what superpositions are, can lack definite spatial locations; but being in a superposition of different spatial locations is presumably still *some* sort of spatial-location property. The idea that everything physical (or physically realized) has a spatial location is also plausible for physical things that are *property-instances*. True, it's often hard to specify the spatial location of a physical property-instance more precisely than by saying that it's located where the object bearing the property is located. For example, we can say that, to a first approximation, (i) Smith's weighing 150 lb. and (ii) Smith's being pregnant are both spatially located where Smith herself is spatially located, though surely (i) and (ii) don't have *precisely* the same spatial location. But imprecise spatial locations, such as (i) and (ii) have, are still spatial locations.

The idea that every physical (or physically realized) thing has a spatial location suggests a second possible conscious mechanism by which the intuition of distinctness might arise in us. For this mechanism to operate is for the intuition of distinctness to arise in us because, as we introspect a current visual sensation of red, we more or less consciously rehearse the following argument:

<u>Argument B</u>

B1. If phenomenal redness is the property of having so-and-so functional organization and rate of firing,[16] then the phenomenal redness of my current visual sensation has a spatial location.
B2. But the phenomenal redness of my current visual sensation doesn't have a spatial location (e.g., in my head, where a neurally realized property might be expected to be).

---

[16] This property, it may be recalled, is assumed to be a physical property of a particular pattern of neuronal firing in, say, the V4 region of the subject's visual cortex, this pattern being a plausible candidate to be, or at least to realize, the subject's current visual sensation.

∴ Phenomenal redness isn't the property of having so-and-so functional organization and rate of firing.

Argument B is formally valid, but how plausible are its premises? Premise B1 is very plausible given that everything physical (or functional and physically realized) has a spatial location. If phenomenal redness is the property of having so-and-so functional organization and rate of firing, then the phenomenal redness of my current visual sensation is located where the particular pattern of neuronal firing in V4 that currently *has* so-and-so functional organization and rate of firing is located. Are there also good grounds for premise B2? I will argue that there are not, so that Argument B fails, and hence that, if the intuition of distinctness arises in us because we more or less consciously rehearse Argument B, it gives us no reason to believe that introspected phenomenal properties really are distinct from whatever physical or physically realized properties we are considering.[17]

Premise B1 would be credible to us at any time. But we experience the intuition of distinctness regarding phenomenal redness only when we are introspecting phenomenal redness. So premise B2 would have to be credible to us only during introspection. Most likely, then, the phenomenal redness of our current visual sensation would have to *seem* to us introspectively *not* to have a spatial location; and this introspective seeming would then lead us to *believe* that the phenomenal redness doesn't have a spatial location. But does the phenomenal redness of a current visual sensation really seem to us introspectively not to have a spatial location? I don't think so. As far as I can tell from conscientious reflection on my own case, the phenomenal redness of a current visual sensation doesn't seem to me introspectively not to have a spatial location. Moreover, its seeming to us introspectively not to have a spatial location would require the phenomenal redness to seem to us introspectively not to be *anywhere*—to be located at *no* place; and the negative universal quantification embedded in the predicate would make this an unprecedentedly sophisticated content for an introspective seeming to have. Finally, it is worth noting that there is some danger of inadvertently inferring that

---

[17] J. J. C. Smart criticizes a superficially similar argument: "The after-image is not in physical space. The brain-process is. So the after-image is not a brain-process" (1959, 150–1). Smart replies that the argument is an *ignoratio*: he wishes to identify the experience of *having* a yellowy-orange afterimage, not the afterimage itself, with a brain process, and the experience *is* in physical space, just as the brain process is.

(i) it *is* the case that the phenomenal redness of a current visual sensation seems to us introspectively *not* to have a spatial location

from the claim that

(ii) it's *not* the case that the phenomenal redness of a current visual sensation *does* seem to us introspectively to have a spatial location.

Claim (ii) is plausible (see section 3.5), but claim (i) doesn't follow from it. It doesn't follow because claim (ii) would be true if introspection tells us *nothing*, one way or the other, about the spatial location of sensations and their phenomenal properties, just as olfaction tells us nothing, one way or the other, about the *colors* of clouds of molecules. But if introspection tells us nothing about the spatial location of sensations and their phenomenal properties, then—contrary to claim (i)—the phenomenal redness of a current visual sensation wouldn't seem to us introspectively to *lack* a spatial location.

3.5 Not Seeming to Have a Spatial Location

If the weaker claim (ii)—that it's not the case that the phenomenal redness of a current visual sensation seems to us introspectively to have a spatial location—is true, then a third possible conscious mechanism by which the intuition of distinctness might arise in us naturally suggests itself. This third mechanism is our more or less consciously rehearsing the following argument:

Argument C

C1. If phenomenal redness is the property of having so-and-so functional organization and rate of firing,[18] then the phenomenal redness of my current visual sensation seems to me introspectively to have a spatial location.
C2. But the phenomenal redness of my current visual sensation doesn't seem to me introspectively to have a spatial location.
∴ Phenomenal redness isn't the property of having so-and-so functional organization and rate of firing.

---

[18] As before, this property is assumed to be a physical property of a particular pattern of neuronal firing in, say, the V4 region of the subject's visual cortex, this pattern being a plausible candidate to be, or at least to realize, the subject's current visual sensation.

Argument C is deductively valid, and premise C2 is just a special case of claim (ii). But what about premise C1? Do those who experience the intuition of distinctness have good grounds for it?

Let us understand a physical *state* to be the possession by an object that is physical (or physically realized) of a property that is physical (or physically realized). Then, if we *perceive* (i.e., see, hear, smell, taste, or feel) a physical state, we certainly expect the physical state to seem to us *sensorily* (i.e., visually, auditorily, etc.) to have a spatial location, even if the location is indefinite or imprecise (e.g., in front of us, overhead, around us, in our mouth). And, given physicalism, this would be true of a current visual sensation of red, if it were somehow possible for me to gaze at Rothko's *Untitled*, while also sneaking a look, via a powerfully magnifying autocerebroscope, at the instantiation of the property of having so-and-so functional organization and rate of firing by the right pattern of firing in V4 of my visual cortex: this physical state of me would seem to me *visually* to have a spatial location—in my visual cortex. However, there is no reason for us to expect—as premise C1 assumes—that a current sensation's being phenomenally red, even if it is a physical state, will seem to us *introspectively* to have a spatial location. There is no reason to think that our capacity for introspection includes *any* ability to represent the spatial locations of sensations, or of their states of having phenomenal properties. Human representational capacities are highly selective in what they can represent. Vision represents objects' colors and shapes, but not their sounds or chemical constitutions—and not even all colors, for butterflies can see colors that humans cannot. Hearing represents objects' sounds, but not their temperatures or chemical constitutions—and not even all sounds, since dogs can hear sounds too high for humans to hear. It is true that the five traditional external senses always represent (if only imprecisely) the location of the property-instances that they represent. But not all human representational systems represent locations; generalized anxiety, for example, seems to represent the existence of danger, but without attributing a location to it. Moreover, the five traditional external senses directly guide our bodily movements or locomotion in the world, so their representing the locations of things, especially in relation to ourselves, has obvious utility. By contrast, our fitness would not obviously be increased if introspection could represent sensations, or their having phenomenal properties, as being located where (if physicalism is true) they actually are—if, for example, introspection could represent a sensation's being phenomenally red as being located in the back of one's head (where the primary visual cortex is), or a toothache's being throbbing as being located in the top half of one's head (where the somatosensory cortex is). There are, then, no grounds for believing premise C1, and Argument C fails. Consequently, if the intuition of distinctness arises in us because, under the right conditions, we more or less consciously rehearse Argument C, then once again it gives us no reason to believe that introspected phenomenal properties really are distinct from whatever physical or physically realized properties we are considering.

Premise C2 is worth a further word or two. I have allowed that C2 is true—that, as I gaze upon Rothko's *Untitled*, the phenomenal redness of my visual sensation doesn't seem to me introspectively to have a spatial location. But, at the same time, the redness of something—a surface—*does* seem to me to have a spatial location—a few feet in front of me. The two claims are consistent because they concern two different kinds of seeming. Premise C2 concerns *introspective* seeming—whereby a current visual sensation or a property of a sensation seems to be a certain way. The second claim concerns *visual* seeming—whereby some non-mental object external to the subject seems to be a certain way.[19] The two claims also concern two different kinds of redness. Premise C2 speaks of *phenomenal* redness—of being red in the sense in which a sensation can still be red even though nothing in the subject's brain or visual environment is red in the ordinary sense applicable to ripe tomatoes and oxygenated blood. The second claim does, of course, speak of being red in the ordinary sense. Finally, the *bearers* of the two kinds of redness are different—a sensation and an external surface, respectively. So: the phenomenal redness of my visual sensation doesn't seem to me, introspectively, to have a spatial location, while the ordinary redness of an external surface does seem to me, visually, to have a spatial location. Bodily sensations present a more troubling challenge to C2 than do perceptual sensations, because a pain can certainly seem to me, introspectively, to be in my left wrist. But the phrase "in my left wrist" should not be taken to imply that my pain is literally located in my left wrist. After all, the same pain can also seem to me, introspectively, to be stabbing; but no one thinks that "stabbing" should be taken to imply that my pain is literally engaged in the action of stabbing. We should treat "in my left wrist" in the same non-literal way we treat "stabbing." The most plausible interpretation of both expressions, when used to report the introspectible phenomenal character of a sensation, is that they report the sensation's *telling* us something—that some stabbing, perhaps, is occurring in my left wrist.[20]

---

[19] Its seeming to me visually that something is red is my having a visual sensation that represents that something is red; see also section 3.7.

[20] Here I assume the representationalism about phenomenal properties introduced in section 3.7.

3.6 Phenomenal Features of Phenomenal Properties

A fourth possible conscious mechanism that might be thought to produce the intuition of distinctness in us is the more or less conscious rehearsal of reasoning from the premise that the introspected phenomenal property has some introspectible feature that is lacked by the particular physical (or functional) property under consideration. For example, phenomenal redness seems introspectively to have the very general feature of *being a phenomenal property*, the more specific feature of *being a visual-phenomenal property* (as opposed to, say, an olfactory-phenomenal property), and the still more specific feature of *being a color-phenomenal property* (as opposed to, say, a shape-phenomenal property). Let us continue to imagine the thinker as attending to the phenomenal redness of a visual sensation caused by viewing Rothko's *Untitled*. Then, according to the present hypothesis, the intuition of distinctness arises in us because we more or less consciously rehearse reasoning that could be expressed in English, at least approximately, as follows:

Argument D

D1. This property (i.e., phenomenal redness) of my current visual sensation has the feature of being a visual-phenomenal property.
D2. The property of having so-and-so functional organization and rate of firing doesn't have this feature.
∴ This property isn't the property of having so-and-so functional organization and rate of firing.

The expression "this property" that occurs both in premise D1 and in the conclusion should be taken to correspond to the first-person *subject-concept* that one would use to *refer* to phenomenal redness when rehearsing the argument. A subject-concept that refers to a property should be distinguished, of course, from a *predicative concept* that can be used to attribute the property to something. The expression "the property of having so-and-so functional organization and rate of firing" is, as before, just a placeholder for the physical property under consideration, some plausible candidate for identification with phenomenal redness. The feature that D1 attributes to phenomenal redness, that of being a visual-phenomenal property, is only an example of a feature that the first premise of such reasoning might ascribe to a phenomenal property; obviously other phenomenal features would serve as well. Premise D1 is presumably something the thinker knows by introspection.

The conclusion of Argument D follows from its premises given the logical principle that, necessarily, for any x and any y, if x and y don't have exactly the same properties, then x is not one and the same thing as y.[21] This logical principle is uncontroversial, so whether Argument D gives the thinker reason to believe its conclusion depends on whether the thinker is warranted in accepting premise D2.

At first sight, D2 seems obvious. But underlying our sense of D2's obviousness is presumably the following train of thought: "The only features had by such physical properties of neural circuits as having a certain functional organization and rate of firing are physical features, presumably those expressible in the proprietary terminology of the neurosciences. But being a visual-phenomenal property obviously isn't one of these physical features. So being a visual-phenomenal property isn't one of the features had by the physical property of having a certain functional organization and rate of firing." And this train of thought is defective. Its second premise—that being a visual-phenomenal property isn't a physical feature—can't be true if physicalism is true. So either the thinker begs the question against physicalism by just assuming the premise or the thinker has some prior warrant for it. But what could the thinker's warrant for it be? Because it would have to be something available to *everyone* who has the intuition of distinctness regarding phenomenal redness, the thinker's warrant would presumably be an *antecedent* intuition of distinctness to the effect that *being a visual-phenomenal property* couldn't possibly be whatever physical or physically realized feature the thinker considered as a candidate for identity with it. But in that case a problematic explanatory circularity would afflict the hypothesis we are currently considering—that the intuition of distinctness regarding phenomenal redness gives us reason to believe that phenomenal redness is distinct from having so-and-so functional organization and rate of firing *because* (i) the intuition arises from our more or less conscious rehearsal of Argument D, and (ii) Argument D is good. For if the thinker's reason for endorsing premise D2 of Argument D had to rely on an antecedent intuition of distinctness regarding being a visual-phenomenal property, then Argument D would be good only if the antecedent intuition of distinctness gave the thinker reason to believe that being a visual-phenomenal property is distinct from whatever

---

[21] The logical principle is usually called "Leibniz's Law," though I have seen this term used differently. A commoner, but logically equivalent, formulation of Leibniz's Law is this: necessarily, for any x and any y, if x is one and the same thing as y, then x and y have exactly the same properties. Leibniz's Law is also known as the Principle of the Indiscernibility of Identicals.

physical or physically realized feature the thinker was considering. But how *any* intuition of distinctness could give someone reason to believe the content of the intuition is precisely what the hypothesis we are currently considering is meant to explain. This hypothesis would therefore have the same deficiency as a hypothesis that sought to explain the operation of a perpetual motion machine by positing a second perpetual motion machine inside the first one. In both cases, the original hypothesis would require for its success something we do not have, namely, a second—and successful—hypothesis with the same explanatory goal as the original hypothesis. And to propose the *same* hypothesis over and over again—an infinite sequence of rehearsals of variants of Argument D—would be as implausible empirically as an infinite series of nested perpetual motion machines.

I conclude that, if the intuition of distinctness arises in us because we more or less consciously rehearse Argument D, the intuition gives us no reason to believe that introspected phenomenal properties really are distinct from whatever physical or physically realized properties we are considering.

3.7 The Homogeneity of Phenomenal Properties

If you attend to the phenomenal redness of the visual sensation produced in you by Rothko's *Untitled*, you will probably be struck by a certain *homogeneity* (or continuity, or smoothness) of the phenomenal redness, a certain *grainlessness*. At the same time, you know that neural firings are events involving neurons, which are made of molecules. And so it seems hard to understand how any merely physical or physically realized functional property of an assemblage of neurons could be homogeneous in the way in which phenomenal redness is. Wouldn't a physical or physically realized functional property of an assemblage of neurons have to be grainy—the discontinuous sum, so to speak, of the physical properties of the individual molecules that make up the assemblage—and hence *not* homogeneous? If a physical or physically realized functional property would have to be grainy, then phenomenal redness couldn't be a physical or physically realized functional property.[22] These reflections suggest another possible conscious mechanism that might be hypothesized to produce the intuition of distinctness in us. If this mechanism operates, then, as we attend to the phenomenal redness

---

[22] This apparent homogeneity also seems to be a problem for panpsychism (see, e.g., Goff et al. 2022, in section 4.4.2 "The Structural Mismatch Problem").

of a visual sensation, we more or less consciously rehearse the following argument:

Argument E

E1. This property (i.e., phenomenal redness) of my current sensation is homogeneous.
E2. The property of having so-and-so functional organization and rate of firing[23] isn't homogeneous.
∴ This property isn't the property of having so-and-so functional organization and rate of firing.

As above, the expression "this property" should be taken to correspond to the first-person subject-concept that the arguer would use, in rehearsing the argument, to refer to the phenomenal redness of his or her current visual sensation. And the logical principle by which the premises entail the conclusion is again Leibniz's Law. Both premises have some plausibility, in light of either introspection (for premise E1) or general knowledge (for premise E2).[24]

Let us look more closely at premise E1. It is presumably true, and known by introspection to be true, for *some* sense of "homogeneous." But introspection doesn't tell us what that sense is, that is, the nature of the relevant kind of homogeneity. A good starting point for an inquiry into its nature is the following *natural conception* of homogeneity: if the color of a thing is homogeneous, then (i) the thing in question is (or has) a *surface* of some kind, and (ii) its color is homogeneous in the sense that between no two colored regions on the surface is there a region that lacks the color.[25] But while the natural conception is an attractive account of the homogeneity of

---

[23] As before, this property is assumed to be a physical property of a particular pattern of neuronal firing in, say, the V4 region of the subject's visual cortex, this pattern being a plausible candidate to be, or at least to realize, the subject's current visual sensation.
[24] Argument E may sound like Wilfrid Sellars's so-called Grain Argument, but in fact it's different. For Sellars, the homogeneity of phenomenal color was *not* established on the basis of introspection (Lycan 1987, 94).
[25] We would probably count the redness of a physical surface encountered in daily life as homogeneous in this sense so long as no non-red sub-regions were visible to the naked eye under normal conditions of observation, even though, with the aid of a magnifying glass, we could make out sub-regions of the surface that were not red. But for the phenomenal redness of a sensation to count as homogeneous, the redness would, I think, have to be *ultimately* homogeneous, so that between no two red regions was there be any non-red region at all. For if it weren't ultimately homogeneous, then at a small enough scale (perhaps discernible by someone paying special attention and trained to introspect) it would be grainy, which would be compatible with its being a physical or physically realized functional property.

the ordinary color of an everyday physical object, for example, a child's toy, it's not easy to see on reflection how the conception could be carried over to apply to the homogeneity of the phenomenal color of a sensation. An initial difficulty is that the natural conception defines the homogeneity of a thing's color in terms of regions of a *surface*. But what could be the relevant surface in the case of a homogeneously red sensation? The brain contains neither an internal movie screen—obviously—nor (relevant) colored surfaces of any other physical kind. Is there more room for maneuver if we allow that dualism of some kind might be true? But substance dualism has traditionally denied that immaterial minds are spatially extended, which seems to rule out an immaterial surface. And it's entirely unclear how property dualism—the view that physically composed brains have immaterial as well as physical properties—could allow for a sensation to have a surface. The suggestion that I am overlooking the obvious idea that a visual sensation has (or somehow involves) a *phenomenal* surface merely promises the chief advantage of theft over honest toil—getting something for nothing—unless it's accompanied by some explanation of what a phenomenal surface would be; "It's a surface—just not a material one" tells us nothing.

There is a second and even more serious difficulty with trying to make the natural conception apply to the homogeneity of the phenomenal redness (say) of a sensation. The natural conception requires that the surface in terms of which the homogeneity of redness is defined be *red*; but there seems to be no suitable sense of "red" available. Only material surfaces can be red in the sense in which everyday physical objects can be called "red," but in the case of a phenomenally red sensation no relevant material surface is red. And it beggars belief that the surface (somehow) involved in a phenomenally red sensation should be red in a sense of "red" *entirely unrelated* to the sense in which a material surface can be red; that suggestion would make our use of the same word in the two cases a sheer coincidence. A better suggestion acknowledges the double life of "red," and of other color terms, but proposes that there are two related senses of "red": (i) a basic sense and (ii) a derivative sense, and, correspondingly, two different but related kinds of redness. According to this suggestion, "red" in the basic sense expresses a property of *sensations*, while "red" in the derivative sense expresses a distinct but related property of *material objects*, roughly, the property of being disposed to produce, in normal observers under normal conditions, visual sensations that are red in the basic sense. This familiar suggestion, however, plausible though it is if we confine our attention to the case of color and other so-called secondary qualities, faces a serious problem and cannot, therefore, supply the natural conception of the homogeneity of color with what it needs in order for it to be applied to the homogeneity of a sensation's phenomenal redness, namely, a satisfactory sense in which the surface involved (somehow) in a phenomenally red sensation can be called "red."

The problem with the familiar suggestion arises because, while the homogeneity of phenomenal redness is an introspectible feature of sensations, it is far from being the only introspectible feature of sensations; and "red" (plus other color terms) are far from being the only terms that we apply both to sensations and to everyday material things. If introspection tells us that visual sensations can be homogeneously red, and hence red, then it also tells us, *in just the same way and with equal force*, that sensations have all sorts of other phenomenal properties: it tells us that visual sensations can be *round* (e.g., an afterimage can be round), that the bodily sensations felt during anxiety can be *fluttering* and *in the chest*, that pains can be *burning*, or *sharp*, or *stabbing*, or *throbbing*, that olfactory sensations can be *citrusy*, and so on. And all the italicized terms are, of course, like "red," also and indeed much more frequently applied to everyday material objects or events. Therefore, just as we must ask in what sense a visual sensation (as opposed to a children's toy) can be called "red," we must also ask in what sense sensations of other kinds (as opposed to everyday material objects or events) can be called "round," or "fluttering," or "in the chest," or "burning," or "sharp," or "stabbing," or "throbbing," or "citrusy." Furthermore, because these questions apparently concern multiple different instances of a single phenomenon, they probably have a uniform answer; it *could* be that calling a visual sensation "red" is an entirely different beast from calling a visual sensation "round" or a pain "sharp," and so forth, but it is far less likely.[26] So if the familiar suggestion—to distinguish a basic from a derivative sense of any term applied both to material objects and to sensations—gives the correct account of the sense in which a sensation can be called "red," then it probably also gives the correct account of the senses in which sensations can be called "round," or "fluttering," or "in the chest," or "burning," or "sharp," or "stabbing," or "throbbing," or "citrusy"—which is to say that, probably, for each

---

[26] If one endorses the traditional distinction between primary qualities (e.g., redness) and secondary qualities (e.g., roundness), then one may feel comfortable declining to extend the third suggestion to "round" and the rest. But one is still left with the problem of explaining the sense or senses in which both after-images and coins are "round." It is an unacknowledged cost of the traditional distinction that it prevents a uniform treatment of "red" and "round," even though the redness and the roundness of an after-image are on a par introspectively, and "red" and "round" apparently live the same double life.

of these expressions there are two related senses: (i) a basic sense and (ii) a derivative sense, and, corresponding to these two senses, two different but related properties. For example, there is probably a basic sense of "burning," as in "a burning pain," in which "burning" expresses a phenomenal property of sensations, a distinctive way in which a bodily sensation can feel, and a derivative sense of "burning," as in "a burning log," in which "burning" refers to the disposition to produce, in normal observers under normal conditions, bodily sensations that are burning in the basic sense.

However, if a distinction between a basic and a derivative sense of such expressions as "burning," "fluttering," and "in the chest" is highly implausible, then so is a distinction between a basic and a derivative sense of "red." And a distinction between a basic and a derivative sense of such expressions as "burning," "fluttering," "in the chest," and so forth *is* highly implausible. It entails claims such as the following concerning the *derivative* senses of the expressions in question:

- to say that human lungs are "in the chest" is to say not that they are located inside the ribcage but that they are disposed to produce, in normal observers under normal conditions, bodily sensations that are "in the chest" in the basic sense;
- to say that razor blades are "sharp" is to say not that they are good at cutting but that they are disposed to produce, in normal observers under normal conditions, bodily sensations that are "sharp" in the basic sense;
- to say that balls are "round" is to say not that they are objects bounded by a surface consisting of all points at a given distance from the point constituting its center but that they are disposed to produce, in normal observers under normal conditions, bodily sensations that are "round" in the basic sense;
- to say that the leaves of a tree are "fluttering" is to say not that they are rapidly moving a small distance back and forth but that they are disposed to produce, in normal observers under normal conditions, bodily sensations that are "fluttering" in the basic sense.

Such claims are hard to believe. So we should, at the very least, avoid commitment to them if we can. And fortunately we can: there is a better way of understanding our use of such terms as "red," "burning," and "in the chest" to describe sensations than the one provided by the familiar suggestion—and there is in consequence a better way of understanding the nature of the homogeneity of a sensation's phenomenal color than the one provided by pressing into service the natural conception of the homogeneity of a thing's ordinary color.

Both these better ways presuppose an unorthodox version of *representationalism* about the phenomenal properties of sensations. Both orthodox and unorthodox versions of representationalism agree in presupposing that sensations are descriptive mental representations, and therefore have intentional content.[27] They both hold that *perceptual* sensations represent current states of one's environment, while *bodily* sensations represent current conditions in, or on the surface of, one's body. Beliefs are also descriptive mental representations, of course, but sensations are held to differ from beliefs in at least two important ways (see, e.g., Tye 1995a, chs. 4 and 5). First, sensations belong to a distinctive *system* (or perhaps to distinctive *systems*) of representation—which is to say that each sensation is a permissible combination of certain semantic constituents, and the semantic content of each sensation is determined, in accordance with certain principles, by (i) its semantic constituents and (ii) their mode of combination in the sensation. But because the semantic constituents of sensations need not have the same contents as the semantic constituents of beliefs, the expressive power of sensations need not coincide with that of beliefs, and (I assume) diverges from it dramatically. Second, sensations and beliefs play different causal roles within the overall cognitive economy of the mind and/or have different teleofunctions. For example, a *visual sensation* as of something red and round in front of one (i) is normally caused by retinal stimulation (with no mediating sensation), (ii) is never inferred from a belief, and (iii) tends only to produce beliefs with (roughly) the same content as itself. By contrast, a *belief* that something in front of one is red and round (i) is never normally caused *directly* by stimulation of the retina (a visual sensation almost always mediates), (ii) can be inferred from other beliefs (e.g., from the belief that a reliable informant has said that something in front of one is red and round), and (iii) can help to produce beliefs with many different contents, depending on what other beliefs one has.

Both orthodox and unorthodox representationalism *also* agree that the phenomenal character of a sensation is determined by the sensation's having the intentional content that it has. But they part company over how exactly

---

[27] More precisely, they presuppose that sensations are *at least* descriptive mental representations; some sensations, most plausibly bodily sensations such as pain, may also be *directive* representations, with the job, also, of producing, via behavior, the outcomes that they represent. The terminology of descriptive and directive representations is due to Ruth Millikan (see, e.g., Millikan 2004, ch. 6).

to articulate this idea—over what exactly they identify the phenomenal character of a sensation with.[28]

According to orthodox representationalism, a sensation's phenomenal character is identified with the intentional content that the sensation has (see Tye 1995a; Dretske 1995; Lycan 1996). Michael Tye, for example, explicitly identifies a sensation's phenomenal character with the sensation's "Poised Abstract Nonconceptual Intentional Content" (or "PANIC"), holding therefore that a sensation's phenomenal character just *is* its PANIC (1995a, 137). And he further identifies specific aspects of a sensation's phenomenal character, that is, its specific phenomenal properties, with specific aspects of the sensation's intentional content. On this view, a sensation's intentional content is *what* the sensation represents. Since the question "What does the sensation represent?" can be answered by saying "That something is red and round," the sensation's phenomenal character is that something is red and around. And since, if a sensation represents that something is red, it can be said to represent redness, so that redness is part of what it represents, the phenomenal redness of a visual sensation is simply redness.[29] Perhaps a sensation's phenomenal redness is an *instance* of redness—an *actual* instance if the sensation is veridical, but a *merely possible* instance if the sensation is hallucinatory; or perhaps a sensation's phenomenal redness is redness understood as a *universal*.[30]

According to unorthodox representationalism, however, a sensation's phenomenal character is identified not with the representational content that it has but with *its having* this representational content—it is the sensation's property of *representing, in the distinctive way in which sensations represent (see above), that so-and-so*, where "that so-and-so" expresses *everything* that the sensation represents. And a particular phenomenal property of a sensation is the sensation's property of *representing, in the distinctive way in which sensations represent, that so-and-so*, where "that so-and-so" expresses

---

[28] Brad Thompson seems to have been the first to make this distinction in print—and with admirable clarity—calling orthodox representationalism "content-based representationalism" and unorthodox representationalism "vehicle-based representationalism" (2008, 395).

[29] A sensation that represents that something is red can be said to represent redness in a sense of "represents" in which a sensation *still* represents property P, even if, because the perceiver is hallucinating, nothing in the perceiver's sensory environment actually has P. In a second sense of "represents," however, "what a representation represents" refers to an existing and actual thing that is represented. So if at dusk on the trail I mistake a small bush for a bear cub, then what I represent in this second sense is a small bush; in the first sense of "represents," what I represent is a bear cub.

[30] Thompson clearly distinguishes—and cogently objects to—these options (2008, 397–405).

something that the sensation represents. Unorthodox representationalism therefore takes a visual sensation's phenomenal redness to be the sensation's property of representing, in the distinctive way in which sensations represent, that something before one is red, and it takes a visual sensation's phenomenal roundness to be the sensation's representing, in a certain distinctive way, that something before one is round. And what goes for the phenomenal redness and phenomenal roundness of perceptual sensations goes also for the phenomenal fluttering-ness, in-the-chest-ness, burningness, and sharpness of bodily sensations. A sensation's phenomenal fluttering-in-one's-chest-ness (as experienced during anxiety) is its representing, in a certain distinctive way, that something in the region of one's chest is rapidly moving a small distance back and forth. A pain's phenomenal burning and being in one's right eye is the sensation's representing, in a certain distinctive way, that there is burning in the region of one's right eye. A pain's phenomenal sharpness and being in one's back is its representing, in a certain distinctive way, that there is cutting or puncturing in the region of one's back; and so on.[31]

Henceforth I shall simply assume the truth of unorthodox representationalism. I shall not argue for the theory, except insofar as my uses of it to solve problems count in its favor.[32] Nor shall I defend it against its detractors (e.g., Levine 2001, ch. 4), though I recommend Michael Tye's defense of his orthodox position (2000, chs. 4, 5, and 6), and Christopher Hill's (2009) defense of the general representationalist approach.[33]

---

[31] I say "region of one's chest," and not just "chest," because I doubt that sensations represent bodily parts understood as having *functions* (e.g., mouth, arms, feet), suspecting instead that they represent bodily-part-shaped sub-volumes of a single, continuous, body-shaped volume of space. I intend "region of one's chest" to denote such a sub-volume.

[32] Papineau points out that standard arguments for representationalism cite facts that could equally be explained by his rival view that introspectible phenomenal properties, rather than being identical to (hence necessarily identical to) properties of representing, are *intrinsic* properties of subjects that *contingently* represent (2021, 40–5). Papineau's rival view may initially appear less parsimonious than unorthodox representationalism, since committed to properties of representing *and* to intrinsic properties; but actually my unorthodox representationalism is also committed to intrinsic properties of subjects—those that (narrowly) *realize* subjects' properties of representing. Where the two views disagree is over whether it is intrinsic or representational properties *that we introspect*. Presumably no one knows how introspective access to phenomenal properties enhances biological fitness; but explaining how it does so appears somewhat easier if phenomenal properties are properties of representing, because introspective access to properties of representing might enable some kind of fitness-enhancing meta-cognition that introspective access to intrinsic properties would not.

[33] Let me comment on Papineau's (2021) recent critique of representationalism. I entirely share his mystification at the apparent implication of orthodox representationalism that the phenomenal redness of a hallucinatory sensation of a ripe tomato is somehow constituted by uninstantiated redness (see 2021, 57–67). But he also argues that phenomenal properties can't be representational properties (as my unorthodox representationalism maintains), since instances of phenomenal properties have a kind of local causal efficacy that instances of representational properties can't have because they supervene on historical and environmental facts

Unorthodox representationalism was introduced with the promise that it would yield a better way of understanding our use of such terms as "red" to describe sensations as well as material objects than the suggestion that "red," for example, has two senses, a basic sense in which it expresses a property of sensations, and a derivative sense in which it expresses a distinct but related property of material objects, roughly, that of being disposed to produce, in normal observers under normal conditions, sensations that are red in the basic sense. Unorthodox representationalism naturally suggests that there is only one sense of "red" and of all the other terms with which we routinely describe both sensations and material objects. It's just that, when we apply these terms to sensations, which are representations, we use them to express the property of *representing* the property that they express when applied to material objects. The resulting expressions might be compared to expressions such as "baby photos," used to describe photos *that represent* babies (contrast "baby hamsters," which denotes hamsters that *are* babies), or "disaster movies," used to describe movies *that represent* disasters, or "sad stories," used to describe stories *that represent events that are* sad. Our characterizations of bodily sensations may seem at first sight not to conform to the pattern manifested by these examples; we say "pain in the shoulder," not "in the shoulder pain." But this difference presumably reflects the fact that prepositional phrases used adjectivally follow rather than precede the nouns they qualify when representation is not at issue; for example, we say "The coin in my pocket is a dime," not "The in my pocket coin is a dime."[34]

Unorthodox representationalism was also introduced with the promise that it would yield a better way of understanding the homogeneity of a sensation's phenomenal color. And so it does: it entails that the homogeneity of a current visual sensation's (say) phenomenal redness is the sensation's *representing*, in a certain distinctive way, that some surface in front of one is homogeneously red, that is, red all over in the sense that between no two red regions is there a non-red region that is visible to the naked eye under normal

---

(2021, 72; 67–71). By parity of reasoning, however, it seems to follow—implausibly—that states of *believing* can't be representational properties either. To avoid this upshot, Papineau must hold that while phenomenal properties seem to us introspectively to have local causal efficacy, states of believing don't. To me, however, both phenomenal properties and states of believing seem introspectively to be in exactly the same causal and explanatory boat.

[34] I take the main claim in this paragraph from Tye (1995b, 225). Interestingly, in the earlier sections of this paper, Tye sounds like an unorthodox representationalist; but in the final section, when he turns explicitly to his account of phenomenal character, his orthodox representationalism is clear.

conditions of observation (see also Clark 1989 for a version of this claim).[35] But if a homogeneously red sensation merely *represents* that some surface before one is homogeneously red, then evidently the sensation doesn't *itself* need to be, or to involve, a surface that is homogeneously red. There is an immediate intuitive resistance to the suggestion that the homogeneity of a current visual sensation's phenomenal redness is a mere representational property; but such resistance is just an instance of the intuition of distinctness, hence to be expected, and cannot be appealed to without begging the question.

Let me explain the upshot for Argument E of this lengthy discussion. Here, once again, is Argument E:

Argument E

E1. This property (i.e., phenomenal redness) of my current sensation is homogeneous.
E2. The property of having so-and-so functional organization and rate of firing isn't homogeneous.
∴ This property isn't the property of having so-and-so functional organization and rate of firing.

The argument's first premise, E1, is plausibly true if the homogeneity of a current visual sensation's phenomenal redness is understood to be the property of representing, in a certain distinctive way, that some surface in front of one is homogeneously red; but not otherwise, since if the homogeneity is understood as essentially involving a surface or something surface-like, serious difficulties ensue. But because premise E1 must be read as claiming that the phenomenal redness of one's current sensation has a certain representational property, then, to avoid equivocation, premise E2 must be read as claiming that the property of having so-and-so functional organization and rate of firing *lacks* this very same representational property. But someone rehearsing Argument E, qua someone having the intuition of distinctness, has no warrant for endorsing E2 when read in this way. For all that such a person knows introspectively or a priori, and without relying on the intuition of distinctness, the physically realized property of having so-and-so functional

---

[35] Why do I add "that is visible to the naked eye under normal conditions of observation"? Because I lean slightly toward the view that a homogeneously red visual sensation represents the sensed object accurately, even if the object, though red all over, can be seen *not* to be red all over if viewed with a magnifying glass.

organization and rate of firing might well *have* the property of representing, in the right distinctive way, that some surface is homogeneously red. It depends on what the *nature* of representing turns out to be, and that is not a question that can be answered a priori or introspectively. Argument E, therefore, fails, because it includes an unsupported premise. And so, if the intuition of distinctness arises because we more or less consciously rehearse Argument E, then the intuition gives us no reason to believe that introspected phenomenal properties really are distinct from whatever physical or physically realized properties we are considering.

Before leaving Argument E behind, let me try to reduce the apparent plausibility of premise E2 if it is read—as I have claimed it *shouldn't* be read—as claiming that the physically realized property of having so-and-so functional organization and rate of firing lacks homogeneity when homogeneity is conceived as essentially involving a surface or something surface-like, and hence that the physically realized property is grainy. If E2 is read in this way, then any reason for endorsing it would have to proceed from some true generalization about the graininess of *all* physical, or physically realized functional, properties of systems of physical particles; for the intuition of distinctness arises no matter which physical or physically realized functional property the subject has in mind. It's not clearly true, however, that even all the *physical* properties of an assemblage of neurons are grainy. Consider, for example, the *mass* of such an assemblage, a mass of 10^{-4} g, say. Intuitively, the mass of such an assemblage is no more grainy than would be the mass of an identically shaped object made of non-particulate matter. True, the mass of such an assemblage of neurons has a *distribution* throughout the assemblage, and this distribution may not be even; but the mass of an identically shaped object made of non-particulate matter could also be unevenly distributed throughout the object, and it wouldn't on that account be grainy.[36] And it's clearly *not* true that all physically realized functional properties of an assemblage of neurons are grainy. An assemblage of neurons could, for example, have the physically realized functional property of playing a certain mediating causal role between two other assemblages of neurons. But this property would no more be the discontinuous sum of the properties of the assemblage's component particles than would a steel bottle opener's defining functional property of a *being a bottle opener* be the discontinuous sum of the

---

[36] Recall, too, that the mass of a neuronal assemblage is a little less than the sum of the masses of its component particles, because there are interatomic forces, and mass and energy are equivalent in general relativity.

properties of the bottle opener's component particles. *Being a bottle opener* is the functional property of *being something with the function of helping one to remove caps from bottles*, and that very same functional property could presumably belong to an object in a possible world in which it couldn't be grainy because it was made of non-particulate matter.

I acknowledge a residual temptation to think that any physical or physically realized functional property of an assemblage of neurons *must* be grainy. The temptation may, however, arise from the combination of two dubious assumptions. The first assumption is that we can think of all macroscopic physical objects as vast clouds of fundamental physical particles floating in a void, with tiny *gaps* between the particles (think of oranges packed into a box). The second assumption is that any *property* of a macroscopic physical object is a sort of aggregate or discontinuous sum of intrinsic physical properties of the object's component particles—in something like the way in which the greyness of a drystone wall is a sort of aggregate of the greyness of the individual rocks that make up the wall.[37] More precisely, the second assumption says that a macroscopic object's having a property just is its component particles' having their respective intrinsic properties. From these two assumptions it follows that any property of a macroscopic object is grainy, for although the object's component particles have their intrinsic properties (whatever those properties are), the tiny *gaps* between particles do not. But the second of the two assumptions generating this conclusion is refuted by many cases of physically realized functional properties, as noted in the previous paragraph. And the first assumption—in particular, the part about gaps between particles—seems unlikely to be vindicated by physics. There are interpretations of quantum field theory according to which it posits no particles at all (see, e.g., Kuhlmann 2020). Moreover, even if particles exist, quantum field theory doesn't in general assign definite locations to them. And, finally, even if particles had definite locations, there aren't really gaps—complete absences of anything physical—between them, because they produce physical fields that explain the operation of forces between particles.

3.8 The Directness of Phenomenal Knowledge

Let us now consider a sixth possible conscious mechanism that might produce the intuition of distinctness in us. This mechanism is our more or

[37] A drystone wall is made of flattish, irregularly shaped rocks without mortar between them.

less consciously reasoning about a special feature of our *introspective knowledge* of the phenomenal properties of our current sensations, rather than about the phenomenal properties themselves. If I know through introspection that my current sensation is phenomenally red, then my knowledge seems not to arise from perception, that is, from the use of any of my five traditional senses.[38] Even though phenomenal redness is a property of my current *visual* sensation, I don't *see* that my sensation is phenomenally red. In fact, in introspecting my visual sensations I don't *see* them at all, and obviously the four other traditional senses are irrelevant; I simply find myself believing that my current sensation is phenomenally red—and in such cases, presumably, believing constitutes knowing. My introspective knowledge that my current sensation is phenomenally red differs in this regard from my knowledge of non-phenomenal facts about myself, for example, my knowledge that I am 5'10" tall, lightly bearded, or mostly made of water; for such knowledge always arises either from perception alone or from perception plus inference. But my introspective knowledge that my current sensation is phenomenally red also differs from *your* knowledge that my current sensation is phenomenally red; for if *you* know that my current sensation is phenomenally red, you have to have made a non-deductive (and possibly non-conscious) inference from what you have perceived of my talk, behavior, or perhaps even brain-state. We can therefore say that my introspective knowledge that my current sensation is phenomenally red is *direct*, where I know *directly* that p iff two conditions are met:

(1) my knowing that p has not arisen from perception alone, or from perception plus inference;
(2) at least given current technology, no one else can come to know that p in this same non-perceptual way.

The *directness* of my introspective knowledge that my current sensation is phenomenally red is not, of course, the same thing as its *infallibility*; I consider the claim that such knowledge is infallible in the next section.

Now, if the sixth possible conscious mechanism operates, then the intuition of distinctness arises in us because we reason, more or less consciously, along the following lines:

---

[38] By "perception," I will henceforth mean the use of one or more of the five traditional senses, that is, vision, hearing, touch, taste, and smell, even though psychologists also recognize other senses.

Argument F

F1. I know directly (i.e., through introspection) that my current visual sensation is phenomenally red.
F2. I don't know directly that my current visual sensation has so-and-so functional organization and rate of firing.[39]
∴ Phenomenal redness isn't the property of having so-and-so functional organization and rate of firing.

The expression "is phenomenally red" should be taken to correspond to a first-person predicative concept—a phenomenal concept—of phenomenal redness. Premise F1 seems obvious on reflection, as we have seen. Premise F2 seems equally obvious. Perhaps I don't know *directly* that my current visual sensation has so-and-so functional organization and rate of firing because I don't know it *at all*, being entirely ignorant of cognitive neuroscience. But even if I do happen to know it, I don't know it directly, for my knowledge has to have arisen from some presumably highly sophisticated combination of perception and inference.

But Argument F still fails, so that if the intuition of distinctness arises in us because we more or less consciously rehearse Argument F, then the intuition gives us no reason to believe that the phenomenal properties we are introspecting are distinct from whatever physical or physically realized properties we are considering. And Argument F fails because it's logically possible for both of its premises to be true while its conclusion is false. In the same way, it's logically possible for me to know that my drink contains alcohol, but not to know that my drink contains C_2H_5OH, even while alcohol = C_2H_5OH (as it actually is). I might fail to know that my drink contains C_2H_5OH, despite alcohol's identity with C_2H_5OH and my knowing that my drink contains alcohol, either because I lack the concept corresponding to "containing C_2H_5OH," so that I can't even *believe* that my drink contains C_2H_5OH; or because I have this concept, but don't *in fact* believe that alcohol = C_2H_5OH (even though I could); or because, though I do believe that alcohol = C_2H_5OH, I fail to put two and two together. Alternatively, imagine a mercury-filled glass thermometer, with its bulb placed in boiling water, that is only calibrated to show temperatures in degrees Fahrenheit. Even though 212°F is the very

---

[39] As before, the property of having so-and-so functional organization and rate of firing is assumed to be a physical property of a particular pattern of neuronal firing in, say, the V4 region of the subject's visual cortex, this pattern being a plausible candidate to be, or at least to realize, the subject's current visual sensation.

same temperature as 100°C, the thermometer represents the water's temperature as 212°F, but it doesn't represent the water's temperature as 100°C.

Another way to put this objection is to say that Leibniz's Law has no application to Argument F's premises because these premises don't jointly entail that a certain epistemic feature—that of being directly known—*is* possessed by phenomenal redness but *is not* possessed by the property of having so-and-so functional organization and rate of firing (or vice versa if the epistemic feature is that of *not* being directly known). But this is not because there are no such epistemic features; there are. But, for all that the premises of Argument F show, phenomenal redness and the property of having so-and-so functional organization and rate of firing don't differ with regard to these features—which becomes clear when it is made explicit which predicative concepts figure in the relevant knowledge-constituting beliefs. For suppose I am introspecting the phenomenal redness of a current visual sensation. Then I know directly, of phenomenal redness, that a current visual sensation of mine has it—by virtue of my having an introspective belief to that effect whose constituent predicative concept is a first-person, phenomenal concept of phenomenal redness; that I have such knowledge is, of course, the truth expressed idiomatically by premise F1. But if phenomenal redness *is* the property of having so-and-so functional organization and rate of firing, then I *also* know directly, of the property of having so-and-so functional organization and rate of firing, that a current visual sensation of mine has *it—also* by virtue of my having an introspective belief to that effect whose constituent predicative concept is a first-person, phenomenal concept of phenomenal redness (= the property of having so-and-so functional organization and rate of firing). Conversely, and obviously, I *don't* know *directly*, of the property of having so-and-so functional organization and rate of firing, that a current visual sensation of mine has it by virtue of my having an *introspective* belief to that effect whose constituent predicative concept is a non-phenomenal concept[40] of the property of having so-and-so functional organization and rate of firing; that I lack such knowledge is, of course, the truth expressed idiomatically by premise F2. But if phenomenal redness *is* the property of having so-and-so functional organization and rate of firing, then I *also* don't know directly, of phenomenal redness, that a current visual sensation of mine has it by virtue of my having an introspective belief to that effect whose constituent predicative concept is a non-phenomenal concept

---

[40] That is, a concept acquired, in this case, from exposure to the proprietary terminology of cognitive neuroscience.

of the property of having so-and-so functional organization and rate of firing (= phenomenal redness).

As we've just seen, the identity of phenomenal redness with the property of having so-and-so functional organization and rate of firing entails that there is a good sense in which the physical property of having so-and-so functional organization and rate of firing *can* be directly known by me to belong to a current visual sensation of mine. But since the knowing is direct, the property can't be so known by anyone other than the sensation's owner, for example, by you. How so, one might ask, if this property is a physical property? Are not all physical properties public, hence knowable by everyone? But the publicity of a property requires at most that everyone have *some* way of knowing that something has the property; it doesn't require that everyone have *every* way of knowing that something has the property. And other people (e.g., you) *do* have *a* way—a third-person, scientific way—of knowing that the property of having so-and-so functional organization and rate of firing belongs to a sensation of mine. You just don't have the direct way, made possible by *my* capacity for introspection, that I have.

But one might still wonder how direct introspective knowledge of phenomenal properties could possibly work—especially if such properties are physical or physically realized. To allay the suspicion that it couldn't work, or at least couldn't work if phenomenal properties are physical or physically realized, I will now tell a plausible story about *how* we gain introspective knowledge that our current sensations have the phenomenal properties that they have.[41] If the story is true, then such introspective knowledge meets the two conditions the meeting of which was stipulated above to be sufficient for being direct knowledge; and—crucially—it meets these conditions even if phenomenal properties turn out to be physical or physically realized properties.[42]

---

[41] In principle, knowledge of the phenomenal properties of our current sensations could be non-introspective. For example, you might infer that you feel on edge from observing your own fidgeting in a mirror. Less plausibly, you might be hooked up to a super-advanced fMRI scanner—in effect, an autocerebroscope—that informs you in real time that you are in a certain neurophysiological state which you know to constitute excellent evidence that your current visual sensation has a certain phenomenal property. Of course, our everyday knowledge of our current sensations' phenomenal properties isn't gained from autocerebroscopes, or even from mirrors.

[42] In section 5.3, I develop a hypothesis about the nature of introspection that is consistent with this story. It is also worth reiterating something from Chapter 1: though we speak of both introspective awareness *of* phenomenal properties and introspective awareness *that* our sensations have phenomenal properties, I doubt there are two fundamentally different kinds of introspection. I think the only representational outputs of introspection are states of believing, which, when true, normally constitute instances of knowing, so that introspective awareness *of* can somehow be understood in terms of introspective awareness *that*.

My story draws upon the *reliabilist* tradition in epistemology, according to which—roughly—what makes one's true belief into knowledge is the fact that the belief was produced by a belief-forming mechanism that is *reliable*, which I shall understand for present purposes to mean that the mechanism generally produces beliefs that are true. Reliabilism is controversial, of course, as are all views about knowledge, but here I will assume that it is at least on the right lines. According to my story, then, one knows through introspection that, say, one's current visual sensation is phenomenally red by being caused to *believe* that one's current visual sensation is phenomenally red by the *fact* that one's current visual sensation is phenomenally red—and caused to believe it not flukily but via an internal belief-forming mechanism that meets two conditions:

(i) it's reliable enough, in the right way, for the beliefs it produces, when they are true, to count as knowledge; and
(ii) it's not a belief-forming mechanism by which the belief that one's current visual sensation is phenomenally red is *inferred* from any of one's conscious mental representations (e.g., conscious mental representations of one's environment, or of oneself, or of one's properties, or of one's current sensation, or of *its* properties).

When condition (ii) is met, one's acquisition through introspection of the belief that one's current visual sensation is phenomenally red is not mediated by any of one's "conscious mental representations." By "mental representations," I mean not only beliefs, including perceptual beliefs, but also sensory representations (i.e., sensations, on my unorthodox representationalist view) and whatever representations are deployed, offline, in conceiving or imagining that something is the case. By "conscious" mental representations, I mean mental representations of which one *can* be conscious under everyday conditions; one needn't always *in fact* be conscious of them. My story imposes condition (ii) on the posited internal belief-forming mechanism because our everyday introspective beliefs about the phenomenal properties of our current sensations seem to me—and presumably also to others—clearly to meet the condition. As far as I can tell from my own case, or from others' reflections on their own cases, such everyday introspective beliefs are not inferred from any intermediate conscious mental representations; the only conscious mental representations that ever seem to be involved in coming to form beliefs about the phenomenal properties of my current sensations are (i) the current sensations themselves, with their phenomenal properties, and (ii) my introspective beliefs about them.

It might be objected that in introspection I infer that, say, my current pain is stabbing from my pain's *feeling that way* or *feeling like that* (or perhaps from a conscious belief that my pain feels that way or feels like that). But, I ask in reply, what could my pain's "feeling that way" or "feeling like that" be? It couldn't be my pain's stabbing, since surely I don't infer that my current pain is stabbing from my pain's stabbing (or from a conscious belief that my pain is stabbing); we don't seem to ourselves to do so, and anyway doing so would be bizarrely circular. Nor could my pain's "feeling that way" or "feeling like that" be something like my pain's burning or throbbing, for why on earth would I infer that my current pain is *stabbing* from its *burning* or *throbbing* (or from a conscious belief that it is burning or stabbing)? If I did infer that my current pain is stabbing from my pain's feeling that way or feeling like that (or from a conscious belief that it does), then, I suggest, my pain's feeling that way, or feeling like that, would have to be a sensation *of* phenomenal stabbingness, in the sense of a sensation *that represents* phenomenal stabbingness, the "of" signifying representation, as it does in the expressions "a sense of danger" and "a tale of woe," which expressions can be glossed, respectively, as "a sense *that represents* danger" and "a tale *that represents* woe." On such a view, I would infer that my current pain is stabbing from a sensation of phenomenal stabbingness in much the same way in which I infer that the painted canvas is red from a visual sensation *of* (i.e., a sensation representing) redness. But as far as I can tell from my own case, or from others' reflections on their own cases, there simply are no sensations of sensations in the sense of sensations that represent sensations or their phenomenal properties. Nor, as far as I can tell from my own case, or from others' reflections on their own cases, are there any *feelings* of sensations in the sense of feelings *that represent* sensations or their phenomenal properties.[43] Nor, finally, are there any *appearances* of phenomenal properties in the sense of ways in which one's phenomenal properties *sensorily appear* to one in introspection. To be sure, there are such things as sensory appearances, since, according to my unorthodox representationalism, phenomenal properties are just such appearances; but they are not sensory appearances of *phenomenal* properties. For example, phenomenal redness is a sensory appearance of (non-phenomenal) redness, and the stabbingness of a pain is

---

[43] A feeling of pain is simply a pain, the "of" here meaning "that is," as it does in "the misery of living," so that, if there is no pain, there is no feeling of pain. Of course, the word, "feeling," can also refer to an *act* of feeling, that is, to an act in which one *senses* something by *touching* it, as in feeling lumps in one's abdomen or feeling the coolness of marble. There are obviously no feelings of pains in this sense.

a sensory appearance of (non-phenomenal) stabbing in some bodily region, such as would be produced by a hypodermic needle. But though in this way phenomenal properties *are* sensory appearances, they don't *have* sensory appearances.[44]

Saul Kripke famously claimed that in the case of pain, and other sensations, we can't make a distinction between appearance and reality. But he sometimes made it sound as though he thought that, while pains *have* an appearance, their appearance and their reality are somehow rolled into one, so that *being* in pain and its *appearing* to one that one is in pain are the very same thing (Kripke 1980, 151–2; cp. 154). I agree that in the case of pain, and other sensations, we can't make a distinction between one's being in pain and its sensorily appearing to one that one is in pain. But the reason we can't make such a distinction is *not* that one's being in pain and its sensorily appearing to one that one is in pain are somehow rolled into one. The reason is rather that, as I have been insisting, pain *has no* sensory appearance to the subject of the pain—which is to say that there is no such thing as its sensorily appearing to one that one is in pain.[45]

If my story about how we know through introspection that our current sensations have their phenomenal properties is to serve my purposes, it must, as promised, entail that the knowledge is direct, while not ruling out the possibility that phenomenal properties are physical or physically realized. It can easily be seen to meet these conditions. My introspective knowledge that my current sensation is phenomenally red is direct in the intended sense iff

---

[44] I mean that they don't have *first-person* appearances, appearances to the people whose sensations possess the phenomenal properties. Phenomenal properties arguably do have *third-person* appearances, appearances to *observers* of the people whose sensations possess the phenomenal properties. For example, the right sort of pain-behavior (e.g., spasmodic movement and vocalization) can plausibly be regarded as a *third-person* appearance of phenomenal stabbingness; it is how the phenomenal stabbingness of someone's pain appears to someone else observing the person in pain. Hill and McLaughlin express a view somewhat similar to mine when they write (1999, 448): "Sensory states are self-presenting states: we experience them, but we do not have sensory experiences of them." I would prefer to say that sensory states are not presented at all, rather than that they are self-presenting; I see no sense in which they are self-presenting. And Hill and McLaughlin also write this (1999, 452): "The reference-fixing property that is associated with a phenomenal concept is identical with the property to which the concept refers." I accept that the phenomenal concept, PHENOMENAL REDNESS, refers in every possible world to the property that in the actual world = phenomenal redness. But I deny that PHENOMENAL REDNESS, when tokened in my head, refers to phenomenal redness *because* I somehow *associate* it with a mental description, "the property that in the actual world = phenomenal redness"; surely this would be a circular account of how PHENOMENAL REDNESS has its reference fixed (even if descriptivism were true).

[45] Pain perhaps has a *propositional* or *intellectual* appearance to the subject of the pain. If so, then we can distinguish between one's being in pain and its *propositionally* or *intellectually* appearing to one that one is in pain.

(1) my knowledge has not arisen from perception alone, or from perception plus inference;
(2) at least given current technology, no one else can come to know that my current sensation is phenomenally red in this same nonperceptual way.

Suppose my story is correct. Then introspection is a way in which I can come to know that my current visual sensation is phenomenally red that, because it's accomplished by an internal belief-forming mechanism that involves no inference from conscious mental representations, does not require perception; so clause (1) is satisfied. It is also a way in which I can come to know that my current visual sensation is phenomenally red, but in which no one else can come to know that my current visual sensation is phenomenally red. For the internal mechanism in *me* that causes *me* to believe that my current visual sensation is phenomenally red, because it's not in *you*, can't cause *you* to believe that my current visual sensation is phenomenally red—or at least it can't unless a technology is developed for linking my brain to your brain in just the right way; so clause (2) is satisfied too. Finally, my story requires of phenomenal properties only that they be capable of triggering the operation of the internal belief-forming mechanism. Since physical or physically realized properties could be such triggers, phenomenal properties can turn out to be physical or physically realized as far as my story is concerned.

There is, however, an objection. My story indeed entails that introspection is a way in which I can come to know that my current visual sensation is phenomenally red, but in which someone else *can't* come to know the same thing. According to the objection, however, the kind of impossibility expressed by the "can't" implied by my story is too weak. For the story entails only that it is *technologically impossible* for someone else to come to know the same thing in this way, not that it is *logically impossible*: the story allows as logically possible that someone else could come to know the same thing if we had the technology to link my brain to the other person's brain in just the right way.[46] However, the objection insists, introspection is in truth a way in

---

[46] It is a tricky question what exactly the other person would come to know. The other person would presumably form a belief partly constituted by a *predicative* phenomenal concept of the same type as the predicative phenomenal concept that partly constitutes my belief. What is not clear is whether the *subject-concept* partly constituting the other person's belief would be of the same type as the subject-concept that partly constitutes my belief. For what it's worth, I suspect that the other person would report their belief by saying, "*My* current visual sensation is red."

which I can come to know that my current visual sensation is phenomenally red, but in which it is not even *logically* possible for someone else to come to know the same thing; and this logical impossibility is essential to the way in which my introspective knowledge of the phenomenal redness of my current visual sensation is mine alone (or *privileged*, as it has often been put). So my story of how I can come to know that my current visual sensation is phenomenally red doesn't explain what it needs to explain, namely, the logical impossibility of someone else coming to know the same thing in the same introspective way in which I myself come to know it.

I answer, however, that we have no reason to accept the objection's assumption that introspection is a way in which I can come to know that my current visual sensation is phenomenally red in which it is *logically* impossible for you to come to know the same thing. Certainly we cannot infer logical impossibility from the *inconceivability* of your coming to know that my current visual sensation is phenomenally red in the same introspective way in which I come to know it myself. For it *isn't* inconceivable—we need only imagine, as we already did, that the belief-forming mechanism that causes me to believe that my current visual sensation is phenomenally red is wired up to your brain so as to cause you too to form the belief that my current visual sensation is phenomenally red. And I know of no other reason to accept the assumption.

Any residual sense that the objection's assumption is true may arise from a natural tendency to conflate it with a certain (true) claim from which it does not in fact follow. The true claim is this:

(1) It is logically impossible for other people to acquire the same knowledge that I have when I know introspectively that my current visual sensation is phenomenally red *if* they would have to do so *only* by making a priori valid deductive inferences from premises that they already accept (e.g., premises about my brain or behavior, or about the neural causes and effects of their *own* visual sensations).

I am inclined to endorse claim (1) on the philosophical grounds that, no matter how much information you have about my brain and behavior or yourself, you can never validly deduce a priori the conclusion that my current sensation is phenomenally red, even if in fact it is; and if a conclusion isn't validly deducible a priori from certain premises, it is logically necessary that it isn't so deducible, so that its valid deducibility a priori would be logically impossible. But many people no doubt endorse claim (1) without reasoning in this way, on the grounds that, when they try, as best they can, to imagine knowing *everything* physical about someone else, they don't feel any logical push toward the conclusion that the other person has a sensation with a certain phenomenal character. Claim (1) is the intuitive source of the traditional skeptical problem of other minds, as well as (more or less) the true premise underlying the Knowledge Argument (on which, of course, see section 2.4).

But now suppose that one forgot all about the "if" clause in (1), perhaps because one thoughtlessly assumed—in the present context, question-beggingly—that the "if" clause specified the *only* possible way in which other people could acquire the same knowledge that I have when I know introspectively that my current visual sensation is phenomenally red. In that case, one would endorse claim (2):

> (2) It is logically impossible for other people to acquire the same knowledge that I have when I know introspectively that my current visual sensation is phenomenally red.

And claim (2) is awfully close to the claim that introspection is a way of coming to know that one's current visual sensation is phenomenally red in which it is not even logically possible for someone else to come to know the same thing—which is the key assumption of the objection I have been discussing to my story about how we come to know through introspection that our sensations have their phenomenal properties.

3.9 Infallible Phenomenal Knowledge?

I turn now to a seventh possible conscious mechanism that might be thought to produce the intuition of distinctness in us. Like the sixth, it exploits an apparent peculiarity of our introspective knowledge of phenomenal properties. We seem to ourselves to be *infallible* with regard to the phenomenal properties of our current sensations: it seems to us that we couldn't possibly be wrong in thinking, introspectively, that a current sensation has a certain phenomenal property. For example, if we *think* (introspectively) that we're now in agonizing pain, then, it seems, we must now *be* in agonizing pain; we couldn't be mistaken. So if you tell your dentist that the drilling really hurts, and she says, "No, it doesn't!" you'll assume that she's either joking or crazy; you won't consider the possibility that she is right and you are wrong.

If the seventh mechanism operates, then the intuition of distinctness arises because we notice the infallibility of our beliefs about the phenomenal properties of our current sensations and then more or less consciously rehearse the following argument:

Argument G

G1. It couldn't happen that I *think* introspectively that I now have a phenomenally red sensation while in fact I *don't* now have a phenomenally red sensation.
G2. If the phenomenal redness of my current visual sensation just was the property of having so-and-so functional organization and rate of firing,[47] then it *could* happen that I think introspectively that I now have a phenomenally red sensation while in fact I don't now have a phenomenally red sensation.
∴ Phenomenal redness isn't the property of having so-and-so functional organization and rate of firing.

The expression "It couldn't happen that . . ." in premise G1 should be interpreted to mean "It's *logically* impossible that . . .," that is, "It couldn't happen that . . ., no matter how different were the laws of nature, or the initial conditions of the universe, or the actual circumstances." So the expression should not be interpreted to express some kind of merely *physical* impossibility, as it would if it were taken to be equivalent to such claims as "It's incompatible with the laws of nature that . . .," or "It's incompatible with the laws of nature and the initial conditions of the universe that . . .," or "It's incompatible with the laws of nature and the actual circumstances that . . ."[48] There are two reasons for requiring the stronger interpretation of "It couldn't happen that . . ." as expressing logical impossibility.

First, we feel that we can make *no sense at all* of the idea of our being introspectively mistaken about the phenomenal properties of our current sensations. We feel very differently, of course, about the possibility of, say, a mercury thermometer's giving an incorrect reading; we may think that such

---

[47] As before, this property is assumed to be a physical property of a particular pattern of neuronal firing in, say, the V4 region of the subject's visual cortex, this pattern being a plausible candidate to be, or at least to realize, the subject's current visual sensation.
[48] In my terminology, therefore, "naturally (or physically) impossible" isn't *equivalent* to "inconsistent with the laws of nature (or of the physical sciences)."

a thing physically couldn't happen—that is, would be incompatible with the laws of nature and the thermometer's actual construction—but we can still make sense of the idea of its happening.

Second, one important argument for premise G2 requires that the expression "it could happen that . . ." in the consequent of G2 be taken to express logical possibility—in which case, to ensure that the argument's conclusion follows validly from its premises, the expression "It couldn't happen that . . ." in premise G1 must be taken to express logical *im*possibility (the logical possibility of error would be *consistent* with its merely *physical* impossibility). According to the argument for premise G2 that I have in mind, if my current sensation's being phenomenally red just was its having so-and-so functional organization and rate of firing, then (i) my *thinking introspectively* that I now have a phenomenally red sensation would be one physically realized state of affairs, while (ii) my actually now *having* a phenomenally red sensation would be a second and (let us suppose) wholly distinct physically realized state of affairs.[49] But one physically realized state of affairs cannot *logically* necessitate a second wholly distinct physically realized state of affairs. A balloon-pricking, for example, can at best in some sense *physically* necessitate a balloon-bursting; for what makes it impossible for a balloon-pricking to occur *without* a subsequent balloon-bursting is the holding, in the actual circumstances, of certain natural laws, whose failure to hold would not be (according to the argument) logically impossible. Therefore, if my current sensation's being phenomenally red just was its having so-and-so functional organization and rate of firing, then (i) my thinking introspectively that I now have a phenomenally red sensation could, at best, in some sense *physically* necessitate (ii) my now having a phenomenally red sensation. The necessitation would be, at best, in some sense *physical* because it would be *logically* possible for those natural laws to fail to hold in virtue of which, given the actual circumstances, state of affairs (i) necessitates state of affairs (ii). In short, what physicalism seems to rule out is the truth of premise G1 when "It couldn't happen that . . ." means "It's logically impossible that . . ."; physicalism would permit the truth of G1 if "It couldn't happen that . . ." were understood as expressing physical

---

[49] Two states of affairs are wholly distinct iff they are not only distinct but also non-overlapping. I mean to rule out the possibility mooted by the second objection discussed in the immediately following paragraph.

impossibility in the sense of incompatibility with the natural laws and the actual circumstances.[50]

Before I develop my own objection to Argument G, let me mention two objections on which I will not be relying. The first objection aims to refute premise G1 (and other claims like it) by describing logically possible circumstances in which one's introspective beliefs about the phenomenal properties of one's current sensations are allegedly mistaken (see, e.g., Churchland 1988, 77–8). But the proposed counterexamples are never entirely convincing; and even if they were, they would serve only to refute the universal thesis that *all* of one's introspective beliefs about the phenomenal properties of one's current sensations can't possibly be mistaken. Argument G, however, doesn't need this universal thesis; all it needs is a single case of an introspective belief about the phenomenal character of a current sensation that—very plausibly, anyway—couldn't (logically) possibly be mistaken. And premise G1 surely seems to describe such case, given the imagined circumstances in which Argument G is rehearsed, circumstances in which the arguer is inspecting Rothko's *Untitled* at point-blank range under ideal conditions of illumination without distraction.[51] The second objection on which I will not rely disputes premise G2, suggesting that it might after all be *logically* impossible for the first of the two distinct physical or physically realized states of affairs to obtain without the second. The idea would be that, if one's introspective belief that a current sensation is phenomenally red somehow *includes* the phenomenally red sensation *as a constituent*, then it would be logically impossible for that very belief to exist without its being true (for an early presentation of this view, see Pollock 1974, 71–9). The objection would be effective if its central suggestion can be developed in enough detail to be convincing (see, e.g., Papineau 2007); but the question of whether it can is a difficult one.[52]

---

[50] I am supposing that the actual circumstances would include certain brain mechanisms that connect (i) and (ii); see below. Since the operation (and indeed existence) of these mechanisms would be contingent, the natural or physical necessitation by (i) of (ii) could not be absolute or unconditional; hence the need to mention the actual circumstances.

[51] To be clear, my view is that, under the imagined circumstances, error is both logically possible and naturally or physically possible in the sense of being compatible with the laws of nature; but that error is also *not* naturally or physically possible in the sense of being compatible with the laws of nature and actual circumstances, which include the existence and operation of certain brain mechanisms connecting the visual sensation and the introspective belief about it.

[52] But see section 5.6.2, where I tentatively propose a "mixed-media model" of introspective beliefs according to which they contain sensations as constituents.

My objection to Argument G is that we have no reason to believe premise G1: the only plausible candidate for a reason to believe it turns out to be inadequate. Premise G1 claims that a certain state of affairs couldn't—logically—obtain. But no philosopher to my knowledge has ever even tried to show that attempts to describe this state of affairs contain, or lead to, a formal contradiction; and it's hard to see how such a demonstration could go. What makes G1 plausible to us, I suggest, is instead the following little argument from what one cannot imagine:

> (A) One can't *imagine* one's thinking introspectively that one now has a phenomenally red sensation while in fact one doesn't now have a phenomenally red sensation.
> (B) Whatever one can't imagine must be logically impossible.[53]
> ∴ It's logically impossible for one to think introspectively that one now has a phenomenally red sensation while in fact one doesn't now have a phenomenally red sensation.

I think that premise (A) of this argument is true if, but only if, the imagining in question is *sympathetic* in Thomas Nagel's sense (1974, 446, note 11). When we imagine something sympathetically, what we imagine is *our being in a mental state* (or combination of mental states); and we imagine our being in a mental state by "put[ting] ourselves in a conscious state resembling the thing [i.e., the mental state] itself." I take it that to put oneself in a conscious state resembling a mental state M is to *simulate* being in M, that is, to put oneself in a mental state that has some but not all of the effects that actually being in M would produce, or that has weaker versions of the same effects, or that has some combination of fewer and weaker effects. For example, to sympathetically imagine one's believing that a grizzly bear has reared up in front of one is to simulate *having* this belief—which may cause mild anxiety but won't cause the panic or flight or freezing that would result from actually believing that a grizzly bear has reared up in front of one. And presumably *simulating* being in M is realized by some of the same brain mechanisms that realize our *actually* being in M.

Now I say that premise (A) is true *if* imagining one's being in the relevant combination of mental states (i.e., thinking introspectively that one now

---

[53] Here, and elsewhere, I use "logically impossible" in a broad sense, as a synonym for "metaphysically impossible." Logical impossibility in this broad sense is neither physical impossibility of any kind nor epistemic impossibility of any kind nor the property of being provably false.

has a phenomenally red sensation while not now having such a sensation) is sympathetic imagining. For, I submit, if one *tries* imaginatively to conjure up this combination of mental states in oneself, one finds one cannot do it. But premise (A) is true *only if* the imagining is sympathetic imagining. For one *can* imagine being in the relevant combination of mental states if the imagining is non-sympathetic. When one imagines something non-sympathetically, what one imagines is a state of affairs, whether mental or non-mental; and one imagines the state of affairs by *mentally representing* the state of affairs in some off-line way, so as to produce some but not all of the effects that would result from, say, one's *believing* that the state of affairs obtains. So one can non-sympathetically imagine one's being in the relevant combination of mental states by mentally representing, in the appropriate off-line way, *that one is in* the stated combination of mental states (rather than by *simulating being* in the combination of mental states). Indeed, one can non-sympathetically imagine one's being in the relevant combination of mental states as easily as one can non-sympathetically imagine that *someone else* is in the relevant combination of mental states. In attempting neither imaginative act does one run into a formal contradiction or experience the sense of psychological blockage one experiences in trying to conceive that, say, a bachelor is married. It is true that, in considering someone else's mental condition, one might *slip* into trying to *imagine being* the other person in the relevant combination of mental states, which would require trying (but failing) to imagine sympathetically one's being in the combination of states; but this failure wouldn't show that one can't *non-sympathetically* imagine that someone else is in the combination of states.

Premise (A), then, when read as speaking of sympathetic imagining, is true. But the little argument for premise G1 still fails, because premise (B) of the little argument is false: it's not true that whatever one can't imagine sympathetically must be logically impossible. Premise (B) is in fact false, whether imagining is sympathetic or non-sympathetic; but unless it applies to sympathetic imagining, it can't combine with premise (A) to entail the little argument's conclusion. Some philosophers think that the imaginability of something entails its logical possibility; but even if they are right, it doesn't follow that the *un*imaginability of something entails its logical *im*possibility. And in fact it's perfectly possible for something that one can't imagine—whether sympathetically or non-sympathetically—still to be logically possible. For it may be that the reason why one can't imagine something is that imagining it is *physically impossible* in one of the senses distinguished above, that of being incompatible with the laws of nature and the actual circumstances, the relevant actual circumstances in the present case being the brain's relatively permanent neuronal organization. Suppose that the imagining is *sympathetic*; then the *physical* impossibility, in the sense specified, of simulating being in mental state *M* doesn't entail the *logical* impossibility either of *simulating* being in or (crucially) of *actually* being in *M*. Suppose now that the imagining is *nonsympathetic*; then the *physical* impossibility in the same sense of *imaginatively representing* the state of affairs doesn't require for its explanation, hence doesn't entail, that the state of affairs is *logically* impossible.

But is imagination not *boundless*? How *could* it be physically impossible, in the sense of being incompatible with the laws of nature and the actual circumstances, to imagine thinking introspectively that one now has a phenomenally red sensation while in fact one doesn't? The answer is that imagining, of any kind, is a psychological activity that must be subserved by some mechanism; and the operation of this mechanism, and its limitations, cannot be determined a priori. Given that my car's braking system is as it actually is—in excellent condition—and that I am not driving downhill, it would be incompatible with the laws of nature for me to apply the brakes without the car's slowing down; so applying the brakes without the car's slowing down is physically impossible in the sense I intend. But, for all we know a priori, one's sensations of red and one's introspective beliefs about such sensations may be so wired up that, given that they *are* so wired up, it would be incompatible with the laws of nature for the introspective belief to be false. Let me now flesh out this possibility in what I hope is a somewhat plausible way.

It's very plausible that, unless one's attention is elsewhere, now having a phenomenally red sensation automatically causes one, via some neural mechanism that arises in the course of normal neurophysiological development, to form an introspective belief that one now has a phenomenally red sensation.[54] Now suppose that it would be incompatible with the laws of nature and the existence of such a neural mechanism for an introspective belief that one now has a phenomenally red sensation to be caused in any *other* way. On this supposition, one can't *actually* think introspectively that one now has a phenomenally red sensation while not now having such a sensation; such a combination of mental states would be physically impossible in the sense of being incompatible with the laws of nature and the actual existence of the envisaged neural mechanism. But because sympathetically imagining one's being in a mental state is *simulating* being in the mental state, so that the same brain

---

[54] The next section (3.10) briefly addresses the possibility that one's attention might be elsewhere.

mechanisms that realize actually being in a mental state are active when one sympathetically imagines being in the mental state, one can't sympathetically imagine being in any mental state—or in any *combination* of mental states— that one can't actually be in. So one can't *sympathetically imagine* thinking introspectively that one now has a phenomenally red sensation while not now having such a sensation; doing so would also be physically impossible in the sense of being incompatible with the laws of nature and the existence of the envisaged neural mechanism. Any attempt to sympathetically imagine thinking introspectively that one now has a phenomenally red sensation while not having such a sensation would be doomed to fail.[55] One might attempt the feat in either of two ways, the two ways differing with regard to which of the two relevant mental states one tries to sympathetically imagine being in first. One might attempt it by *first* trying (successfully) to sympathetically imagine thinking introspectively that one now has a phenomenally red sensation, and *then* trying (but unsuccessfully) to sympathetically imagine one's *not* now having a phenomenally red sensation. Or one might attempt it by *first* trying (successfully) to sympathetically imagine *not* now having a phenomenally red sensation, and then trying (but unsuccessfully) to sympathetically imagine thinking introspectively that one now has a phenomenally red sensation.[56]

So the only argument for premise G1 of Argument G—the little argument—fails, so that we have no reason to believe the premise. I conclude that Argument G fails too, and hence that, if the intuition of distinctness arises from our more or less consciously rehearsing it, then the intuition gives us no reason to believe that introspected phenomenal properties are distinct from the physical or physically realized properties that we are considering as candidates for identity with the phenomenal properties.

3.10 Subjectivity

Joseph Levine (2001, 84) speaks of "the subjectivity of conscious experience, the fact that my qualia [i.e., the phenomenal properties of my sensations] are 'for me' in a cognitively substantive and determinate way."[57] He might equally

---

[55] Given that, in the current state of neuro-technology, one can't destroy or temporarily disable the envisaged neural mechanism.
[56] The ideas in this section about different kinds of imagining, and about the role of simulation in imagining, make a reappearance in the next section (3.10) and then again in section 5.5.
[57] In this section, I will ignore Levine's "in a cognitively substantive and determinate way." His view (2007, 157–8) is that, in thinking introspectively of a phenomenal property, we form a

well have said that, when one introspects a sensation, its phenomenal properties seem to be given (or presented) *to one*. Also, he clearly takes for-me-ness, as we may call it, to be a feature of *instances* of phenomenal properties (e.g., a feature of the phenomenal sharpness of the twinge in my neck right now), rather than a feature of phenomenal properties as types or kinds. And he would probably agree that for-me-ness is an *essential* feature of instances of phenomenal properties—so that, for example, the phenomenal sharpness of the twinge in my neck just now didn't just *happen* to be for me but couldn't have existed without being for me (in the intended sense of "for me").

I accept that for-me-ness is, on some construal of what it is, an essential feature of instances of phenomenal properties. It suggests an eighth possible conscious mechanism that might be thought to produce the intuition of distinctness in us. If this mechanism operates, then, as we introspectively notice the essential for-me-ness of our sensations' phenomenal properties, we more or less consciously rehearse the following argument:

Argument H

H1. The phenomenal redness of my current visual sensation is essentially for me.
H2. If phenomenal redness were the very same property as having so-and-so functional organization and rate of firing,[58] then the phenomenal redness of my current visual sensation would not be essentially for me.
∴ Phenomenal redness ≠ the property of having so-and-so functional organization and rate of firing.

Our first task is obviously to ask what, exactly, the essential for-me-ness of the phenomenal redness of my current visual sensation *is*.

A first suggestion might be that the phenomenal redness of my current visual sensation is "essentially for me" in the sense that my current

conception of it "with substantive and determinate content." If we do, then I would construe our doing so as a case of our introspective knowledge of phenomenal features of phenomenal properties, as discussed in section 3.6. If that construal is correct, then Frank Jackson's Mary would gain introspective knowledge not only of phenomenal redness but also of at least one phenomenal feature of phenomenal redness when she is finally able to see a red rose.

[58] As before, this property is assumed to be a physical property of a particular pattern of neuronal firing in, say, the V4 region of the subject's visual cortex, this pattern being a plausible candidate to be, or at least to realize, the subject's current visual sensation.

phenomenally red visual sensation is *essentially mine*, so that it not merely isn't but couldn't have been *someone else's* (or *no one's*) phenomenally red sensation. But there is clearly more to the essential for-me-ness of the phenomenal redness of my current red sensation than its being essentially mine in this sense. Lots of things (e.g., my current smile, my current cold) are essentially mine in this sense but are not "for me" in the same way that the phenomenal redness of my current visual sensation seems introspectively to be "for me."

A second suggestion: the phenomenal redness of my current visual sensation is "essentially for me" in the sense that the phenomenal redness is *essentially represented* (in introspection) *by me*—so that my current visual sensation couldn't possibly have been phenomenally red *without my thinking introspectively that* my current visual sensation is phenomenally red. If this second suggestion is correct, then what premise H1 says is that the phenomenal redness of my current visual sensation *necessitates* my thinking introspectively that I now have a phenomenally red sensation—where "necessitates" has to mean "metaphysically necessitates," because whatever is essential in the philosopher's sense is presumably metaphysically, and not just physically, necessary. But there's nothing special about my current visual sensation, so if premise H1 were true, then (on the present suggestion) that would be because, necessarily, if one has *any* sensation with *any* phenomenal property, then one thinks introspectively that one has such a sensation. Let us call this general claim the *necessity of introspective belief thesis*.

Some philosophers have certainly endorsed this thesis.[59] But there is some reason to think that, as it stands, it is too strong to be true. Certain everyday occurrences can, with some plausibility, be described as counterexamples to it—as cases in which people have sensations with certain phenomenal properties but do not think introspectively that they are having sensations with those phenomenal properties. Here is one such plausible case:

> I have the habit of listening to loud music through earbuds as I iron clothes. One day, I set my phone to play a favorite song, with a view to savoring a

---

[59] The thesis has traditionally been called the *self-intimation* thesis. It may be contrasted with the infallibility thesis of section 3.9, which says that, necessarily, if one believes one has a sensation with a certain phenomenal property, then one does have a sensation with that phenomenal property.

passage of glorious virtuosity toward the end of its keyboard solo. I then work on pressing a shirt of pure cotton. The next thing I know the song is over, and I have no recollection whatever of having heard any of the keyboard solo, let alone the particular passage I wanted to savor.[60]

What happened? It's possible, of course, consistently with the necessity of introspective belief thesis, that I thought introspectively that my auditory experience during the keyboard solo had a certain phenomenal character, but that I promptly forgot all about it; after all, sooner or later we forget the phenomenal character of virtually all of our introspected sensory experiences. And yet the forgetting must be hypothesized to have been total, and to have occurred almost immediately. Is it so easy so quickly to forget an experience so completely? Perhaps it is, if the experience has little or no emotional valence; but the auditory experience in question, if I had been aware of it, would have had a strong positive valence—it would have *delighted* me. It also seems possible, however, that the reason why I have no recollection of having heard any of the keyboard solo is that, though I had the auditory experience I intended when I set the phone, and the experience had the complex auditory phenomenal character I expected it to have, still, because my attention was elsewhere—I was concentrating too closely on ironing the troublesome cotton shirt without scorching it—I didn't form an introspective belief to the effect that I was having an experience with the complex auditory phenomenal character it actually had. Conditions were present (earbuds in, phone on, volume up high, no ambient sound, normal ears and auditory cortex) that, under ordinary circumstances, are *sufficient* for auditory experiences of very loud, very brash music.

I will not pursue further the question of what happens in cases of the sort I have described; it's a question for empirical psychology and ingenious experimentation. But to insure against the risk of such counterexamples, let us assume that the necessity of introspective belief thesis can be, and has been, so qualified as to take account of the possibility that, because one's attention is elsewhere, one might have a sensation with a certain phenomenal property and yet not think introspectively that one has it. Even if the thesis is qualified

---

[60] I like my case a little better than the standard example, introduced by David Armstrong (1981), of the long-distance truck driver who suddenly realizes that he is quite unable to recall his visual experience of the road during the past few minutes, even though he has successfully driven his truck over that period. Readers can reproduce my case for themselves in relative safety.

in this way, however, there is, I claim, no reason to endorse it, and therefore no reason to endorse premise H1 as interpreted by the present suggestion; the only argument for the (qualified) necessity of introspective belief thesis that is known to me fails.[61] That argument, in the specific guise of an argument for H1 as interpreted by the present suggestion, is an argument from unimaginability:

> (A*) One can't *imagine* one's now having a phenomenally red sensation without introspectively thinking that one now has a phenomenally red sensation.
> (B) Whatever one can't imagine must be logically impossible.
> ∴ It's *logically impossible* for one now to have a phenomenally red sensation without introspectively thinking that one now has a phenomenally red sensation.

Obviously, this argument for premise H1 closely resembles the little argument for premise G1 that was discussed in the preceding section (3.9). Its weaknesses, too, are very similar to those of the earlier argument, so my analysis of it can be brief.

Premise (A*) is true if, but only if, the imagining in question is sympathetic (i.e., if, but only if, one is imagining one's being in a certain mental state M by simulating being in M). For if one tries imaginatively to simulate being in the relevant combination of mental states (now having a phenomenally red sensation, while not introspectively thinking that one now has a phenomenally red sensation), one finds one cannot do it. On the other hand, one can non-sympathetically imagine one's being in this combination of states by mentally representing, in the appropriate off-line way, *that* one is in the combination of states. Thus, one can readily conceive that the following two claims are true simultaneously: (i) I now have a phenomenally red sensation and (ii) I do not introspectively believe that I now have a phenomenally red sensation. Claims (i) and (ii) don't formally contradict one another, and in conceiving of their joint truth one has no sense of psychological

---

[61] Perhaps someone might conclude that the phenomenal redness of one's current sensation is necessarily introspected from the premise that it is in fact introspected, plus the triviality that, if it's introspected, then, necessarily, it's introspected; but I doubt that many people are tempted by this modal fallacy, since no one—well, hardly anyone—concludes that trees are necessarily perceived from the premise that they are in fact perceived, plus the triviality that, if they're perceived, then, necessarily, they're perceived.

blockage such as one has in trying to conceive that, say, Jim is married and a bachelor.[62]

As we have already seen, however, premise (B) is false: being in mental state M can be logically possible even though being in M is sympathetically unimaginable. For being in M might be sympathetically unimaginable because sympathetically imagining being in M is physically impossible, in the sense of being incompatible with the laws of nature and the actual circumstances; but the *physical* impossibility, in this sense, of *sympathetically imagining* being in M doesn't entail the *logical* impossibility of *actually* being in M. And here is how it could turn out to be physically impossible, in the relevant sense, sympathetically to imagine now having a phenomenally red sensation without introspectively thinking that one now has a phenomenally red sensation (even when one's attention isn't elsewhere). As suggested in section 3.9, it's very plausible that, unless one's attention is elsewhere, now having a phenomenally red sensation automatically causes one, via some neural mechanism that arises in the course of normal neurophysiological development, to form an introspective belief that one now has a phenomenally red sensation. On this supposition, then, it's physically impossible (unless one's attention is elsewhere) *actually* to have a phenomenally red sensation now without thinking introspectively that one has a phenomenally red sensation now—physically impossible in the sense of being incompatible with the laws of nature and the actual existence of the envisaged neural mechanism. But because sympathetically imagining one's being in a combination of mental states is *simulating* being in the combination of mental states, so that the same brain mechanisms are active that realize actually being in the combination of mental states, if it's physically impossible for one *actually* to be in a combination of mental states, then it's physically impossible for one to *simulate* being in, and hence *sympathetically to imagine* being in, the combination of mental states. So it's physically impossible (unless one's attention is elsewhere) for one sympathetically to imagine now having a phenomenally red sensation without thinking introspectively that one now has a phenomenally red sensation now.

Let me make a final comment of a quite different kind. I rather doubt that we, the people, when we insist that the phenomenal redness of a current sensation is essentially for us, are in fact claiming that the phenomenal redness is essentially introspected. For the essential for-us-ness of the phenomenal

---

[62] Nor does the situation change if one adds the qualifying claim that (iii) one's attention isn't elsewhere.

redness of a current visual sensation seems to be an introspectible, occurrent feature of the phenomenal redness. It's not clear, however, that the modal feature of *not possibly existing unless introspected* could be an introspectible, occurrent feature of anything.

Let me turn now to a third and final suggestion regarding what feature, or features, of a sensation one is noting when one judges introspectively that a current visual sensation is essentially for one. The suggestion appeals to unorthodox representationalism, introduced in section 3.7 as a working hypothesis. Unorthodox representationalism, it will be recalled, holds that a sensation is a distinctive kind of mental representation, like a belief in that its job is to represent how the world actually is, but unlike a belief in its representational format and in the role it plays in the overall economy of the mind. And it holds that a phenomenal property of a sensation is the sensation's property of representing, in the distinctive way in which sensations represent, that so-and-so, where "that so-and-so" expresses some particular thing that the sensation represents. The third and final suggestion, then, is that, when one judges introspectively that a current visual sensation is essentially for one, one is noting two distinct ways in which the subject—oneself—enters into the sensation.

According to this suggestion, the *first* part of what I am noting when I judge introspectively that the phenomenal redness of a current visual sensation is essentially for me is that my sensation is essentially an episode of *my* sensing—of *my* sensorily representing—that something is red, so that I am not only *doing* the representing, but also going to *use* the representation. The *second* part of what I am noting, according to the third suggestion, is that the sensation sensorily represents that the red something *stands in some spatial relation to me*. That is, in having a visual sensation, I am sensorily representing that something is *F* and at some spatial location relative to me, for example, that something is red, rectangular, and *two meters directly in front of me*.[63] But we should beware overintellectualizing, or otherwise aggrandizing, one's sensation's reference to oneself: it is not a reference to one's Self. When one's visual sensation represents that something is red, rectangular, and two meters directly in front of one, the content of the sensation's semantic constituent that refers to oneself is, I speculate, something like *this*

---

[63] What I have in mind, of course, is the rectangular surface of Rothko's *Untitled*. My talk of "two meters" as a measure of distance is not to be taken seriously; I have no idea how the magnitudes of distances are represented by vision—possibly by using the lengths of body parts as units.

roughly-human-trunk-shaped thing.[64] One's non-visual perceptual sensations also seem to represent things as spatially located in relation to oneself. Olfactory sensations surely represent odors as *here*, that is, as located where the sensing subject is located, or perhaps to the subject's left or right. Auditory sensations represent sounds (or objects that produce sounds) as close to or distant from the subject, as above the subject, as passing from left to right in front of the subject, and so on. The situation with bodily sensations is a little different, because, unlike perceptual sensations, bodily sensations don't represent conditions fully external to the body, but rather conditions in, or on the surface of, one's body. But if, inasmuch as one's sensations represent oneself, one's body (speaking loosely) *is* oneself, then bodily sensations also represent things as spatially located in relation to oneself. A stabbing pain in my left foot, for example, represents stabbing as *occurring in* a certain (foot-shaped) sub-volume of this roughly-human-body-shaped thing.[65]

What is the impact of the present suggestion on Argument H? If premise H1—that the phenomenal redness of my current visual sensation is essentially for me—is interpreted in accordance with the present suggestion, then it is true and can be known to be so introspectively. However, when premise H2—that if phenomenal redness *were* the very same property as having so-and-so functional organization and rate of firing, then the phenomenal redness of my current visual sensation would *not* be essentially for me—is interpreted in the same way, then, qua subject of introspection rehearsing Argument H, I would have no reason to think the premise true. The reason is simply that, for all I can know qua subject of introspection, my current visual sensation might be an episode of *my* sensing that something red is two meters in front of *me*, an episode that is physically realized by a brain-state of mine with so-and-so functional organization and rate of firing—in which premise H2 would be false. That my current sensation is not such an episode of sensing cannot be shown either by a priori reasoning accessible to everyone who has the intuition of distinctness or (unless we assume without

---

[64] I suspect that the trunk has a special importance because I notice that, when I turn my head to the left and look straight ahead at an object, so that the object is now in the center of my visual field, the object still seems to me, visually, to be to *my* left, even though it's not to the left of my *head*; it is, however, still to the left of my trunk. The location of sensed objects in relation to me seems also not to depend on where my arms and legs are; for example, the cup to my left still seems to be to my left if I place my left hand to *its* left.

[65] Sensorily representing that there is stabbing in a certain region of my body is a *necessary* condition for my having a stabbing pain in my left foot, but it's not *sufficient*. A sufficient condition would have to include pain's affective dimension. I have a representationalist account of what this affective dimension is, but it is not germane to the present discussion.

argument that the intuition of distinctness has probative force) by appeal to my intuition of distinctness. I might draw upon some prior and independent argument against regarding my current visual sensation as physically realized by one of my brain-states; but in that case my intuition of distinctness would be providing no additional reason to endorse the conclusion of Argument H. I conclude, therefore, that, if the intuition of distinctness arises in us because we more or less consciously rehearse Argument H, then once again the intuition gives us no reason to believe that the phenomenal properties we are introspecting are distinct from whatever physical or physically realized properties we are considering.

3.11 Non-conscious Mechanisms

Until now, I have considered possible *conscious* mechanisms that might produce the intuition of distinctness in us, thereby making it the case that the intuition gives us reason to believe that the phenomenal properties we are introspecting are distinct from whatever physical or physically realized properties we are considering. For such mechanisms to operate is for the intuition of distinctness to arise in us because sometimes, when we introspect a phenomenal property of one of our current sensations, we more or less consciously rehearse a good argument for the conclusion that the introspected phenomenal property is not the physical or functional property that we are considering as a candidate for identity with the phenomenal property. In the present section, I turn my attention to possible *non-conscious* mechanisms that might produce the intuition of distinctness in us, also thereby making it the case that the intuition gives us reason to believe that the phenomenal properties we are introspecting are distinct from whatever physical or physically realized properties we are considering. A non-conscious mechanism operates entirely unconsciously, but is reliable in the sense that the (objective) probability that what *seems* to us to be the case, as we have the intuition, actually *is* the case is high, or at least higher, given that the intuition is the output of the mechanism, where this high, or just higher, probability is suitably non-accidental.

The most plausible way to envisage such a mechanism, I suggest, is to suppose that it consists of two devices operating in sequence. The first device determines that an introspected phenomenal property is non-physical, by which I here mean neither physical nor functional and physically realized. The output of this device—a representation that the introspected phenomenal property is non-physical—is then taken as an input by a second device. On receiving this input, the second device notes which physical property the subject is currently considering as a candidate for identity with the introspected phenomenal property, and then outputs the intuition that the phenomenal property is distinct from the physical property. The second device is reliable because if the introspected phenomenal property is non-physical, it can't possibly be identical with the contemplated physical property, which property the device would "know" to be physical because (by hypothesis) the subject is representing it by means of a concept acquired as a result of exposure to the proprietary language of physics. The challenging question is how the first device could possibly work. Since it would be in effect a non-physicality detector, the question is how a non-physicality detector could possibly work. I will consider some proposals regarding how such a detector might be thought to work, and argue, not that the proposed detectors wouldn't work, but that it's highly implausible that our minds actually contain any of them.

If an introspected phenomenal property is non-physical, then it *lacks* something—it *lacks* the feature that physical properties have of being physical. Hence any hypothetical device that is sensitive to the absence of this feature must *somehow* be such that, if the device is activated by a phenomenal property lacking the feature, then it outputs a representation that the phenomenal property is non-physical.[66] But how?

A natural first thought is that the device, when activated by a non-physical phenomenal property, *just does* output a representation that the property is non-physical. This first thought is coherent; but it is tantamount to claiming that the non-physicality of an introspected phenomenal property directly produces a representation that the introspected property is non-physical in accordance with a fundamental law of nature. The law would be fundamental in the sense that its holding wouldn't have a reductive explanation in terms of the simultaneous holding of other, deeper laws governing the operation of constituent sub-mechanisms. The existence of such a fundamental law, however, while possible, is highly improbable. To see why, recall that, for the theoretical purposes of this book, we are understanding physical properties to be those that are expressed, or expressible, by terms drawn from the physical

---

[66] Couldn't the hypothetical system be sensitive to the presence of a positive feature, say, being ectoplasmic? It could; but the problem would remain of how the system managed reliably to reach the desired conclusion that the property detected to be ectoplasmic is non-physical (ectoplasm might be some hitherto unrecognized phase of indisputably physical matter).

sciences. On this understanding, the physicality of a physical property is not an *intrinsic* meta-property of the physical property—not some golden thread running through, and discernible in, every physical property—but instead a highly complex *relational* feature of the physical property. And so the *non*-physicality of a non-physical property is the *absence* of this highly complex relational feature. Therefore, a fundamental law according to which the non-physicality of an introspected phenomenal property directly produces a representation that the property is non-physical would require that the production of this representation depends in a *fundamental* way on (and only on) the *absence* of a certain highly complex relational feature of the introspected property. But no fundamental law of nature whose holding is uncontroversial or seriously contemplated involves the dependence of an outcome on (and only on) the earlier *absence* of a highly complex *relational* feature. So a fundamental law of the hypothesized sort, though still conceivable, would be utterly alien to our prior and very successful conception of how the world fundamentally works.[67] Systems do exist, of course, that can reliably detect the absence of complex relations; for example, some British people can reliably tell that someone is not a member of the Middlesex County Cricket Club (MCCC). But nobody thinks such systems work in virtue of fundamental laws by which the absence of membership in the MCCC directly and alone produces some cognitive response; everybody assumes they work in virtue of elaborate underlying mechanisms (in my example, mechanisms involving conscious reasoning in response to observable features that contingently but reliably indicate not being a member of a county cricket club).

Could an appeal to a fundamental law of this highly implausible kind be avoided? Yes, if there could be an underlying mechanism to account for the operation of the non-physicality detector. To avoid the fundamental law, the device would at a minimum have to yield its representational output as a result of *recognizing* that the introspected phenomenal property is not expressible in the proprietary vocabulary of the physical sciences. But while human minds as wholes could clearly meet this condition, it is fantastical to suppose that human minds contain, as a proper part, a device that does so. For such

---

[67] It would be less plausible than the fundamental physico-phenomenological laws that J. J. C. Smart memorably called "nomological danglers" and whose holding he rejected (1959, 142–3). For the latter would require the fundamental dependence of mental states on orthodox physical states, albeit ones of unimaginable complexity, rather than on the *absence* of a highly complex *relational* feature. A similar consideration also counts against the suggestion that a representation of non-physicality might depend in a fundamental way upon the negative property of *being non-spatial*.

a device would have to be able to determine, for any introspected phenomenal property, that the phenomenal property wasn't as a matter of empirical fact identical with any physical property that the device already "knew" to be physical, presumably because (since there seems to be no other way) it represents the physical property by means of a physical concept. But a device able to do so would have to possess a capacity to assess empirical identity claims that was effectively equivalent to that of a sophisticated scientific investigator, a capacity only ever possessed, as far as we know, by entire human minds. No less implausibly, the device would also have to represent by means of a physical concept every physical property with which any introspected phenomenal property might possibly be identical, a condition that, perhaps, no actual human mind meets.

Now many dualists are theists, and nearly all theists are dualists. So at this point some readers may protest that, no matter how implausible it might be that we contain non-physicality detectors operating naturally and acquired through solely natural means, we might still contain non-physicality detectors operating supernaturally and acquired through supernatural means: God might have created non-physicality detectors, and equipped us with them, miraculously. If we have a *sensus divinitatis* (as some theists think), then perhaps we have a *sensus dualitatis* too.[68] For atheists and agnostics, obviously, the probability that we contain a divinely implanted *sensus dualitatis* is either zero, very low, or inscrutable. But even for those who assign a reasonably high probability to theism, there is not much reason to expect that God would have endowed with us non-physicality detectors. It's logically possible, of course, but it's not to be expected. Even if phenomenal properties are non-physical, and God wanted us to know it, there is no telling whether he would want to make it as *obvious* to us as a reliable intuition of distinctness would make it. For example, that God exists is, if true, a truth of immense importance; but, notoriously, God doesn't make even this truth obvious to us (Drange 1998; Schellenberg 2015). Theists must say that he has his reasons for not making it obvious, and they do; but then perhaps those reasons, or similar ones, would apply to the putative truth that phenomenal properties are non-physical.

Let us set aside putative non-physicality detectors and end by considering a different suggestion for a possible non-conscious mechanism. Imagine a device with a one-track mind: whenever it is activated by a phenomenal

---

[68] There is, I discover, a (late) Latin word, *dualitas, -itatis*, f., meaning twoness, though I was fully prepared, in the tradition of "analysandum," just to invent a Latin word!

property, it outputs a representation that the property is distinct from *P*, where *P* is whatever physical property the subject is currently considering as a candidate for identity with the phenomenal property. So long as (i) every phenomenal property is *in fact* distinct from any physical property, and (ii) the mechanism is never activated by anything but a phenomenal property, the device will always output a truth. For it only ever represents that a phenomenal property is distinct from some physical property, and no phenomenal property *is* a physical property. In effect, the device simply tags any phenomenal property as non-physical, rather like a motion-activated "DANGER" sign that lights up, becoming visible, when someone strolling along a high cliff gets too close to the edge.[69]

It is doubtful that this hypothetical device would reliably detect that phenomenal properties are distinct from contemplated physical properties. Compare a putative milk-freshness detector that works like this: it always outputs "Fresh milk!" when its probe is dipped into liquid from the fridge, but the only liquid ever in the fridge is fresh milk, and the device is never used to test liquid from anywhere but the fridge. Now this device is reliable in the sense that it will never tell you that the milk is fresh when it isn't; but, intuitively, it's not really a reliable milk-freshness detector, even though, given the set-up as described, it can't ever go wrong. Why not? If the liquid that the probe is dipped into *hadn't* been fresh milk, the mechanism would *still* have told you (falsely) that it was fresh milk; the mechanism's output doesn't depend counterfactually on the freshness of the fresh milk (or indeed on its being milk). But the same complaint can be made about the hypothetical device described in the previous paragraph. If the phenomenal property that activated the device *had* been *P*, the mechanism would *still* have said, "That property is distinct from *P*"; the mechanism's output doesn't depend counterfactually on the true nature of the phenomenal property. The mechanism would therefore fail to be suitably non-accidental, as a reliable mechanism would need to be.

On the other hand, perhaps the hypothetical device owes its reliability not to the laws of its internal working but to the fact that it would not have *existed*, where it did in fact exist, had it not been such that it never produced falsehoods. To revert to my analogy with the danger sign on the edge of a dangerous cliff, we are inclined to take the evidently non-natural danger sign as indicating real danger, because the sign would not have existed, in

---

[69] I take the sign to mean something like, "You're in danger."

its actual location, if the cliff had not been dangerous; the authorities would not have ordered a sign to be placed there unless they had deemed the cliff to be dangerous. If so, then whether the hypothetical device is reliable would turn on how it came to be located in our minds. If it came to be located in our minds in such a way that it would not have existed there had it not told the truth, then it would be reliable; but otherwise not. In principle, the device could meet this condition by having been naturally selected for, that is, by having been naturally selected *because* it always told us something *true*. But it's implausible that such a device would have been selected because it always told us something true, since it is far from obvious how *truly* believing that phenomenal properties are not physical properties would enhance our fitness in ways that merely *falsely* believing that phenomenal properties are not physical properties would not.[70] Alternatively, the hypothetical device could conceivably meet the condition—of having come to be located in our minds in such a way that it would not have existed there had it not told the truth—by having been divinely designed with the purpose of instilling certain true beliefs in us. But, as we saw a few paragraphs back, not even theists have much reason to think that God would have endowed us with a device that produces a veridical intuition of distinctness in us.

3.12 Conclusion

The forced march is finally over. In the immediately preceding section (section 3.11) of this chapter, we found no plausible proposals to the effect that the intuition of distinctness arises in us from the operation of a non-conscious psychological mechanism. In the earlier sections (3.2–3.10), we found no plausible proposals to the effect that it arises in us from the operation of a conscious psychological mechanism. The failure, even after extended investigation, to come up with a conscious or a non-conscious psychological mechanism that can plausibly be thought actually to operate in us provides good inductive evidence—without, of course, deductively entailing—that the intuition of distinctness doesn't arise in us from the operation of either a conscious or a non-conscious mechanism. Since the intuition would have

---

[70] Yes, the hypothetical device could have arisen without being adaptive, if, say, the combination of genes responsible for it was also responsible for another trait that was adaptive; but at this point in the dialectic only selection for telling the truth will do, since only selection for telling the truth ensures that the device would not have existed if it had not told the truth.

to arise in one of these two ways in order to give us reason to believe that introspected phenomenal properties are distinct from whatever physical or physically realized properties we are considering as candidates for identity with the phenomenal properties, it follows that the intuition of distinctness gives us no such reason.

4

Previous Accounts of the Intuition of Distinctness

4.1 A Critical Survey

In Chapter 5, I will propose a novel explanation of the intuition of distinctness, consistent with physicalism, that makes it very likely that the intuition of distinctness gives us no reason to think that physicalism is false; and readers may, if they wish, proceed directly to that chapter, since it presupposes no knowledge of the present one. In the present chapter, I provide a critical survey of earlier theories intended by their proponents to explain the intuition of distinctness or plausibly regarded as able to explain it, consistently with physicalism.[1] The survey therefore omits all theories intended to explain the intuitive attractiveness of dualism about mentality in general, or of dualism about such specific aspects of mentality as agency, free will, or rationality.[2] The survey also omits nearly all theories intended *directly* to

---

[1] I do not include U. T. Place's *phenomenological fallacy* in my survey (1956, 48–50). The reason is that Place posited the fallacy for a specific dialectical reason only distantly related to the task of explaining the intuition of distinctness. He summarizes this reason in the paper's abstract:

> It is suggested that we can identify consciousness with a given pattern of brain activity, if we can explain the subject's introspective observations by reference to the brain processes with which they are correlated. It is argued that *the problem of providing a physiological explanation of introspective observations is made to seem more difficult than it really is* by the "phenomenological fallacy," the mistaken idea that descriptions of the appearances of things are descriptions of the actual state of affairs in a mysterious internal environment. (1956, 44; italics added).

Though Place explicitly calls the phenomenological fallacy a "logical mistake" (1956, 49), he always characterizes it in his 1956 paper as a false view rather than as a faulty inference. But in a later paper he describes it as "the fallacy of supposing, for example, that the statement 'X looks green to O' commits us logically and inescapably to the conclusion 'there is a green image in O's mind'" (1959, 72).

[2] Paul Bloom's (2004) theory seeks to explain the appeal of substance dualism. Papineau briefly considers but then rejects a possible explanation of the intuition of distinctness by appeal to Western culture's widespread endorsement of dualism (2011, 15). But cultural endorsement of dualism—substance dualism, presumably—seems to me too general to explain the very particular phenomenon of the intuition of distinctness. A culturally induced conviction that one is, or that one's mind is, an immaterial object doesn't seem to predict the intuition of distinctness.

Phenomenal Properties and the Intuition of Distinctness. Andrew Melnyk, Oxford University Press.
© Andrew Melnyk 2025. DOI: 10.1093/9780198942351.003.0004

explain the sense of an explanatory gap, which, though it certainly concerns the right aspect of mentality—the phenomenal properties of sensations—nonetheless seems clearly to be a different phenomenon from the intuition of distinctness; for example, it arises when we contemplate purportedly reductive explanations of phenomenal properties rather than when we engage in introspection.[3]

As far as I can tell, the theories I survey in this chapter are not rivals to my proposed explanation in the sense that they are incompatible with its truth. They are, of course, rivals in the weaker sense that they address, or could plausibly be taken to address, the same explanandum as my proposed explanation. But in the present state of our ignorance of the intuition of distinctness I would hesitate to insist that we only have a use for one explanation of the intuition of distinctness. Intuitive resistance to physicalism about phenomenal properties is strong and stubborn enough to raise the suspicion that it constitutes a perfect storm—an unusually or even uniquely striking effect of the confluence of multiple factors.

4.2 Armstrong

David Armstrong draws attention to the Headless Woman Illusion:

> To produce this illusion, a woman is placed on a suitably illuminated stage with a dark background and a black cloth is placed over her head. It looks to the spectators as if she has no head. The spectators cannot see the woman's head. But they gain the impression that they can see that the woman has not got a head. (Armstrong 1968, 48; see also Armstrong 1999, 29–30)

The illusionist prevents the spectators from seeing the woman's head by making the woman's head visually indistinguishable from its background; it seems that in order to see an object we must be able to distinguish it from its background. In the version of the illusion reported by Armstrong, the illusionist covers the woman's head with a black cloth that perfectly matches the background, though the bodypainting artist Mirjana Kika Milosevic

---

[3] *Any* explanation of the intuition of distinctness can *indirectly* explain the sense of an explanatory gap if, as I claimed in section 2.3, people have the sense of an explanatory gap because when they contemplate the phenomenal-physical (or phenomenal-functional) type-identity claims that would be required by reductive explanations of phenomenal properties, they resist these identity claims because they have the intuition of distinctness.

produces the same effect on video by applying black make-up to her own head.[4] What happens next? Having experienced the illusion myself by watching Milosevic's video, I'm inclined to think that the spectators don't make an inference from a conscious belief *about their seeing* (e.g., from a conscious belief that they *do not see* a head). Rather, once they are prevented from seeing the woman's head, their visual systems *automatically* represent the woman as having no head, and so the woman *automatically* looks to them to have no head. However, at least if they are adults, they don't *believe* that she has no head, because of their very high prior confidence that all women have heads.

In the Headless Woman Illusion, the spectators are, of course, misled. But the same kind of automatic response on the part of our visual systems does not always mislead. For example, if we are asked to verify that a cardboard box is empty, we look inside the box and (if it is indeed empty) we naturally fail to see anything in the box; but our visual systems automatically go further, representing the box as containing nothing; and, of course, we happily describe ourselves as seeing nothing in the box—which we would not do if the box was simply out of sight.[5] This kind of automatic response yields correct representations in the box example whenever it's true that, if there are objects in the box, we will see them; our not seeing objects in that case entails that there are no objects. The automatic response yields a false representation in the Headless Woman Illusion because the illusionist has contrived things so that it's *not* true that, if the woman has a head, we will see it.

What does the Headless Woman Illusion have to do with physicalism about sensations? Armstrong says that the illusion "may be a useful model, whose employment will . . . explain materialist wavering" (1968, 48). But, unlike me, he seems to take the illusion to result from a conscious inference from a premise about perceiving, for, generalizing from the model, he says:

> In certain cases, it is very natural for human beings to pass from something that is true: "I do not perceive that X is Y," to something that may be false: "I perceive that X is not Y."

On this view, the items from which, and to which, we "pass" are conscious beliefs about our states of perceiving; they are not conscious beliefs about *only*

---

[4] Remarkably, her head seems to disappear: https://www.youtube.com/watch?v=03uqTfhZV-8.
[5] We could also *feel* inside the box, of course, and parallel points would hold.

(or other mental representations of *only*) the items perceived.[6] Accordingly, Armstrong's suggested explanation for materialist wavering seems to be that the wavering materialist makes an inference from one conscious belief about her introspective awareness to another conscious belief about her introspective awareness (1968, 48–9):

> It can now be suggested by the Materialist that we tend to pass from something that is true:
> I am not introspectively aware that mental images are brain-processes
> to something that is false:
> I am introspectively aware that mental images are not brain-processes.

I daresay that plenty of people, physicalists and dualists alike, have reasoned in this sort of way, concluding that introspection tells them that sensations are not physical (or functional) occurrences. But I doubt that such reasoning explains the intuition of distinctness. The intuition of distinctness persists among sophisticated thinkers, including physicalists. But it does not take very much sophistication to see (i) under what condition such reasoning would be unreliable, taking one from a true premise to a false conclusion; and (ii) that, for all we know, that condition is met. The reasoning is reliable on condition that, if mental images *are* brain-processes, then by introspecting one can become *aware* that they are. The reasoning is unreliable if, for some reason, it's not true that, if mental images are brain-processes, then by introspecting one can become aware that they are. But it is obviously possible that introspection just isn't the sort of faculty to comment on whether sensations are brain-processes—or spatially located, or created by God, or whatever. This possibility is obvious because we all know that, for example, vision doesn't comment on pitches, hearing doesn't comment on patterns of light, and neither vision nor hearing comment on the atomic constitution of the world around us. And, without having any understanding of *why* these things are true, we can readily entertain the possibility that something similar is true also of introspection.[7]

The Headless Woman Illusion might, however, be relevant to explaining the intuition of distinctness in a way different from the one apparently

---

[6] That this passing is from, and to, a conscious belief about our state of perceiving is quite consistent with its being automatic, and hence with Armstrong's comment that "we have here one of those unselfconscious and immediate movements of the mind of which Hume spoke" (1968, 48).

[7] For further discussion, see the treatment in section 3.2 of Argument A.

envisaged by Armstrong. The new hypothesis would be that our faculty of introspection is disposed to make the same sort of *automatic response* as that which (I have claimed) our visual system is disposed to make. The idea would be that introspection fails to represent the phenomenal properties of our sensations as being physical properties, and then automatically represents them as not being physical properties, just as, in the model of the Headless Woman Illusion, our vision fails to represent the woman as having a head and then automatically represents her as not having a head. The new hypothesis, if correct, would explain what needs explaining: its seeming to us, as we introspect, that an introspected phenomenal property of a current sensation just couldn't be, or at least isn't, a physical property.

The hypothesis assumes that introspection can output *negative* representations, that is, representations with the content that a phenomenal property is *not* a physical property. It also assumes that introspection is so configured that (given attention) its not representing that a phenomenal property *is* a certain physical property automatically yields a representation that the phenomenal property *isn't* that physical property. But both these assumptions have some independent plausibility. Introspection often seems to tell us that we are *not* undergoing certain sensations; for example—I am happy to report—it seems to me introspectively right now that I am *not* in pain. So introspection seems able to output negative representations. And, it seems, we can plausibly *explain* the output of negative representations of this kind by supposing that (given attention) introspection automatically yields a representation that a sensation (or phenomenal property) doesn't have (or isn't) a certain property whenever it fails to represent the sensation (or phenomenal property) as having (or being) that property.

But the hypothesis also makes a third assumption: that the representational repertoire of introspection includes *physical* concepts of physical properties, for example, a physical concept of a brain-process or of a neural property, where physical concepts are those acquired from exposure to the distinctive theoretical vocabulary of the physical sciences. Unless this is so, introspection cannot output a representation that a current mental image is *not* a brain-process, or that an introspected phenomenal property is *not* a certain neural property. This third assumption is doubtful. For one thing, introspection obviously never uses physical concepts to represent sensations as *having* physical properties.[8] So we don't have *that* evidence for thinking that

---

[8] I say "uses *physical* concepts to represent," because if physicalism is true, then introspection does use *phenomenal* concepts to represent sensations as having what are *in fact* physical properties.

the representational repertoire of introspection includes physical concepts of physical properties. Furthermore, because introspection never uses physical concepts to represent sensations as having physical properties, it differs from vision, the putative model, in this respect: even if *in the circumstances of the illusion* vision doesn't represent the woman as having a head, vision often *does* represent people as having heads. (Indeed, it almost does so *whenever* it represents people as having bodies.) And this difference between introspection and vision looks relevant, because vision doesn't represent an object as lacking a property P *just because* it doesn't represent the object as *having* P; for example, vision doesn't represent a chair as *not composed* of atoms just because it doesn't represent a chair as *composed* of atoms. Some further condition must be met, and a natural suggestion is that the representing faculty must sometimes represent something as *having* P. But in the hypothesized case of introspection this condition is not met.[9] The hypothesis would therefore have to say that the representational repertoire of introspection includes physical concepts of physical properties, but that these concepts are used *only* when introspection represents sensations as *not* having the properties—which is a little hard to believe. And there is a reason for *denying* the third assumption (that the representational repertoire of introspection includes physical concepts of physical properties): not only does introspection never use physical concepts to represent sensations as *having* physical properties but it also never uses physical concepts to represent sensations as, for example, *causing* or *caused by* physical (e.g., neural) events, or indeed to represent such physical events *themselves* as having physical properties.

4.3 Lycan

According to William G. Lycan, the feeling that sensations couldn't be brainstates sometimes arises because people commit the *stereoptic fallacy*:

> We look with one eye at the brain of a human subject who is having a visual sensation [of cyan]. ... With the other eye, so to speak, we imagine *having*

---

[9] That the condition isn't met presumably explains Shaun Nichols's observation that although introspection doesn't represent, say, sudden headaches as *having* causes, it also doesn't represent them as *lacking* causes—so that we can't explain the indeterminist intuition that our choices or decisions lack causes by supposing that (given attention) introspection automatically yields a representation that a sensation doesn't have a certain property *whenever* it fails to represent the sensation as having that property (2012, 295–6).

the intense cyan sensation.... The first eye's view of the subject's brain is nothing the least bit like the second eye's having the cyan sensation; the two views are totally incongruous.... And this seems damning to materialism. (Lycan 1996, 47–8, see also 5–6; and Lycan 1987, 76–7)

And it is fallacious to conclude that materialism is damned, according to Lycan, because doing so presupposes a claim that is unwarranted and false— the claim that, if materialism is true, then the greyish visual sensation one has in *seeing* the brain-state that, according to materialism, is, or realizes, a certain sensation of cyan should have the *same phenomenal character* as the visual sensation of cyan.[10]

Lycan offers no evidence that the (or a) feeling that sensations couldn't be brain-states sometimes arises from the stereoptic fallacy, though of course it might. But I doubt that the intuition of distinctness—the particular phenomenon *I'm* interested in—arises from it. The intuition of distinctness seems to me to arise even when one attends *only* to the phenomenal character of a current sensation; it doesn't seem to require simultaneously imagining one's seeing a brain-state. For it presumably arises in people quite innocent of neurobiology who (like my shockingly ignorant undergraduate self) wouldn't even know how to start imagining their seeing a brain-state, and so wouldn't even try. More seriously, Lycan regards the false assumption that he thinks underlies the stereoptic fallacy as rather obviously false. "Even to call this inference a 'fallacy,'" he says, "is to flatter it" (Lycan 1996, 6). I quite agree. But that makes the stereoptic fallacy a poor candidate to explain the intuition of distinctness, which is had by logically and philosophically sophisticated thinkers, including logically and philosophically sophisticated physicalists who are well marinated in the dialectic of debates about physicalism.

It might be that something like the stereoptic fallacy nonetheless gives rise to an anti-physicalist intuition, but not via Lycan's incongruity between two different phenomenal characters. Suppose we imagine our seeing someone else's being in a brain-state alleged by physicalists to be (or to realize) pain; perhaps we imagine our seeing the "gray cheesy mass" (Lycan 1996, 47) of someone's brain, or perhaps we imagine our seeing a network of neurons through a microscope. Because what we imagine ourselves to be seeing is supposed to *be* pain (or its realizer), we may expect that *we* will have a

---

[10] David Papineau (1993, 177–8) cites Thomas Nagel (1974, 445–6, note 11) as proposing a view like Lycan's. For the record, I read Nagel as trying instead to explain the contingency of the relationship between the physical and the phenomenal—our sense that they *needn't* be identical.

sensation of pain too, in addition to our visual sensation, so that, when we don't have a sensation of pain, we infer that what we imagine ourselves to be seeing can't be (or can't be enough for) pain. Why would we expect that we too will have a sensation of pain in the circumstances described? Two possibilities suggest themselves. The first is that, if a certain brain-state really is (or realizes) pain, then we expect to be able to infer a priori from what we see that the person is in pain, and then further expect (because this is what commonly happens when we see people hurt themselves) that we will sympathetically imagine being in pain ourselves (which imagining is at least a pain-like mental state). The second possibility is that we reason as follows: we are supposedly aware, through vision, of the very same brain-state that we are aware of, through introspection, when we attend to a pain of our own; but when we attend to a pain of our own, we thereby become aware of pain's distinctive phenomenal character; so when we see the very same brain-state in someone else, we should also become aware of pain's phenomenal character.

But neither possibility is a plausible explanation of why dialectically well-girded physicalists—who still have the intuition of distinctness—would expect themselves to have a sensation of pain (or something akin to one) in the circumstance described. Well-girded physicalists almost always deny that, even if a certain brain-state really is (or realizes) pain, there is a valid a priori entailment from the premise that someone is in the brain-state to the conclusion that the person is in pain. Well-girded physicalists also reject the reasoning hypothesized by the second possibility. If we really are seeing a brain-state in someone else that is (or realizes) pain, and attending visually to the right property of the brain-state, then we really are aware of the phenomenal character of someone else's pain—but only in the sense that we are using *physical* concepts to represent the brain-state as having the very properties that in fact constitute its pain-distinctive phenomenal character. We are not, however, representing those properties by using the *phenomenal* concepts that we would use in *introspectively* representing the same properties of one of *our* own brain-states. So we would not become aware of pain's phenomenal character in a way that presupposes *having* a pain with that character.

4.4 Papineau

It is from David Papineau, of course, that I have borrowed the term "the intuition of distinctness," to refer to the phenomenon (described in Chapter 1) that the present book investigates. But Papineau's own description of the psychological phenomenon that he calls, in full, "the intuition of mind-brain distinctness" is stated in this passage (2002, 74):

> There is something very counter-intuitive about the phenomenal-material identity claims advocated by materialists. When materialists urge that *seeing red* (and here you must imagine the redness) is identical to some material *brain property*, it strikes many people that this *must* be wrong.

Papineau doesn't always use "the intuition of distinctness" in strict accordance with this passage; sometimes he uses it for a more general phenomenon, as when, for example, he speaks of "the compelling intuition that the *mind* is ontologically distinct from the material world," where the scope of the intuition is not restricted to phenomenal properties (2002, 3; italics added). Nonetheless, the phenomenon he describes in this passage, despite its full name, is surely a very close relative (at least) of the phenomenon that I have been calling "the intuition of distinctness." It consists of our reaction to phenomenal-physical (or phenomenal-functional) type-identity claims, for by "material" he means "physical or functional" (2002, 15). And—though this isn't immediately obvious—it consists of our reaction to such identity claims under the special circumstance of our being introspectively aware of the phenomenal character of a current mental state. True, he urges readers to "*imagine* the [phenomenal] redness" (my emphasis), rather than to *introspect* a current visual sensation of red. But he thinks that, when we imagine phenomenal redness, "we deploy a phenomenal concept imaginatively," and hence "activate a 'faint copy' of the experience referred to" (Papineau 2002 170); and, as we shall eventually see, his proposed explanation of the phenomenon requires us to be aware of this "faint copy," presumably through introspection. So Papineau clearly regards the psychological phenomenon he describes—his "intuition of mind-brain distinctness"—as including introspective awareness of a phenomenal property of a current mental state.

But how exactly Papineau proposes to *explain* this phenomenon is harder to pin down than might at first appear. On the one hand, he frequently says that the phenomenon arises because we commit what he calls "the antipathetic fallacy." He characterizes this fallacy as

> the argument which moves from the true premise that third-person ways of thinking about conscious experiences do not *use* versions of those conscious experiences, to the false conclusion that those ways of thinking do not *mention* those conscious experiences, but only physical states. (Papineau 1993, 177; italics added and typo corrected)

Now this way of characterizing the fallacy most naturally suggests the following hypothesis to explain the intuition of mind-brain distinctness:

> When thinking about some material property (e.g., being in brain-state B), we notice that doing so doesn't require that we actually *be* in pain (or in any faint version of pain); we notice, that is, that we don't *use* being in pain to think about being in B. We then commit the anti-pathetic fallacy to conclude that thinking about being in B isn't a way of *mentioning* (i.e., thinking about) being in pain—that being in B ≠ being in pain.

But *this* hypothesis is not Papineau's hypothesis—for two reasons. The first is that this hypothesis only has us notice that our thinking about being in brain-state B doesn't require our being in pain; it doesn't have us *compare* our thinking about brain-state B with our thinking about pain. Papineau, however, repeatedly says that the intuition of mind-brain distinctness arises in part because we make just such a comparison (e.g., Papineau 2002, 170). An adequate formulation of Papineau's hypothesis must therefore assign an essential role to this comparison.

The second reason is that the anti-pathetic fallacy, as formulated in the quotation from Papineau above, exemplifies a highly implausible pattern of inference. As Papineau himself writes,

> Most concepts don't use or involve the things they refer to. When I think of being rich, say, or having measles, this doesn't in any sense make me rich or give me measles. (2002, 171)

Precisely for this reason, it is implausible that the anti-pathetic fallacy as formulated above explains the intuition of mind-brain distinctness. For, to explain it, the anti-pathetic fallacy obviously can't be less tempting than the intuition of mind-brain distinctness itself. But how tempting can it be, especially for the "convinced materialists" who, as Papineau rightly says, are nonetheless "likely to feel the pull of this intuition," when most of our everyday concepts are counterexamples to the pattern of inference that it exemplifies (2002, 161)?[11] How tempting can it be for Papineau himself, who freely admits that in his "own case" the intuition of mind-brain distinctness "continues to press, despite any amount of immersion in the arguments of

---

[11] He is also committed to holding that materialists commit the fallacy by his thinking that the intuition of mind-brain distinctness explains why materialists (including himself) deem zombies to be possible (Papineau 2002, 94–5).

the previous chapters," and despite, we might add, his own clear recognition and articulation of the fallaciousness of the anti-pathetic fallacy (2002, 161)?

This objection to Papineau's appeal to the anti-pathetic fallacy might be deemed inconclusive, because there are fallacies that people tend to keep committing even when they have been convinced that the fallacy is indeed a fallacy. Consider, for example, the Monty Hall Problem; very few people who have understood the error that leads to the incorrect answer now find avoiding the error intuitive.[12] But the pattern of inference exemplified by the anti-pathetic fallacy is not like that. We simply have no general tendency to engage in it; if we commit it at all, we do so only in the case of thoughts involving phenomenal concepts. It is as if we only ever commit the fallacy of denying the antecedent when reasoning about our digestions, in which case, regrettably, we cannot help ourselves.

Papineau's hypothesis to explain the intuition of mind-brain distinctness must therefore be interpreted differently. So let us consider Papineau's narrative of how the intuition arises in us:

> When you think imaginatively about a pain . . . [a version of this experience] will be present in you, and because of this the activity of thinking phenomenally *about* pain . . . will strike you introspectively as *involving* the feeling of [pain].
>
> Now compare the exercise of some material concept which might refer to just the same conscious state. No similar feelings there. To think of activation of nociceptive-specific neurons . . . doesn't in itself create any feeling of pain.
>
> So there is an intuitive sense in which exercises of material concepts "leave out" the experience at issue. They "leave out" the pain . . . in the sense that they don't activate or involve [pain]. Now it is all too easy to slide from this to the conclusion that, in exercising material concepts, we are not thinking *about* the experiences themselves. (Papineau 2002, 170; see also Papineau 1993, 176–7)

In this narrative, it seems to me, Papineau in effect proposes a subtly but significantly different hypothesis. Officially, of course, the fallacy ("slide")

---

[12] See https://en.wikipedia.org/wiki/Monty_Hall_problem. I am not myself one of the few.

hypothesized in the final paragraph is an equivocation on the term "leave out," whereby it is first understood as equivalent to "don't activate or involve" and then as equivalent to "don't mention or refer to." But this slide is just the anti-pathetic fallacy as formulated above—which makes no use of the *comparison* between exercises of phenomenal concepts and exercises of material concepts that Papineau stresses ("Now compare . . .") in this narrative. The subtly different hypothesis posits the same equivocation on "leave out" except that "leave out" is first understood as equivalent not to "*don't* activate or involve" but to "*fail* to activate or include." Simply not activating or involving something is not yet to leave out something in the sense of *failing* to activate or include it; for example, my spelling of "equivalent" doesn't involve the letter "z," but it doesn't *leave out* the letter "z"—it doesn't *fail* to involve it—because "equivalent" is not *supposed* to include a "z." When something is left out or fails to be present, it's a defect: something is not there that *should* be there.[13]

On this interpretation of Papineau's hypothesis, then, we infer the *conclusion* that the exercise of a material concept leaves out the feeling of pain in the sense of *not mentioning* it from the *premise* that it leaves out the feeling in the sense of *failing to activate or include* it. But what makes us think that the exercise of a material concept *fails* to activate or include the feeling of pain, rather than merely *not* activating or including it? This, I suggest, is where the *comparison* with our thinking about pain by exercising a phenomenal concept comes in. Because we have noticed that thinking about pain by exercising a phenomenal concept activates or involves a feeling of pain (albeit perhaps a faint version of pain), we come to expect that *all* thinking about pain does the same. Then, when we turn to thinking about the activation of nociceptive-specific neurons while wondering whether, in so thinking, we are thereby thinking about pain, we find that our thinking about the firing of nociceptive-specific neurons does *not* activate or include what it *should* if it really is thinking about pain, that is, that it *fails* to activate or include the feeling of pain.

This new interpretation of Papineau's hypothesis avoids the two difficulties of the first interpretation: it doesn't appeal to the anti-pathetic fallacy as formulated above, and it assigns an essential role to the comparison

---

[13] There is a usage of "should" in which it reflects what there is evidence to expect *will* happen, whether or not it would be a good thing, as in "The terrorist's bomb should have gone off by now." Also, I accept that "fail to" *can* report the mere non-occurrence of something, without presupposing that it should have occurred.

of our thinking about our phenomenal states by exercising a phenomenal concept with our thinking about our brain-states by exercising a material concept. However, it remains an implausible explanation of the intuition of mind-brain distinctness. It requires that very sophisticated thinkers who have the intuition make not one but two rather elementary mistakes. The first mistake is the unwarranted extrapolation involved in expecting that *all* thinking about pain activates or involves a feeling of pain just because our everyday untutored thinking about pain does so. Inductions from a single kind of case certainly *can* be good, but only given a suitably rich background of prior knowledge, and we obviously have no such background regarding our everyday thinking about pain. And it would be implausibly ad hoc to suggest that we are psychologically locked into the extrapolation in this case and no other. The second mistake is to miss the lexical ambiguity in the claim that thinking about brain-states "leaves out" the feeling of pain ("fails to activate or involve" vs. "doesn't mention"). True, the ambiguity is closely related to philosophers' traditional distinction between use and mention, which is not initially obvious to all students; but the traditional distinction *is* obvious to some students and easily explained to the rest. Surely the ambiguity can play no part in explaining why the intuition of mind-brain distinctness "continues to press" on Papineau and other philosophers.

4.5 Robbins and Jack

Philip Robbins and Anthony I. Jack have proposed "an empirically grounded account of how the intuition [of an explanatory gap] arises" (2006, 60). They begin their account by citing psychological evidence that humans possess three psychological capacities, which they call "stances." Two of these stances are familiar: the *intentional* stance, which is the capacity to explain and predict humans' behavior by ascribing to them intentional mental states, such as beliefs and desires (which are usually thought to lack phenomenal character); and the *physical* stance, which is the capacity to predict and explain the behavior of uncontroversially physical systems by treating them as moving from one physical state to another in law-governed ways. The third (and novel) stance, the *phenomenal* stance, is the capacity (i) to ascribe mental states with phenomenal character to other people, (ii) to understand these ascribed phenomenal states, including these states' hedonic value, on the model of one's own phenomenal states, and (iii) to attribute moral significance to the people to whom these states are ascribed (Robbins and Jack 2006, 69–72). Robbins and Jack borrow the terminology of "stances" from Daniel Dennett (1987), but they give the terminology a psychologistic gloss by treating stances as psychological capacities rather than as points of view or heuristics; and, of course, they posit the phenomenal stance in addition to Dennett's intentional and physical stances.

Robbins and Jack first address what they take to be the "explanatory gap concerning the *intentional* mind" (2006, 73; italics added). They seek to explain it by appeal to certain differences—semantic, functional, and neural—between the physical stance and the intentional stance. "These differences," they suggest, "jointly give rise to a problem of cognitive integration: they make it cognitively difficult and demanding—unnatural, to a certain extent—for us to bind information from the physical and intentional domains" (2006, 73). They spell out what they mean as follows (2006, 80–1):

> The problem is essentially one of mental file-keeping . . . . In the physical stance, we think about people qua physical objects, tracking their physical properties and adding this information to file F1; in the intentional stance, we think about people qua intentional agents, tracking their intentional properties and adding the information to a different file, F2. F1 and F2 contain disparate sorts of information, and there is minimal sharing of information between the domains in which the two files are stored. This predisposes us to think that F1 and F2 are about different things.

In this passage, Robbins and Jack posit distinct mental files for the physical and intentional stances in order to explain why we are predisposed "to think that F1 and F2 are about different things," that is, predisposed to think that physical properties and intentional properties belong to different kinds of object. They don't say how this predisposition would account for an "explanatory gap concerning the intentional mind" (Robbins and Jack 2006, 73), that is, a predisposition to think that physical properties couldn't possibly explain intentional properties. But presumably physical properties couldn't possibly explain intentional properties if the physical properties belong to one kind of object and the intentional properties to another. In fact, however, we seem not to be predisposed to think that physical properties and intentional properties belong to different kinds of object. We have no trouble in ascribing *both* physical *and* intentional properties to the *same* kind of object. We attribute intentional properties to *people*, while fully recognizing that people are ordinary physical objects—subject to gravity, able to move other physical objects through contact with them, liable to be knocked over by moving masses, and so on. For example, it is a perfectly natural thought that Jen is *afraid* that *she* will be swept away by the current. The view that people are *purely immaterial* objects—quite without physical properties—is a philosophical, not a folk, view.

Let us now turn to Robbins and Jack's view of "what drives the intuition of an explanatory gap regarding *consciousness*" (2006, 76; italics added). Part of their explanation is that "the same point applies, *mutatis mutandis*, to the physical and *phenomenal* stances" as applied to the physical and *intentional* stances (2006, 75; italics added). But the main component of their explanation is specific to the case of phenomenally conscious mental states, and trades on their claim that, when we exercise the phenomenal stance by ascribing phenomenal states to someone, we attribute moral significance to the person to whom we ascribe the states. Robbins and Jack outline this main component of their explanation as follows:

> First, to think about something as conscious is to think about it as a locus of moral concern. Second, thinking about something as a locus of moral concern is naturally opposed to thinking about it as a *mere* physical object (however complex in structure), since a *mere* physical object is the wrong sort of thing to attract moral concern. (2006, 75–6; italics added)

If both these claims are true, then, whenever we think of a person as phenomenally conscious, we will be naturally disinclined to think of the person in a physicalist way, as an exclusively ("mere") physical object. Are both the claims true? The first is true if the phenomenal stance as defined above exists.[14] The second is plausible: it's plausible that the folk *think* that being a locus of moral concern requires being more (or other) than a physical object. On the other hand, thinking this begs the question against the view that phenomenal states are physical states, since if phenomenal states *are* kinds of physical state, then a mere physical object *can* be a locus of moral concern. But this point doesn't invalidate the explanation; at most, it shows that the explanation applies only to people who don't notice the question-begging.

Robbins and Jack's explanation is officially aimed at accounting for the intuition of an explanatory gap between the physical and the phenomenal. However, it seems incapable in principle of explaining the explanatory gap,

---

[14] In later work, Robbins and Jack present novel psychological evidence for the existence of the phenomenal stance (Jack and Robbins 2012).

at least as I understand the explanatory gap; it promises at best to account for—and indeed may account for—a more general unease about viewing people *both* as being in phenomenally conscious mental states *and* as exclusively physical. As I understand the explanatory gap regarding the phenomenal (section 2.3), it is a certain difference between (i) how people react to familiar reductive explanations of non-phenomenal properties (e.g., of water's boiling at 100°C) and (ii) how people react to purported reductive explanations of phenomenal properties. For example, people find the sketchiest of reductive explanations of water's boiling point fairly convincing, whereas no matter how much neurophysiological detail people are given about someone enjoying a phenomenally red visual sensation, they still feel that no progress has been made toward reductively explaining the sensation's phenomenal redness. On this understanding of the explanatory gap, however, it arises not when we look at, or imagine looking at, a whole human organism, as we might do in everyday life with unaided vision, but when we attend in particular to someone's neurophysiological state. By contrast, Robbins and Jack think of their intentional and phenomenal stances as psychological capacities to cognize—precisely—the whole human organism, as seen with unaided vision; likewise for the physical stance when it is directed on people. For this reason, in their empirical work aimed at providing evidence for the reality of the phenomenal stance, the vignettes that they give to their experimental subjects mostly describe the whole organism and never include neurophysiological detail (Jack and Robbins 2012). Moreover, the conception of the *physical* assumed by Robbins and Jack's talk of the physical stance is a pre-scientific, commonsense one; paradigms of objects that are physical in the sense uppermost in their minds would be rocks or chairs, which behave gravitationally except when acted upon by contact, and which act only by contact. The physical stance as Robbins and Jack understand it, therefore, may have little or nothing to do with the domain of the *neurophysiological*, where causation is biochemical and appears, at any rate, not to involve pushing and pulling (or falling).

The fact that (i) the intentional and phenomenal stances are capacities to cognize the whole human organism and that (ii) the physical stance presupposes a pre-scientific, commonsense conception of the physical means that Robbins and Jack's explanation is also incapable in principle of explaining the intuition of distinctness. (Not that they claim otherwise, of course.) The intuition of distinctness arises not when one uses unaided vision to view a whole human organism but when one *introspects* the phenomenal character of a current sensation of one's own. And the content of the intuition might be that, say, phenomenal redness just couldn't be the firing of certain neurons in the primary visual cortex.

In a later, single-authored paper, Jack proposes a slightly different explanation of the explanatory gap. He cites empirical evidence for the existence of a "reciprocal inhibitory relationship between [two] networks" (Jack 2014, 184). The first network is the *task positive network* (TPN), the regions forming which "are recruited by a variety of non-social tasks, including visual attention, working memory, language, logical reasoning, mathematical reasoning, general problem solving and causal/mechanical reasoning tasks" (2014, 179); Jack believes that "a good characterization of this network is that it is involved in *analytic-empirical-critical* thinking" (2014, 181). The second network is the *default mode network* (DMN), "The midline regions [of which] ... are recruited both when we introspect our own current mental states (e.g. emotions) and when we attribute mental states to others" (2014, 178). Jack interprets the reciprocal inhibitory relationship between the TPN and DMN by proposing "the opposing domains hypothesis," which claims that "the neural antagonism between the TPN and DMN reflects a fundamental cognitive tension between thinking about internal mental states and physical mechanisms" (2014, 186). However, even if the opposing domains hypothesis is true, it has nothing like the resolving power necessary to explain something as specific as the intuition of distinctness. Suppose I attend introspectively to the phenomenal character of an itch. Then, according to the opposing domains hypothesis, my DMN is activated, while activation of my TPN is inhibited (though not totally shut down, because Jack says that the DMN and TPN can be co-activated), thus making "analytic-empirical-critical thinking" harder for me (2014, 181; italics removed). But "analytic-empirical-critical thinking" is obviously a very broad category indeed. Increased difficulty in such thinking obviously doesn't predict the very particular psychological fact about me that I am unable to make anything of the thought that the phenomenal character of my itch just is a certain physical or functional property.[15]

---

[15] I can't make everything Jack says fit together. For he writes:
> Psychopaths don't seem to have any problem perceiving an explanatory, epistemological or conceivability gap. In one experiment we presented scenarios based on Nagel's bat (1974), Jackson's Mary (1986) and Chalmers's philosophical zombie (1996). Virtually everyone perceived these gaps, and there was no clear correlation with psychopathy. (Jack 2014, 195)

But Jack holds that (i) psychopaths are incapable of, or at least deficient in, taking the phenomenal stance, and that (ii) the DMN is the neural basis of the phenomenal stance (Jack 2014, 190).

4.6 Fiala, Arico, and Nichols

Brian Fiala, Adam Arico, and Shaun Nichols seek "to illuminate the source of the explanatory gap," that is, "to illuminate why physicalist explanations of consciousness leave us feeling as if something has been left out" (2011, 97). They first propose a view about the different psychological processes by which we attribute sensations (what they call "conscious states") to things:

> We suggest (1) that there are two cognitive pathways by which we typically arrive at judgments that something has conscious states, and (2) that these pathways correspond to a system 1/system 2 distinction. On the one hand, we propose a "low-road" mechanism for conscious-state attributions that has several characteristic system 1 features: it is fast, domain-specific (i.e., it operates on a restricted range of inputs), and automatic (i.e., the mechanism is not under conscious control). On the other hand, there are judgments about conscious states that we reach through rational deliberation, theory application, or conscious reasoning; call this pathway to attributions of conscious states "the high road." (Fiala et al. 2011, 91)

They call their specific view of how the "low-road" mechanism works the "AGENCY model"[16]:

> According to this model, we are disposed to have a gut feeling that an entity has conscious states if and only if we categorize that entity as an AGENT, and typically we are inclined to categorize an entity as an AGENT only when we represent the entity as having certain features. . . . Previous research has identified three features that reliably produce AGENT categorization: that the entity appears to have eyes, that it appears to behave in a contingently interactive manner, and that it displays distinctive (non-inertial) motion trajectories. (Fiala et al. 2011, 91–2)

Given (i) and (ii), the opposing domains hypothesis would seem to imply that, contrary to the quotation, psychopaths *would* have difficulty "perceiving an explanatory . . . gap," because, with less activation of the DMN, there is less reciprocal inhibition of the TPN.

[16] They should be understood as using the upper-case term "AGENT" in a technical sense that may not correspond closely to everyday uses of "agent," and that is certainly less rich than philosopher's typical uses of "agent" in discussions of practical rationality and free will (Arico et al. 2011, 331–2).

114 INTUITION OF DISTINCTNESS

Fiala, Arico, and Nichols give the following sketch of how their view that there are two psychological processes by which we typically attribute sensations illuminates the source of the explanatory gap:

> People's natural inclination to judge that broadly physicalist accounts of consciousness "leave something out" depends on a cognitive architecture involving two distinct processes [i.e., the low-road mechanism and the high-road mechanism]. In typical cases of consciousness attribution, the two processes produce harmonious outputs and lead to unsurprising attributions. However, in the case of the explanatory gap, we claim, one of the relevant cognitive processes fails to produce any output, thus leading to the disharmonious sense that the neural description is fundamentally incomplete as an explanation of consciousness. (Fiala et al. 2011, 99)

An illustrative example adds a little detail:

> Consider Jenny, who is in the grip of physicalism about consciousness. Using high-road reasoning, she could apply the hypothesis that consciousness is identical to a certain kind of brain process, in which case Jenny's high road would produce the output that specific brain processes or brain regions *are* conscious experiences. For example, Jenny might believe that consciousness is identical to populations of neurons firing in synchrony at a rate between 40 Hz and 60 Hz; on this basis she could infer (using the high road) that specific brain regions that are firing synchronously are conscious experiences. If Jenny knew that Jimmy's brain had regions that were firing synchronously between 40–60 Hz, she could infer (using the high road) that Jimmy's brain states are conscious experiences. However, since this description of Jimmy's brain does not advert to any of the featural cues that trigger AGENCY categorization, Jenny's low road is not activated, and thus remains silent on whether the synchronously firing neurons are conscious. (Fiala et al. 2011, 96–7; in-text citation removed)

So much for exposition of the explanation proposed by Fiala, Arico, and Nichols. I have three comments on it.

First, the explanation proposed by Fiala, Arico, and Nichols and the explanation that I will propose in Chapter 5 have different explananda. As their illustrative example makes clear, their explanandum typically arises in third-person cases: Jenny has the sense of an explanatory gap, but it arises as she thinks about *Jimmy's* sensations; she is not attending introspectively to her *own* sensations. By contrast, the explanandum of my proposed explanation is the intuition of distinctness, which arises only in first-person cases, because people must be attending introspectively to their own sensations for it to seem to them that an introspected phenomenal property of a current sensation just couldn't be a physical or functional property. So the explanation proposed by Fiala, Arico, and Nichols and the explanation that I will propose are not direct rivals. I am, of course, committed to an *indirect* explanation of the explanatory gap, because I suggested in section 2.3 that people have the sense of an explanatory gap because their intuition of distinctness makes them resist the phenomenal-physical (or phenomenal-functional) type-identity claims that would be required for reductive explanations of phenomenal properties. But the explanation of the explanatory gap proposed by Fiala, Arico, and Nichols seems logically consistent with my indirect explanation of it and would be non-redundant if the mechanism it posits *intensified* a sense of an explanatory gap that arose initially from the intuition of distinctness.

Second, Fiala, Arico, and Nichols make it less than ideally clear why exactly one's low road is not activated on those occasions when one has the sense of an explanatory gap. The key sentence in their tale of Jenny and Jimmy is this (Fiala et al. 2011, 96–7): "since this description of Jimmy's brain does not advert to any of the featural cues that trigger AGENCY categorization, Jenny's low road is not activated." Obviously they are right that the description *of Jimmy's brain* doesn't advert to any of the featural cues that trigger AGENCY categorization; but so what? Jenny can hardly be unaware that Jimmy does in fact exhibit these featural cues (eyes, contingent reactions, and non-inertial motions), if only because she knows full well that he is an ordinary human being. Is the thought, then, that this knowledge is not present to Jenny's mind while she has the sense of an explanatory gap—so that, if it were brought to her attention, she would lose the intuition? Or is the thought perhaps that AGENCY categorization is triggered visually, so that Jenny's low road is not activated because she is not *looking* at Jimmy (or imagining looking at him)? Fiala, Arico, and Nichols remark that "if Jenny were to view a picture of Jimmy (or Jimmy himself), her low road would be activated by the presence of the relevant featural cues" (2011, 97, note 9). But their remark is problematic. The explanation they propose says that the sense of an explanatory gap arises because the high road is activated while the low road is not. So if viewing Jimmy would trigger activation of the low road, then the intuition ought to disappear if Jenny views Jimmy; but surely it would not disappear if she viewed Jimmy.[17]

Finally, Fiala, Arico, and Nichols don't need their AGENCY model in particular in order to give the kind of explanation that they do of the sense of an explanatory gap. The heart of their explanation is that "one of the [two] relevant cognitive processes fails to produce any output, thus leading to the disharmonious sense that the neural description is fundamentally incomplete" (Fiala et al. 2011, 99). But the cognitive process that fails to produce any output does not have to take any particular form, so long as it yields ascriptions of sensations under everyday conditions; so though it might operate as the AGENCY model claims, it also might not.[18] And surely *some* such cognitive process exists, because anyone who sees a person accidentally drop a house brick on their bare foot immediately ascribes sensations of pain to the unfortunate person. As well as being immediate, such ascriptions also seem to be automatic and not to result from conscious inference.

4.7 Elpidorou and Dove

Andreas Elpidorou and Guy Dove have proposed an intriguing explanation of "the psychological observation that consciousness appears to be other-than-physical when we consciously deliberate about the ontological status of consciousness" (2018, 199; italics removed). Their explanandum is therefore at least a close relative of the intuition of distinctness.[19] Their explanation appeals to the controversial but empirically supported thesis—called by them "conceptual embodiment"—that even the thinking of thoughts that involve *physical* concepts involves the activation of sensory and motor representations that have associated phenomenal characters, so that typically there is something it is like to think a thought even if the thinker employs only physical concepts in doing so (2018, 182–6). In particular, they claim

[17] It's unclear why a mere picture of Jimmy—a still photo, say—would trigger activation of the low road, since a picture would naturally show that Jimmy has eyes but not that he *reacts* contingently and *moves* non-inertially (though it would remind Jenny that he is a normal human being).
[18] Evidence for the model has been presented (Arico et al. 2011), though doubts have also been voiced (Jack and Robbins 2012).
[19] Sometimes (e.g., Elpidorou and Dove 2018, 192) they say that their explanandum is "the appearance of contingency"—the appearance that the physical and phenomenal are not necessarily connected. Even though the appearance of contingency (if the appearance is veridical) entails the distinctness of the phenomenal and the physical (given the necessity of identity), it is not the same as the appearance of distinctness.

that physical concepts are "multimodal in precisely this sense: Not only do [physical concepts] encode a rich array of experientially derived information (information that was derived from more than one sense modality), but also their employment involves the simultaneous and selective engagement of multiple sensorimotor and affective neural systems" (2018, 189). Elpidorou and Dove seek to explain the fact that phenomenal properties appear non-physical by appeal to a "contrast between the *multimodal* character of physical concepts and the *unimodal* character of phenomenal concepts" (2018, 192; italics added). They present their explanation as follows:

> When we carefully consider a conscious experience, say, the experience of seeing red, we recognize that we need to think of it unimodally. However, when we think of neural stimulation, we recognize that we are able to think of it multimodally. The employment of a physical concept has a potentially multimodal complexity that is lacking from the employment of a phenomenal concept. The appearance of consciousness' special and elusive status appears then to be a straightforward consequence of the phenomenological difference involved in the employment of the two types of concepts. The idea here is simple: We have come to associate multimodality with physical objects and events. When this multimodality is absent, however, from our employment of phenomenal concepts, it is natural for us to think that the referents of phenomenal concepts cannot be physical objects and events. Consequently, it is natural for us to think that phenomenal and physical concepts do not co-refer. (2018, 191)

This explanation doesn't trade on the claim that employing a phenomenal concept involves phenomenology whereas employing a physical concept does not; it trades on the claim that the phenomenology of employing a phenomenal concept is unimodal, whereas the phenomenology of employing a physical concept is multimodal.

It is not obvious, however, that the physical concepts most relevant to consciousness' appearance of non-physicality—neural concepts—really are multimodal. It is plausible that *some* physical concepts *aren't* multimodal. For example, shortly after Wilhelm Röntgen's discovery of X-rays in 1895 there was only one way to detect the presence of X-rays—by observing the faint green glow from a fluorescent screen.[20] At that time, therefore, people's

[20] See https://en.wikipedia.org/wiki/X-ray.

concept of X-rays presumably *didn't* "encode a rich array of experientially derived information (information that was derived from more than one sense modality)." And because X-rays had a neutral emotional valence and no obvious connection to action, it also seems unlikely that "[the] employment [of the concept of X-rays] involve[d] the simultaneous and selective engagement of multiple sensorimotor and affective neural systems" (Elpidorou and Dove 2018, 189). What about neural concepts? They too have a neutral emotional valence and no obvious connection to action; and, for most people employing a neural concept, it may be that the only sensation activated is that of seeing a generic image of a brain scan.[21] It is perhaps because of such considerations as these that in the long quotation above Elpidorou and Dove claim only that the "employment of a physical [e.g., a neural] concept has a *potentially* multimodal complexity" (191) rather than an actually multimodal one (italics added). But their retreat to merely potential multimodality makes it less plausible that their proposed explanation accounts for the intuition of distinctness. First, awareness of the merely potential multimodality of a physical concept may be too sophisticated a cognitive achievement to figure in an explanation of a widespread and reflexive intuition. Second, their—admittedly attractive—motivating idea, which they call "Difference in Introspective Phenomenology" (2018, 179), was to explain the intuition of distinctness by appeal to current, actual phenomenological differences between the employment of physical and phenomenal concepts, not merely potential ones.

Regarding the example of X-rays, it might be replied that, even in the immediate aftermath of their discovery, people could also gain information about them through language—by *hearing* true spoken sentences about X-rays—so that the employment of the concept of X-rays might activate *auditory* as well as visual sensations; and the same sort of thing could obviously be said about neural concepts. But if this reply is accepted, then the other essential claim of the proposed explanation—that phenomenal concepts are unimodal—is endangered, for we can employ phenomenal concepts in learning about the phenomenal properties of other people's visual sensations by *hearing* the people utter true sentences that report the (visual) phenomenal character of their sensations.

There are further reasons to doubt that phenomenal concepts are unimodal. As we have seen, Elpidorou and Dove claim that, when concepts are

---

[21] There is obviously also a question about how to individuate "modes" for the purpose of evaluating claims of *multi*modality.

multimodal, "their employment involves the simultaneous and selective engagement of multiple sensorimotor and affective neural systems" (2018, 189); the sensations induced by the activation of *these* systems are not, of course, ways of *detecting* the referents of multimodal concepts. On the face of it, though, many phenomenal properties have a positive or negative emotional valence and are intimately connected to action, so that the employment of phenomenal concepts of these properties should be expected to "involve [. . .] the simultaneous and selective engagement of multiple sensorimotor and affective neural systems" and hence to be multimodal. Obvious examples of such phenomenal properties are being a pain (because pain often goes along with fear, tension, and such movements as wincing or flinching) and being nausea (because nausea goes along with the muscular contractions that constitute vomiting). Less obvious examples might be phenomenal blueness (because blue is said to recede) and phenomenal redness (because red is said to suggest danger or excitement). A second reason to doubt that phenomenal concepts are unimodal is that we ascribe phenomenal properties to other people's sensations on the basis of *looking* at other people. For example, people in severe pain have a look—a visual appearance—that the neurotypical can recognize and that triggers (among other things) a phenomenal-concept-involving ascription of pain; the look is a matter both of facial expression and overall posture. On the face of it, therefore, the employment of a phenomenal concept of pain might be expected to involve the activation of certain *visual* sensations and hence to be multimodal.

I have been expressing reservations about Elpidorou and Dove's claim that phenomenal concepts are unimodal, whereas neural concepts are multimodal. But a further and perhaps more serious doubt about their proposed explanation arises even if we grant this claim. Their proposed explanation continues:

> When this multimodality is absent, however, from our employment of phenomenal concepts, it is *natural for us to think* that the referents of phenomenal concepts cannot be physical objects and events. (Elpidorou and Dove 2018, 191; italics added)

Let's suppose that it's true, and that we notice, that our employment of phenomenal concepts is unimodal, while that of physical concepts is multimodal. Is it really "natural for us to think that the referents of phenomenal concepts cannot be physical objects and events"? This thought would be natural if it followed given an intuitively plausible general principle. But the principle that, if we think of X unimodally but think of Y multimodally, then X ≠ Y cannot be said to be intuitively plausible. Indeed, it might easily be thought intuitively *implausible*, because the yet more general principle that, if we think of X and Y in different ways, then X ≠ Y is clearly false, since how we think about Dr. Jekyll differs from how we think about Mr. Hyde, and yet Jekyll is Hyde. The thought would also be natural if we had a brute psychological tendency to have the thought whenever we notice the alleged contrast between phenomenal and physical concepts. But Elpidorou and Dove provide no evidence that we have such a tendency; for example, they cite no manifestations of it in other contexts. They are at liberty, of course, simply to postulate such tendency, without offering independent evidence of its existence. But I think we have a smidgin of evidence *against* it. I suggested above that, shortly after the discovery of X-rays, physicists had a concept of X-rays that was unimodal, because X-rays could only be detected in one way, had a neutral emotional valence, and had no direct connection to action. If we imagine ourselves in the shoes of these physicists, we don't seem to feel at all inclined to the thought that X-rays *couldn't* be a certain kind of atom, say, even though our employment of a concept of atoms is presumably multimodal.

4.8 Molyneux

Bernard Molyneux offers an elaborate account of why "proposed identifications between mental and physical phenomena typically give rise to how-possibly questions," thus leaving us "mystified" (2015, 239 and 258). This account might therefore seem to be aimed at explaining the sense of an explanatory gap; and nowhere is the account said to be aimed instead at explaining the intuition of distinctness.[22] But because an earlier version of the account was explicitly aimed at explaining the intuition of distinctness (see Molyneux 2011), and also because the account is intriguing, I will discuss it. My main objection to the account does not require taking a stand on whether the account's explanatory target is the sense of an explanatory gap or the intuition of distinctness or indeed some third thing.

Molyneux's account appeals to the ways in which *identification*—the formation of a belief to the effect that an a posteriori identity claim is true—is

---

[22] In fact, the expression "intuition of distinctness" does not even appear in Molyneux (2015).

PREVIOUS ACCOUNTS OF THE INTUITION OF DISTINCTNESS 121

rationally constrained by Leibniz's Law, the logical principle that, if $x = y$, then x and y have exactly the same properties (2015, 240). According to Molyneux, Leibniz's Law rationally constrains identifications in two different ways, depending upon which of two situations the thinker is in. In the first situation, we are considering or already believe the claim that $x = y$, but we believe that x has, while y doesn't have, property P. We therefore have the makings of an objection, grounded in Leibniz's Law, to the claim that $x = y$—a valid argument for the conclusion that $x \neq y$. So, if we wish to endorse, or to continue endorsing, the claim that $x = y$, we must avoid the objection, and to avoid the objection we must abandon the (conjunctive) belief that x has, while y doesn't have, property P. In the second situation, we already believe that $x = y$, and that x has P, but we lack the belief that y has P too. There is no *objection* here to the claim that $x = y$, but we are rationally required by Leibniz's Law to form the further belief that y has P (2015, 256).

Molyneux's fundamental insight is that the rational constraint that Leibniz's Law imposes on identifications has the potential to generate an *infinite regress*. It has this potential because, under a certain condition, the rational constraint imposed by Leibniz's Law requires making a second identification, which, given the same condition, requires making a third identification, and so on indefinitely, the potential regress reflecting the logical fact that, if $x = y$, then every property of x is identical with some property of y, and every property of every property of x is identical with some property of some property of y, and so on indefinitely (Molyneux 2015, 249–50). The condition giving rise to this infinite regress has two parts. The first part concerns our prior ascriptions of properties to x (qua x) and to y (qua y)—where we *ascribe* a certain property to, say, water (qua water) iff we believe that water has the property, using the folk concept of water to think about water, though using a folk *or* scientific concept to think about the *property*. The first part of the condition giving rise to the infinite regress is that we regard our prior ascriptions of properties to x (qua x) and to y (qua y) as both *correct* and *complete*—whether x and y are either the entity or entities mentioned in the *original* identification or the entity or entities (e.g., the property or properties) mentioned in our *subsequent* identifications (2015, 257). Our prior ascriptions of properties to x (qua x) are *correct* iff every such property-ascription is true; and they are *complete* iff they ascribe to x (qua x) every property that x in fact possesses. Likewise, of course, for our prior ascriptions of properties to y (qua y). The second part of the condition giving rise to the infinite regress is that in the *second* identification, and indeed in every subsequent identification, a property is identified with a *named* property (rather than with some or other property).

To see how an infinite regress arises when this two-part condition holds, let us review the two situations in which identification is rationally constrained by Leibniz's Law. Suppose, first, that we are considering or already believe the claim that $x = y$, but that we believe that x has, while y doesn't have, property P, so that we have an objection to the identity claim grounded in Leibniz's Law. How to respond consistently with believing that $x = y$? Abandoning the belief that x has P is ruled out by our regarding our prior ascriptions of properties to x (qua x) as correct. So we must instead abandon the belief that y doesn't have P, and adopt in its place the belief that y *has* P. But to continue regarding our prior ascriptions of properties to y (qua y) as complete, we must adopt the belief that P is (non-trivially) identical with some property that we have *already* ascribed to y (qua y). And since (by the second part of the two-part condition) we must identify P with a *named* property that we have already ascribed to y (qua y), we must believe that P = Q, where Q is the particular property we have selected. But then we are again in one of the two situations in which an identification is rationally constrained by Leibniz's Law—only now with regard to the identification of P with Q. Suppose, second, that we believe that $x = y$, and that x has P, but we lack the belief that y has P too. Given Leibniz's Law, we must start believing that y has P. But the only way in which we can start to believe that y has P consistently with regarding our prior ascriptions of properties to y (qua y) as complete is to adopt the belief that P is (non-trivially) identical with a property that we have already ascribed to y (qua y). And, exactly as in the first situation, since we must identify P with a named property that we have already ascribed to y (qua y), we must believe that P = Q, and we are once more in one of the two situations in which an identification, this time of P with Q, is rationally constrained by Leibniz's Law.[23]

---

[23] *Must* we be in one of the two situations with regard to the identity claim that P = Q? Molyneux thinks so, on the grounds that otherwise we wouldn't distinguish between P and Q in the first place. However, this rationale may confuse (i) distinguishing *property* P from *property* Q with (ii) distinguishing our *concept* of P from our *concept* of Q. Surely we somehow do the latter, perhaps non-consciously; otherwise the claim that P = Q would strike us as trivial. But we might have two predicative concepts, between which *concepts* we distinguish, even though they both express the very same property, and even though we believe, of P as such, all and only what we believe of Q as such. Distinguishing between the two concepts may be a matter of each concept's having a different functional role, where the difference between the two roles doesn't require our believing, of P as such, something that we don't believe of Q as such. But the issue obviously requires a fuller discussion. A second issue is whether, as an infinite regress requires, *every* property has at least one property.

Now though Molyneux holds that being rationally constrained by Leibniz's Law has the *potential* to generate an infinite regress, he doesn't think that it must, or does, *in practice*. Sometimes an infinite regress in practice is avoided because the *first* part of the two-part condition is not met: we are prepared to *revise* our prior ascriptions of properties to *x* (qua *x*) and to *y* (qua *y*), either by correcting or by adding to our prior ascriptions, so that we aren't forced to adopt any further identity claim such as that P = Q (see Molyneux 2015, 257, where he cites the identification of water with H_2O as an example). But an infinite regress in practice can also be avoided because the *second* part of the two-part condition is not met: rather than forming the belief that property P is identical with a named property, Q, that we have already ascribed to *y* (qua *y*), we instead form the existentially quantified belief that *there is a property of y that is (non-trivially) identical with P* (2015, 244–6; and see 258, where he again cites the identification of water with H_2O as an example, though under different imagined conditions). To form the existentially quantified belief is to accept what Molyneux calls a "semi-solution" to the problem of making our identifications conform to the constraints imposed by Leibniz's Law, and forming such a belief is consistent with (though it does not require) regarding our prior ascriptions of properties to *y* (qua *y*) as complete (2015, 245). But the potential regress is blocked, because we are not thereby placed, with regard to a novel identity belief, in one of the two situations in which an identification is rationally constrained by Leibniz's Law.

Because Molyneux allows that semi-solutions are available in the case of phenomenal-physical identifications, it cannot be infinite regress alone, and as such, that on his view accounts for why phenomenal-physical identity claims give rise to how-possibly questions, and consequent mystification, while undisputed scientific identity claims do not.[24] What, therefore, is the relevant difference between semi-solutions in the case of phenomenal-physical identifications, which *do* give rise to how-possibly questions and mystification, and semi-solutions in the case of undisputed scientific identifications, which do not? Molyneux's answer is that, when we contemplate undisputed scientific identifications, we *don't* regard our prior ascriptions of properties to *x* (qua *x*) and to *y* (qua *y*) as both correct and complete,

---

[24] In an earlier paper, by contrast, Molyneux sought explicitly to account for the intuition of distinctness; and his explanatory hypothesis appealed to the idea of *glimpsing an infinite regress*. "When we experience deep-seated misgivings about identifying the physical and the phenomenal," he wrote, "it is because we are glimpsing the infinitely hard problem—a problem arising from the combination of appropriately related conceptual schemes together with the logic of Leibniz's Law" (Molyneux 2011, 227). This idea *seems* to be absent in his 2015 account.

whereas, when we contemplate phenomenal-physical identifications, we *do* regard our prior ascriptions of properties to x (qua x) and to y (qua y) as both correct and complete (2015, 251–5 and 258).

How exactly this difference is relevant to the generation of how-possibly questions and consequent mystification, according to Molyneux, is a question to which I will return. But I have already presented enough of Molyneux's account to be able to state my main objection to it. As we have just seen, his account assumes that, when we contemplate phenomenal-physical identity claims, we regard our prior ascriptions of properties to x (qua x) and to y (qua y) as both correct and complete. But this assumption, I say, is unwarranted and implausible. In the case of phenomenal-physical identity claims, the relevant prior ascriptions fall into two classes (Molyneux 2015, 251). In the first class are our *third-person* beliefs to the effect that certain physical or physically realized items (e.g., human brain-states or properties of such brain-states), conceived by means of scientific concepts, possess certain physical or physically realized properties (e.g., neurophysiological or computational-representational properties), also conceived by means of scientific concepts. In the second class are our *introspective* beliefs to the effect that certain phenomenal states or phenomenal properties, conceived by means of phenomenal concepts, have certain phenomenal properties, also conceived by means of phenomenal concepts. The assumption of Molyneux's account to which I object, then, is that we do in fact regard both our third-person beliefs and our introspective beliefs as correct and complete. Molyneux argues for this assumption, in effect, by inferring it from the premise that we *should* regard our beliefs of these kinds as correct and complete (given that we meet certain conditions which we do meet). I reject this premise, on the grounds that it wrongly assumes a wall of evidential separation between (i) our best science and (ii) our philosophical attempts to solve the mind-body problem. The considerations I shall adduce could be endorsed by anyone; but they are very widely endorsed by physicalists, who are therefore most unlikely to regard both their third-person and their introspective beliefs as correct and complete. Hence Molyneux's proposed account is most unlikely to explain the mystification that *physicalists* feel in the face of phenomenal-physical identity claims, a mystification that they do not feel in the face of undisputed scientific identity claims.

Let me start with our third-person beliefs. These beliefs, we may assume, belong to the current scientific consensus. Each such belief is therefore supported by empirical evidence, which gives us reason to think that it is correct. Fair enough; but it does not follow that we may not abandon such beliefs, as

Molyneux's account requires. For we often have, and we can always imagine having, *evidence* for a phenomenal-physical identity claim, and this evidence might be stronger than the evidence for a third-person belief with which (given other well-supported beliefs) it conflicts. Therefore, when faced with the choice between accepting the identity claim and maintaining the third-person belief, the rational response may be to deem the third-person belief to be incorrect, and therefore to abandon it. As regards whether we should regard our third-person beliefs as complete, Molyneux writes that "if it [i.e., "empirical science"] finds no property, the philosopher of mind has no business insisting upon it" (2015, 253). Insistence would be out of place, I agree; but insistence is not the issue. The issue is whether, in the search for overall epistemological coherence, physicalists, or people imaginatively adopting a physicalist position, could reasonably ascribe a property to some physical or physically realized item that our best current science has not yet ascribed to it; and the answer, as far as I can see, is that they could.

One might suspect that physicalists couldn't, since physicalists are committed to the completeness of our third-person beliefs. After all, physicalism says that *all* properties are physical or physically realized. Don't we have to have *discovered* a property before we can know that it is physical or physically realized? In fact, we don't. Physicalism is a universal generalization, supportable by inductive extrapolation from a large and varied sample of properties for each of which we have non-extrapolative evidence that it is physical or physically realized (Melnyk 2003, 256–60). So having evidence for physicalism does not require having a complete list of properties, for each of which we have non-extrapolative evidence that it is physical or physically realized; it does not require having discovered every single property. Physicalists are not committed to the completeness of our third-person beliefs.

Admittedly, the fact that our best current science hasn't *yet* ascribed more than a certain number of physically realized properties to a physical or physically realized item provides *some* evidence that the item has no further physically realized properties. But the evidence is weak; for there are many possible reasons why science might not yet have discovered a physically realized property, including the inevitable scarcity of scientific resources, bad luck, and, of course, error. Moreover, science's track-record of steadily generating new discoveries is evidence for thinking that such discoveries will continue, and hence that science *hasn't* yet discovered all the physically realized properties; and surely the scientific investigation of physically realized computational-representational properties of brain-states is at best in its adolescence. Finally, because, as noted above, we often have evidence *for* a phenomenal-physical identity claim, we often thereby have indirect evidence for property-ascriptions that are not part of our current best science; and this indirect evidence may well outweigh the net evidence, if any, that we have for thinking that our current best science has omitted no physically realized property. Suppose, for example, that I have excellent correlational evidence for the proposition that a visual sensation of red is a certain brain-state, and the evidence of common experience that a visual sensation of red can be accurate or inaccurate. I thereby have evidence that a certain brain-state (is a representation that) can be accurate or inaccurate—a property-ascription that might not already be part of our current best science.

Let me turn now to our introspective beliefs. We are right, I concede, to regard our introspective beliefs as generally *correct*—not because we can't possibly mistake a severe itch for a pain on a particular occasion, but because, unless we regard our introspective beliefs as generally correct, we're not engaged in the project of trying to discover the place of the phenomenal in the physical world. For introspection provides our only reason for believing in sensations and their phenomenal properties in the first place; we have gone eliminativist if we cease to regard our introspective beliefs as generally correct (Molyneux 2015, 252–3). Our introspective beliefs' *completeness*, however, is another matter. Molyneux suggests that we should regard our introspective beliefs as complete because "conscious states are *self-intimating*—i.e., if one's experience is F, it seems to one that it is F" (2015, 252; italics added). Suitably modified (e.g., to take due account of the role of attention), the thesis of self-intimation is plausible: if I wake up tomorrow morning with a severe toothache, ask myself whether I feel okay, and am not distracted, then I'm bound to form the introspective belief that I have a severe toothache (see section 3.10). But the thesis of self-intimation is only plausible if its scope is restricted to the properties that we ascribe to ourselves in introspective beliefs by means of phenomenal concepts; for Molyneux's formulation of the thesis to be correct, "F" must be taken to be a phenomenal concept. For physicalism certainly entails that, if pain is a certain brain-state, then every phenomenal property of pain is a physical or physically realized property of the brain-state. But physicalism doesn't entail that, if pain is a certain brain-state, every physical or physically realized property of the brain-state is a *phenomenal* property of pain; for phenomenal properties are properties of which we can become aware from the inside, through introspection, and physicalism entails nothing about which properties of our physical or physically realized mental states we can, and which we can't, represent introspectively. And we have no idea, empirically, what *proportion* of the physical or physically realized properties possessed by brain-states plausibly identifiable with sensations we represent introspectively. The thesis of self-intimation therefore provides neither conceptual nor empirical grounds for regarding our introspective beliefs as complete. Consequently, if we believe that pain is a certain brain-state, and we know that the brain-state consumes such-and-such a quantity of glucose per second (say), then we may and should form the belief that pain uses that quantity of glucose per second.

I promised to return to the question of how exactly, according to Molyneux, our regarding our third-person beliefs and our introspective beliefs as correct and complete gives rise to how-possibly questions, and consequent mystification, when we contemplate a phenomenal-physical identity claim. One part of the answer is that Molyneux views compliance with Leibniz's Law in an identification as the *explaining away of apparent differences* between x and y, that is, as explaining why x appears distinct from y in a manner consistent with maintaining that x really is y (2015, 241). This view opens up the possibility that the special difficulty that arises in phenomenal-physical identifications is *explanatory*—that we are mystified because something can't be explained. However, it is not at all clear that Molyneux is right to view compliance with Leibniz's Law in an identification as *always* being the explaining away of apparent differences between x and y. His view is plausible when identifiers are in the *first* of the two situations distinguished above, in which we are considering or already believe the claim that $x = y$, but believe that x has, while y doesn't have, property P. For this situation is reasonably described as one in which it seems to us that $x \neq y$ because x and y apparently differ. But his view is not plausible when identifiers are in the *second* situation distinguished above, in which we already believe that $x = y$, and that x has P, but merely lack the belief that y has P too. For in this situation there is no *apparent difference* between x and y to be explained away, nor therefore any sense in which it *seems* to us that $x \neq y$. Rather, we have failed to infer a logical consequence of our existing beliefs, a kind of failing presumably common in our daily lives; and if we correct our error, by inferring to a new belief, nothing that previously seemed to be the case turns out not really to have been the case, and so no appearance turns out to have been deceptive. What if aspiring identifiers of phenomenal and physical items are *always* in the *first* of the two situations? What if, that is, for *any* identity claim that they consider, they *always* have the makings of an objection grounded in Leibniz's Law? But Molyneux does not claim that this is so and indeed seems to deny it (2015, 256); in any case, such a claim is hardly obvious and would need to be argued for.

Another part of the answer to the question of how exactly, according to Molyneux, how-possibly questions, and consequent mystification, are supposed to arise when we contemplate a phenomenal-physical identity claim is that compliance with Leibniz's Law when contemplating a phenomenal-physical identity claim must result (on pain of infinite regress) in a semi-solution: at some point, rather than forming the belief that property P is identical with a named property, Q, that we previously ascribed to y (qua y), we must instead form the existentially quantified belief that some (unspecified) property of y is (non-trivially) identical with P. But then, obviously, we need to know how exactly adding in the inevitability of accepting a semi-solution gets us to how-possibly questions and mystification. Here is the passage in which Molyneux gives his fullest answer to this question:

> The answer is that I can finitely discharge any quantificational placeholder in the water/H_2O semi-solution. E.g., when I leave a placeholder that covers for water's lacking M [a certain micro-structural property], I anticipate that, later, I may discharge it by either (i) subtracting M from H_2O [i.e., by ceasing to ascribe M to H_2O qua H_2O] or (ii) adding M to water [i.e., by ascribing M to water qua water]. And there are other options. The fact that I do not yet know which option is right means I have how-*actually* questions to answer. (2015, 258)

When addition and subtraction are prohibited [i.e., when we regard our prior ascriptions of properties as correct and complete], in contrast, attempts to finitely discharge a placeholder result in the reimposition of another placeholder. That's because, given the prohibition, a placeholder can only be discharged by identifying discriminable properties. Yet those properties, in being discriminable themselves, must also have their differences explained away, which, given the prohibition, requires that *their* discriminable properties be identified, and so on. Sooner or later we must abandon the regress. But that means leaving a placeholder in lieu of the next identification.

> In leaving a placeholder I promise that this can all be worked out somehow. But I can conceive of no finite way in which it could. So where, with water and H_2O, I had how-actually questions to answer, with consciousness and physical states, I have how-possibly ones. This is why, according to the present account, the latter problem leaves me mystified. (Molyneux 2015, 258)

Let me try to reformulate what is being claimed in this passage. A *placeholder*, for Molyneux, is an existentially quantified identity claim to the effect that *some* property of y = P. And a placeholder is *discharged* iff it subsequently turns out that the existentially quantified identity claim can be withdrawn, *either* because x turns out after all *not* to have P *or* because y turns out after all to *have* P.[25] It follows that the discharge of a placeholder requires a *revision* of our prior ascriptions of properties to x (qua x) and to y (qua y). So if we regard all our prior ascriptions of properties to x (qua x) and to y (qua y) as *unrevisable*, because correct and complete, as we do regard them, according to Molyneux, in the case of a phenomenal-physical identification, then we cannot consistently regard the discharge of a placeholder as possible; we have to regard ourselves as, so to speak, stuck with the placeholder; a placeholder is, in principle, the best we can do. But if we *don't* regard all our prior ascriptions of properties to x (qua x) and to y (qua y) as correct and complete, as we don't in the case of undisputed scientific identifications, then in such cases we are at liberty to regard the discharge of a placeholder as possible ("I can finitely discharge," (258) as Molyneux puts it).

So far, so good: there is a difference between phenomenal-physical identifications and undisputed scientific identifications. But how exactly does this difference yield the two different kinds of question that we are promised in the quoted passage—a how-possibly question in the first case, but a mere how-actually question in the second? And what are the questions, exactly? How-possibly *what*? How-actually *what*? It is not obvious how Molyneux does or would respond to these queries. Since he holds that compliance with Leibniz's Law in identifications is the explaining away of apparent differences between x and y, his story already includes one question, "How could x and y be identical, given their apparent differences?" But *this* question confronts us in both phenomenal-physical and undisputed scientific identifications. Moreover, *this* question seems clearly to be a how-possibly, rather than a how-actually, question. For if I ask how smoking causes lung cancer, I am asking how something comes about that I have no reason to think *couldn't* come about, and there is no prima facie case for the thing's impossibility; I am merely asking a how-actually question. But if I ask how more exercise causes a gain in weight, I am asking how something comes about that I *do* have reason to think couldn't come about, and there *is* a prima facie case for the thing's impossibility; I am asking a how-possibly question. And apparent

---

[25] Here I simply generalize from Molyneux's example of water/H_2O, neglecting the "other options" of which he speaks.

differences between x and y obviously constitute a prima facie case that x can't be y. Finally, in both phenomenal-physical and undisputed scientific identifications the *answer* that is given to *this* (how-possibly) question takes exactly the same form—that of an existentially quantified identity claim; the answer, one might therefore think, is equally good, or equally bad, in each case.

The difference between the two cases articulated in the previous paragraph concerns whether the aspiring identifier in each case can consistently accept the possibility of *transcending* this answer in a certain way; and, as we saw, the aspiring identifier can consistently accept this possibility in the second but not in the first case. But this difference doesn't seem to necessitate a reformulation or reevaluation of the *original* question ("How could x and y be identical, given their apparent differences?"): in both cases it *remains* a how-possibly question. Molyneux may perhaps think that the original question somehow becomes *more of a* how-possibly question in the phenomenal-physical case, on the grounds that in that case (but not in the other) the prima facie case that x can't be y turns out to be stronger. But the prima facie case that x can't be y seems to me unchanged: it still consists, and consists only, of the fact that x and y seem to differ in their properties. The fact that the aspiring identifier can't consistently accept the possibility of transcending the answer given—the existentially quantified identity claim—doesn't seem to entail that there is more reason to think that x couldn't be y. After all, the aspiring identifier has *already* explained how x could be y, given that x seems to have P while y seems to lack it: P is (non-trivially) identical to some property that actually y has.

An earlier passage sheds further light:

> If there is no way to fully explain away the differences, then the physicalist won't be able to correctly conceive of one. The best she can do is to offer a semi-solution. Yet in offering a semi-solution where she can think of no full solutions, the physicalist (a) claims that though the identificanda appear to differ, there is some coherent way to explain away the differences, yet (b) can conceive of no *specific* way of explaining away the differences (for if she could then she would have at least one full solution to offer). The result is a how-possibly question: *How could it possibly be the case that x and y are identical when there is no conceivable way to explain away their differences?* (Molyneux 2015, 254)[26]

---

[26] By "identificanda" Molyneux means x and y when the question is whether $x = y$; there may not be *two* entities, as the Latinate plural of his coinage suggests.

The how-possibly question is said to result from a tension between (a) and (b)—between thinking that "there is some coherent way to explain away the differences" and being able to "conceive of no *specific* way of explaining away the differences." I agree that these two things are in tension, and that anyone committed to a semi-solution must think that there is a coherent way to explain away the differences between x and y. But it doesn't seem right to describe the physicalist as being unable to *conceive* of a specific way of explaining away the differences. For *being able to conceive of something* is construed in recent discussions of the mind-body problem as *deeming something consistent with what one knows a priori*. But Molyneux's imagined physicalist has presumably ascribed several neurophysiological (say) properties to the particular brain-state she wishes to identify with pain (say); and she cannot rule out a priori that property P is identical with any one of these properties; so in one good sense she *can* conceive of specific ways of explaining away the differences. But in that case what is it that she *can't* do with regard to specific ways of explaining away the differences?

Perhaps the answer is that she can't *rationally choose* a specific way of explaining away the differences, because her choice of a specific way is underdetermined by all possible evidence. If P is (non-trivially) identical to some property that brain-state B has, and hence, by the assumption that the physicalist's prior property-ascriptions are complete, identical to some property that she has already ascribed to B (qua B), and if she has already ascribed to B (qua B) just three properties, say, Q, R, and S, then either P = Q, or P = R, or P = S. But, also by the assumption that her prior property-ascriptions are complete, she must already have *all the possible evidence* relevant to the question of which of these specific identity claims is true. For any relevant evidence would consist in such facts as that instances of P are perfectly correlated with instances of Q, or that P and Q have same causal profiles. But these facts are the possession by P and Q of certain metaproperties, and her property-ascriptions—assumed to be complete—ascribe not only all properties to states but also all meta-properties to properties (and indeed all meta-meta-properties to meta-properties, and so on). The physicalist is committed, then, to holding that (i) there is a determinate fact of the matter regarding whether P = Q, or P = R, or P = S, but (ii) no one of these specific identity claims is superior to its rivals *even in light of all possible evidence*. Noting this commitment, she might well be mystified how the choice between competing hypotheses could thus be underdetermined by all *possible* evidence—underdetermined even when she already has all the evidence she could in principle get (Newton-Smith 1978). And, of course, no such underdetermination would arise in the case of undisputed scientific identifications, where she would not regard her prior property-ascriptions as complete. Even if my suggestion is plausible, however, it doesn't vindicate Molyneux's contention that phenomenal-physical identifications, but not others, give rise to how-possibly questions, or that they give rise to a special class of how-possibly questions. All that follows from my suggestion is that, in phenomenal-physical identifications, the *answers* that can be given to the kind of how-possibly questions that *all* identifications, according to Molyneux, must confront generate a unique perplexity.

Whatever the merits of my suggestion, let me reiterate my main point that Molyneux's elaborate and intriguing account does not, I fear, explain anything, because it requires the assumption, argued above to be unwarranted and implausible, that we in fact regard our third-person and introspective beliefs as both correct and complete.

4.9 Sundström

Pär Sundström has argued that, if physicalism is true, then—it is most plausible to think—"our exceptional resistance" to phenomenal-physical (or phenomenal-functional) property-identity claims "is fully explained by our having an erroneous understanding of consciousness or its physical basis" (2018, 682; italics removed). The crucial premise in his argument for this contention is a claim he calls "Anthropological Law":

> It is anthropological law [sic] that: if (a) some hypothesis of the form x = y is true, and (b) a typical human subject S has sufficiently good reason to accept it, and (c) S has an error-free understanding of x/y associated with both the x-concept and the y-concept, then S does not have the kind of resistance that we in fact have to the supposition that [consciousness property] C = [physical or functional property] P. (2018, 688)

Assume that Anthropological Law is true, that C = P, and that we have sufficiently good reason to believe that C = P. Then, since we *do* have the kind of resistance in question to the supposition that C = P, it must be that we *don't* have an error-free understanding of C/P associated with both our C-concept and our P-concept—which erroneous understanding therefore explains the resistance.

In support of Anthropological Law Sundström presents evidence that is inductive in the narrow sense of constituting positive instances of the alleged law—cases that satisfy both the antecedent and consequent of the statement of the alleged law—in the absence of any negative instances. Sundström can easily point to many positive instances, while there are no uncontroversial negative instances. Nonetheless, his case for Anthropological Law is weak. It has a serious rival: the claim—let's call it "Anthropological Law Minus"— that what Anthropological Law claims to be true of *every* case of considering an identity hypothesis is in fact true of every case *except* those cases where a phenomenal property is hypothesized to be identical to a physical or functional property. Anthropological Law Minus predicts every positive instance that Sundström cites as evidence in support of Anthropological Law (obviously he cites no positive instance in which a phenomenal-physical or phenomenal-functional identity hypothesis is considered); but it doesn't permit the derivation of Sundström's contention that "our exceptional resistance" to phenomenal-physical (or to phenomenal-functional) identity claims "is fully explained by our having an erroneous understanding of consciousness or its physical basis."

Now it would be a poor reply to Sundström *merely* to point out the existence of an empirically equivalent rival to his favored hypothesis; for all hypotheses have empirically equivalent rivals, even the ones that we single out for acceptance. But Anthropological Law Minus is not just any old empirically equivalent rival. It differs from, say, the silly hypothesis that what Anthropological Law claims to be true of every case of considering an identity hypothesis is in fact true of every case except those where the identity hypothesis was first proposed on a Tuesday. For it would be unreasonable—a kind of inductive-logical sulk—to refuse to extrapolate from Sundström's sample to identity hypotheses first proposed on a Tuesday, even though his sample (let us suppose) includes no identity hypotheses first proposed on a Tuesday, and even though it could—just about!—be true that identity hypotheses first proposed on a Tuesday are the sole exceptions to an otherwise universal generalization. The refusal to extrapolate to identity hypotheses first proposed on a Tuesday would be unreasonable because nothing in our background knowledge gives us any reason to suspect that an identity hypothesis's having been first proposed on a Tuesday makes any difference at all to what explains any resistance we might feel to an identity hypothesis. Anthropological Law Minus, however, is not like the silly hypothesis; it would not be an inductive-logical sulk to refuse to extrapolate from Sundström's sample to identity hypotheses in which a phenomenal property is claimed to be identical to a physical or functional property. For we have two grounds for suspecting that cases where a phenomenal property is hypothesized to be identical to a physical or functional property are exceptional.

The first ground arises because there is a good prima facie empirical case for a comprehensive doctrine of physicalism, grounded in well-known scientific successes of the past hundred years in condensed matter physics, physical chemistry, biochemistry, cell biology, and so on (Melnyk 2003, ch. 6). Yet, for many scientifically informed philosophers and others, this empirical case is outweighed by their resistance to identifying phenomenal properties with physical or functional properties; they are led to a view of the fundamental nature of contingent reality according to which everything whatsoever is physical or physically realized—with the lone exception of phenomenal properties! The fact that resistance to identifying phenomenal properties with physical or functional properties can have this cognitive effect suggests that it is very strong, and quite possibly stronger than the resistance felt in any of the historical cases that Sundström implicitly takes to support his proposed Anthropological Law. The second ground for suspicion is that the most significant form taken by resistance to identifying phenomenal properties with physical or functional properties is surely the intuition of distinctness, which, however, arises in the special context of attending introspectively to a phenomenal property of a current sensation while considering the identity claim that that very property is literally one and the same thing as a certain physical or functional property. This fact presumably distinguishes the resisted identification of phenomenal properties with physical or functional properties from all of Sundström's historical examples of resisted identity hypotheses, where resistance was not associated either with the special context of introspection or with anything like it.

Though Sundström contends that "our exceptional resistance" to phenomenal-physical (or to phenomenal-functional) property-identity claims "is fully explained by our having an erroneous understanding of consciousness or its physical basis," he doesn't address the question of *how* an erroneous understanding of consciousness or its physical basis would produce resistance to the claim (2018, 682; italics removed). But it would presumably do so by misleading people into taking to be *true* what is in fact a *false* premise in some otherwise good argument against the identity hypothesis, and therefore mistakenly taking the argument to provide good reason to reject the identity hypothesis. In that case, however, dualists and physicalists— whom we might expect to feel resistance to phenomenal-physical (or phenomenal-functional) identity claims to different degrees—would tend to disagree systematically about the nature either of phenomenal properties or of physical (or functional) properties, this disagreement being both prior and additional to the main disagreement over whether phenomenal properties are physical (or functional) properties. However, though there is endless squabbling over the force of the standard anti-physicalist arguments that appeal to phenomenal properties, I see no sign of the sort of systematic disagreement over the correct understanding of phenomenal or physical (or functional) properties envisaged by Sundström's explanation.

Sundström's explanation is not actually aimed at accounting for the intuition of distinctness in particular; it's aimed at accounting for a general resistance to phenomenal-physical (or to phenomenal-functional) property-identity claims. Perhaps a version of the explanation could be devised to account for the intuition of distinctness, but it would have to explain why the intuition arises in the special context noted above. As things currently stand, however, Sundström's explanation provides no rival to the explanation of the intuition of distinctness proposed in the next chapter.

4.10 Conclusion

So much for earlier theories that were intended to explain the intuition of distinctness, or that might plausibly be taken to explain it, in a manner fully consistent with physicalism. Their failings yield no general morals, I think, except that the task of constructing a successful such theory is a difficult one. With some trepidation, then, I turn in the next chapter to my own attempt to do better.

5
What, Then, Does Account for the Intuition of Distinctness?

5.1 Rehearsal of Defective Arguments?

In this chapter, I propose a novel explanation of how the intuition of distinctness arises in us—and also indirectly (if the arguments of Chapter 2 are correct) a novel explanation of why some people take an otherwise inexplicably dismissive or uncomprehending attitude toward physicalism, why many people experience the intuition of revelation, why many people feel that there is an "explanatory gap," and why some people resist powerful objections to standard anti-physicalist arguments on rather obscure grounds. If this novel explanation is correct, then the intuition of distinctness gives us no reason to think that physicalism is false but is instead (if physicalism is true) a systematic error to which we are inevitably prone (though see section 5.6.1).[1] But though we (probably) can't make it go away, we can at least ignore it in good conscience.

The novel explanation is worked out explicitly enough, I hope, that it avoids any appearance of the miraculous.[2] But it is still highly speculative, and I do not go so far as to claim that it is true. I claim only that it might be true, in the sense that it is not ruled out by anything we already know, that it has the virtue of predicting the intuition of distinctness as I have characterized it, and that it has some initial plausibility. In section 5.2 and in subsequent sections, I work toward a full presentation of the novel explanation. First, however, in the balance of the present section, I sketch a much simpler explanation of the intuition of distinctness.

---

[1] Because I do not deny that phenomenal properties exist, but I do hold that they seem nonphysical but aren't, I count as a *weak illusionist* in David Chalmers's terminology (2018, 49).

[2] Sidney Harris's well-known cartoon (http://www.sciencecartoonsplus.com/pages/gallery.php) features two scientists in front of a chalkboard inscribed with many equations plus "And then a miracle occurs"; one of them says to the other, "I think you should be more explicit here in step two."

According to this simpler explanation, the intuition of distinctness arises from some kind of unconscious or semi-conscious rehearsal of the tempting but (according to me) defective introspection-based arguments surveyed in sections 3.2 through 3.10 of Chapter 3.[3] The explanation doesn't require that every person who has the intuition of distinctness rehearses the same defective argument, or set of defective arguments. It doesn't even require that the same person, on the different occasions when they have the intuition, is always rehearsing the same defective argument, or set of defective arguments. An obvious objection is that this simple explanation couldn't account for the intuition of distinctness in people who, like me, are convinced that the introspection-based arguments surveyed in sections 3.2 through 3.10 are defective. But the objection is inconclusive. For reflection on criticisms of the arguments may only eliminate their attractiveness temporarily, and old temptations may re-emerge after an interval despite oneself. Also, because the arguments are numerous, their defects often subtle, and their defectiveness not very intuitive, one may find it nearly impossible to keep the criticisms of *all* the arguments in one's mind at the same time. So even if one tried to rid oneself of the intuition of distinctness by working through each argument one at a time, reminding oneself of its defects, it would take time to work through every argument, and by the time one had reminded oneself of the defects of the last of the arguments, it might be that one's intuition of distinctness was now due to one's unconscious or semi-conscious rehearsal of the first of the arguments, whose defects were no longer present to one's mind. And if, to eliminate this possibility, one returned to the first argument to remind oneself of *its* defects, it might be that one's intuition of distinctness was now due to one's unconscious or semi-conscious rehearsal of one of the later arguments.[4] However, I will not discuss this suggested explanation any further.

---

[3] I cite the introspection-based arguments discussed in Chapter 3, rather than the standard anti-physicalist arguments discussed in Chapter 2, because Chapter 2 argued that the appeal of the latter arguments rests in part on the intuition of distinctness. It would be circular to explain the intuition of distinctness in terms of unconscious reliance on tempting arguments whose appeal is itself explained, in part, by the intuition of distinctness itself.

[4] Whenever I reconsider Anselm's ontological argument for the purpose of teaching introductory philosophy, I can't shake off the feeling that it is sound, even though no specific formulation satisfies me. This may be because I can't keep the refutations of all the specific formulations of the argument before my mind at the same time.

5.2 The Novel Explanation Introduced

The novel explanation of how the intuition of distinctness arises in us assumes two major hypotheses. According to the *first* hypothesis, our introspection[5] of phenomenal properties is *conceptually encapsulated*: the beliefs about our current sensations and their properties that introspection generates are constructed out of a sharply limited repertoire of concepts (namely, phenomenal concepts).[6] And though this repertoire can be expanded, it cannot be expanded to include concepts that we acquire as a result either of perception (e.g., by noticing a hitherto unfamiliar kind of cactus) or of exposure to new vocabulary (e.g., by learning the specialized terminology of cognitive neuroscience). And because introspection is encapsulated in this way, even though it can generate beliefs that our sensations have phenomenal properties, and therefore, if phenomenal properties *are* physical or functional properties, beliefs that our sensations have properties *that are in fact* physical or functional, it cannot generate beliefs whose predicative concepts express these physical or functional properties *but aren't phenomenal concepts*. According to the *second* major hypothesis, however, believing that an introspected phenomenal property just is a certain physical or functional property requires that introspection *can* generate beliefs of precisely this sort. So believing that an introspected phenomenal property just is a certain physical or functional property requires an impossibility.

Just as our sensations have phenomenal properties, our thoughts have content properties, such as a belief's property of having the intentional content that today is Tuesday; but we don't experience an intuition of distinctness with regard to the content properties of our thoughts.[7] So if a proposed explanation of the intuition of distinctness entails that, contrary to fact, we do, then the explanation can't be correct (Chalmers 2018, 10). My novel explanation avoids this entailment by denying that our capacity to become aware from the inside of our thoughts and their content properties is also

---

[5] In Chapter 1, I explain briefly how I intend my use of "introspection" in this book to be understood.

[6] Throughout this book, to simplify the exposition, I assume that such phenomenal concepts as our phenomenal concept of phenomenal redness are semantically primitive and unstructured. I should not be surprised, however, if they turn out not to be, as Robert Schroer has very interestingly proposed (see Schroer 2010). I have not worked out how much of what I claim about phenomenal concepts would in that case remain plausible, but I am optimistic.

[7] I take this observation to support the traditional and independently plausible view that there is no phenomenology distinctive to thoughts or to their having specific contents (see, e.g., Robinson 2005).

conceptually encapsulated. Of course, such a denial entails that this capacity differs importantly from the capacity—that I have been calling "introspection"—to become aware from the inside of our sensations and their phenomenal properties. But, as a recent survey notes, "There is no guarantee that the same mechanism or process is involved in introspecting all the different potential targets [e.g., both sensations and propositional attitudes]" (Schwitzgebel 2019). And it may well be that our capacity to become aware from the inside of our thoughts and their content properties is simply a manifestation of a general-purpose capacity to form beliefs about anything. It is in any case independently plausible that *some* dramatic difference must be posited between (i) our capacity to become aware from the inside of our thoughts and their content properties and (ii) our capacity to become aware from the inside of our sensations and their phenomenal properties; for we need to explain why there are no versions of the Knowledge Argument or Zombie Argument concluding that the content properties of thoughts are neither physical nor physically realized.

I will spell out the two major hypotheses and how they help to explain the intuition of distinctness in section 5.5. First, however, in sections 5.3 and 5.4, I will elaborate on the hypotheses themselves. Section 5.6 defends the novel explanation against three objections.

5.3 Introspection's Conceptual Encapsulation

Some years ago, Jerry Fodor (1984) proposed the hypothesis that our perceptual capacities are psychological modules that are "informationally encapsulated."[8] He claimed that sensory input from the environment (e.g., patterns of retinal stimulation) is first processed by a self-contained computational sub-system—a module—whose outputs are representations of how the perceived environment *looks*. These representations are then taken as inputs in a further computational process whose outputs are all-things-considered beliefs about the perceived environment. These beliefs sometimes have the same truth-conditional contents as the input representations that represent how the perceived environment looks.[9] But sometimes they have different truth-conditional contents; in these latter cases, the input representations

---

[8] On psychological modules, and the evidence for positing them, see Robbins (2017).
[9] Two representations have the same truth-conditional content if and only if they are true (or accurate) under exactly the same conditions.

that represent how the environment looks are in effect deemed to be misleading appearances. Now the computational processes that take as input representations of how the perceived environment looks and yield as output all-things-considered beliefs about the perceived environment can in principle draw upon any belief that the perceiver has, and use it as a premise in their computations. So, for example, if the perceiver believes on the basis of someone's reliable testimony that the wall being viewed is bathed in red light, then the input representation (from the module) that the wall looks pink may be combined with this belief to produce the all-things-considered belief that the wall is white, not pink. By contrast, the module that produces representations of how the environment looks is *not* able to draw upon the perceiver's beliefs and use them as premises in computations.[10] The module does in some sense have access to information not contained in the sensory stimulus (e.g., assumptions about the likeliest distal causes of ambiguous proximal stimuli), and it may even represent this information explicitly; but even if it does, these explicit representations are not among the perceiver's *beliefs* (though a perceiver who happens to be a vision scientist might *also* have beliefs with the same truth-conditional content as these representations). This feature of the module—its lacking access to the perceiver's beliefs—is what Fodor calls its informational encapsulation.

I recall Fodor's well-known hypothesis, not because I necessarily endorse it, but because it is analogous to my hypothesis that introspection is conceptually encapsulated.[11] My hypothesis claims that introspection is a self-contained, special-purpose capacity (possibly but not necessarily computational) whose sole job is to take as inputs one's current sensations and to produce as outputs non-inferential[12] beliefs to the effect that the sensations currently have such-and-such phenomenal properties; I call these beliefs that are outputs of the capacity for introspection "introspective beliefs."[13] If no such special-purpose capacity exists, then my hypothesis is false. Crucially, the hypothesis further claims that—and this is the conceptual encapsulation of introspection—introspective beliefs as I define them are

---

[10] The most plausible interpretation of Fodor's view, I think, is that the representations of how the environment looks are non-concept-involving *sensations*, rather than any kind of *belief.*

[11] Whether sensory systems are encapsulated in something like Fodor's sense seems to be an unresolved question in psychology (see, e.g., Firestone and Scholl 2016). I take this to be *some* indication that it is a live empirical possibility that introspection is encapsulated in my sense.

[12] By "non-inferential," I mean not resulting from *conscious* inference. Unconscious inference is another matter, on which I am silent.

[13] As noted previously, I allow that introspection can also generate beliefs that phenomenal properties have certain (phenomenal) features.

constructed out of a sharply limited repertoire of concepts. By "concepts," of course, I mean certain representational constituents of beliefs, constituents that stand to beliefs in something like the way in which subject-terms and predicates stand to declarative sentences of English. I take the concepts whose repertoire is limited to be *predicative* concepts, concepts analogous to predicates in declarative sentences of English. A predicative concept can be used to think, of something, that it has a certain property; I put this by saying that the predicative concept *expresses* this property. Because introspection can also generate beliefs that phenomenal properties themselves have certain (phenomenal) features, introspective beliefs can presumably also have as constituents phenomenal *subject-concepts*, analogous to subject-terms in declarative sentences of English, which *refer to* (rather than express) phenomenal properties; but my hypothesis says nothing about phenomenal subject-concepts beyond what is implied by its claims about the predicative concepts that help constitute introspective beliefs.[14]

The predicative concepts in introspection's limited repertoire of concepts express phenomenal properties and no other properties. But, of course, if phenomenal properties form a proper subset of physical or functional properties (as physicalism claims), then as a matter of fact these predicative concepts express certain physical or functional properties. If a predicative concept can be used to think, of a certain sensation, that it has a certain property, and if that property is in fact a certain physical property, then the predicative concept can be used to think, of that sensation, that it has that physical property. A predicative concept's expression of a property is purely extensional.

The predicative concepts in introspection's limited repertoire of concepts are the so-called phenomenal concepts. We do not acquire such concepts in either of the two most familiar ways in which we acquire concepts. We acquire many concepts as a result of learning new *words*, either non-technical words used in everyday life or words that belong to the technical vocabulary of some branch of science. It is probably in this way—as part and parcel of learning new words—that we acquired our first concepts of Virgil, or of chicory, or of electricity, or of cadmium, or of (quantum-mechanical) spin.

---

[14] For example, my hypothesis implies that if introspective beliefs' phenomenal subject-concepts turn out to be definite descriptions, they cannot be constructed out of predicative concepts from *outside* the limited repertoire of predicative concepts. I suggest instead that phenomenal subject-concepts are formed from an operator, meaning something like "Being . . .," that operates on phenomenal (predicative) concepts to yield such phenomenal subject-concepts as "Being phenomenally red."

According to my hypothesis, however, phenomenal concepts do *not* arise as a result of learning new words. We also acquire many concepts as a result of perceptual exposure to whatever the concept is of—the object, kind, or stuff that the concept refers to or the property that the concept expresses. It is probably in this way that we acquired our very first concepts of water, or of Mama, or of dogs, before we learned *words* for water, Mama, or dogs; and it is presumably in this way that we acquire concepts of new people we encounter and learn to recognize by sight, for whom we have as yet no name. According to my hypothesis of conceptual encapsulation, however, phenomenal concepts don't arise in this second way either. They do, however, arise in a similar way, only with introspection playing the role of (external) perception. We can acquire a concept of an unfamiliar kind of cactus perceptually, as part of the process of learning to recognize that kind of cactus by sight (Loar 1997).[15] So we must possess some mechanism by which (very roughly) when we view an external object and are not triggered to apply to it a concept that we already possess, we coin a new concept for it. Similarly, according to my hypothesis, we possess some mechanism by which (very roughly) when we are attending introspectively to the phenomenal property of a sensation and are not triggered to apply to the sensation a predicative phenomenal concept that we already possess, we coin a new predicative phenomenal concept for the property.

According to my hypothesis, then, we never acquire phenomenal concepts as a result of learning new words. But it doesn't follow that we never acquire concepts *that express phenomenal properties* as a result of exposure to new words; expressing a phenomenal property is a necessary but not sufficient condition for being a phenomenal concept. Obviously, if physicalism is true, then, by learning the right scientific vocabulary, we can acquire concepts that express phenomenal properties but that aren't phenomenal concepts. But perhaps we can also do so by learning a new word for a color which we have never seen: perhaps, in learning, say, "pervenche," we thereby acquire not only a new concept of an external color (of an interior wall, say) but also a new concept of a phenomenal property, expressible maybe as "the phenomenal property of our visual sensations that pervenche objects as such cause in us when we see them" or as "being of [i.e., representing] pervenche."[16] But if we do, and if the very next day we *see* something pervenche for the first time,

---

[15] We may never learn the cactus's name; it may not even have a name.
[16] Readers may suspect they catch the whiff of an objection here; please see section 5.6.3 for what I hope is an adequate reply.

we may then acquire a *second* concept of this phenomenal property, only this time a genuine phenomenal concept of the phenomenal property (pace Tye 2009).[17]

The concepts in introspection's limited repertoire of concepts are phenomenal concepts; they are *only* phenomenal concepts. Introspection's limited conceptual repertoire can be expanded, because we can acquire new phenomenal concepts. But it cannot be expanded with the addition of concepts acquired either as a result of learning new words or as a result of perceptual (as opposed to introspective) exposure to properties. For example, it cannot be expanded with the addition of concepts acquired as a result of learning the technical vocabulary of, say, physics or cognitive neuroscience.

I have distinguished between concepts that *are* in introspection's limited repertoire from those that are *not* by reference to the different ways in which concepts are *acquired*. This way of distinguishing them has an interesting but surprising consequence for the question of what is to count as a physical or functional property in the context of the intuition of distinctness—or, at any rate, it has this consequence if the hypothesis of conceptual encapsulation helps to explain why we have the intuition of distinctness. The intuition of distinctness, of course, is its seeming to us that an introspected phenomenal property of a current sensation couldn't possibly be any physical or functional property that we happen to be considering. But what are to count, in this characterization, as "physical or functional" properties? The answer, if conceptual encapsulation helps to explain the intuition of distinctness, is this: the physical or functional properties—the properties that, it seems to us, an introspected phenomenal property could not possibly be—are all and only the properties expressed by those of our predicative concepts that we acquired as a result either of perceptual exposure to the properties or of learning new words.[18] But, I now observe, properties expressed by predicative concepts that we acquired as a result of learning new words are not restricted to those expressed by concepts acquired from exposure to the vocabulary of *current* scientific theories; they also include properties expressed by concepts acquired from exposure to the vocabulary of *any* scientific theories—past, present, or future. Therefore, if conceptual encapsulation

---

[17] Merriam-Webster defines "pervenche" thus: "a grayish purplish blue that is duller than average delft, bluer, lighter, and stronger than regimental, and lighter and stronger than average navy blue." So now you know.
[18] Don't forget that a property expressed by one of these concepts may *also* be expressed by a phenomenal concept, and therefore *be* a phenomenal property. Physical and phenomenal properties are not automatically the same—obviously—but neither are they automatically distinct.

helps to explain the intuition of distinctness, we ought *also* to experience the intuition of distinctness when we consider properties expressed by concepts acquired from exposure to the vocabulary of abandoned scientific theories of the *past*, and properties expressed by concepts acquired from exposure to the vocabulary of imagined scientific theories of the *future*. And this prediction is borne out. Those who experience the intuition of distinctness experience it no matter what sort of physical or functional property they consider as a candidate for identity with the introspected phenomenal property. It can be a property posited by classical physics, or by quantum or relativistic physics, or by an imagined physics of the future—or even by an imagined dualistic science of ectoplasm or psychons.[19] It makes no difference: the intuition of distinctness is still experienced.

This point is closely related to a curious feature of the standard anti-physicalist arguments (discussed in Chapter 2) that appeal to phenomenal properties. The plausibility of these standard arguments is invariant not merely under any transformation of how we conceive of the physical but also under the substitution of the *ectoplasmic* (or the *psychonic*) for the physical. Paul Churchland noticed that Frank Jackson's Knowledge Argument is just as plausible if we imagine that Mary, its heroine, instead of learning only the completed physical sciences while confined to the black-and-white room, learns also a completed science of ectoplasm. After her release from the black-and-white room, Churchland (1985) noted, she would *still* learn what it's like to see blue, thus revealing her previous knowledge to be incomplete. And Churchland's point is easily extended to other anti-physicalist arguments that appeal to phenomenal properties. For example, if there is an explanatory gap between the precise neurophysiological state of a person in severe pain and the phenomenal character of the sufferer's simultaneous pain, then there is also an explanatory gap between any imagined ectoplasmic (or psychonic) state of the sufferer and the phenomenal character of the sufferer's simultaneous pain. Likewise, if a zombie world is conceivable, so also is a possible world in which people have minds made out of ectoplasm (or out of psychons) to any specification you please but still don't have phenomenally conscious sensations. This invariance under the substitution of the ectoplasmic (or psychonic) for the physical has sometimes been explained by

---

[19] "Ectoplasm" is a dummy term for the hypothetical stuff that dualists might think constitutes our minds. Psychons are the hypothetical constituents of mind actually posited by the substance dualist and neurophysiologist John Eccles, according to whom "all mental events and experiences . . . are a composite of elemental or unitary mental events, which we may call psychons" (1994, 101).

hypothesizing a radical subjectivism about phenomenal properties—the view that phenomenal properties are essentially *subjective* in some sense in which not only the physical or the functional—past, present, or future—but also the ectoplasmic or psychonic are *objective*.[20] But the invariance can also be explained less extravagantly. Suppose, first, that the properties that (it seems to us) an introspected phenomenal property could not possibly be are precisely the properties expressed by those of our predicative concepts that are *not* acquired in the way in which phenomenal concepts are acquired. Suppose, second, that when people conceive of ectoplasmic (or psychonic) properties, they conceive of them as expressed by concepts that are acquired either as a result of learning new words or as a result of perceptual exposure to (external) properties, that is, *not* acquired in the way in which phenomenal concepts are acquired.[21] Suppose, third, as Chapter 2 argued, that the intuition of distinctness plays an important role in explaining why people find standard anti-physicalist arguments concerning phenomenal properties plausible in the face of apparently powerful objections. Given these three suppositions, people *should* find the standard anti-physicalist arguments plausible, in the face of apparently powerful objections, even when the ectoplasmic (or psychonic) is substituted for the physical.

My hypothesis of conceptual encapsulation, then, is that (i) introspection is a self-contained, special-purpose capacity whose sole job is to take one's current sensations as inputs and to produce as outputs non-inferential beliefs to the effect that the sensations currently have such-and-such phenomenal properties,[22] and that (ii) these non-inferential beliefs—what I call "introspective beliefs"—have as constituent predicative concepts only phenomenal concepts. For the purpose of explaining the intuition of distinctness, however, the most important thing about this hypothesis is that it trivially entails something I will be calling *the inability thesis*:

> We are unable to form introspective beliefs whose predicative concepts are *non-phenomenal* concepts, that is, concepts acquired either as a result of learning new words or as a result of perceptual exposure to properties.

---

[20] The sense of "subjective" may be something like "accessible even in principle from a single perspective only," but I don't know how to make this more precise. Of course, it's not my hypothesis.

[21] In my view, of course, there is no non-empty concept of an ectoplasmic property; but I assume that we can acquire empty concepts, just as we can develop defective hearts.

[22] Or to the effect that phenomenal properties have certain (phenomenal) features.

A non-phenomenal concept can, of course, be of a phenomenal property. To illustrate the inability thesis, suppose that being phenomenally red just is the property (possessed by a certain neural circuit in the V4 region of the visual cortex) of having such-and-such neuronal organization and firing rate, and that I have a concept of that property as a result of exposure to the language of neuroscience. The inability thesis entails that I cannot turn my attention inward, while having a red sensation, and use my *neuroscientific concept* of that property (= phenomenal redness) to form an introspective belief that my current visual sensation has the property—even though, of course, I can and do form an introspective belief that my current visual sensation is phenomenally red by using my *phenomenal* concept of phenomenal redness.[23] Or suppose that the stabbing quality of my current pain just is the property of non-conceptually representing that some part of my body is being penetrated, and that I have a concept of this representational property as a result of exposure to psychological theory. The inability thesis entails that I cannot turn my attention inward, while experiencing a pain, and use my *psychological* concept of this representational property to form an introspective belief that my current pain has the property—even though, of course, I can and do form the introspective belief that my current pain is stabbing by using my *phenomenal* concept of phenomenal stabbingness. It is this inability— to form introspective beliefs whose predicative concepts are acquired either as a result of learning new words or as a result of perceptual exposure to properties—that plays a crucial role in my proposed explanation of the intuition of distinctness.

It will deepen understanding of the hypothesis that introspection is conceptually encapsulated also to note something that the hypothesis does *not* entail. It does not entail that we are unable to form *non*-introspective beliefs, *also* about our current sensations, whose predicative concepts *are* acquired as a result either of learning new words or of perceptual exposure to properties. In order for a belief to be introspective in my intended sense, it must attribute a property to a current sensation. But this necessary condition is not sufficient: a genuinely introspective belief must also be the output of the self-contained, special-purpose capacity that is introspection. So a belief can attribute a property to a current sensation without being an introspective

---

[23] When I speak of "one's using" a concept to form an introspective belief, I don't mean to suggest that one *intentionally* forms the belief by (somehow) deliberately deploying the concept. I assume the formation of introspective beliefs is always automatic given the right conditions, even though one can intentionally turn one's attention inward.

belief. And the hypothesis of conceptual encapsulation does not rule out our possessing (as we surely do possess) a *general-purpose* capacity to form beliefs that can be (i) about anything at all, including therefore our current sensations, and (ii) constructed out of any predicative concepts at all, including therefore those acquired as a result either of learning new words or of perceptual exposure to properties. For example, the hypothesis of conceptual encapsulation does not rule out the possibility of one's believing that one's current, phenomenally red visual sensations have such-and-such neuronal organization, or that one's current stabbing pains are non-conceptually representing that some part of one's body is being penetrated. And physicalists, of course, typically do believe such things, even though they have the intuition of distinctness. Such non-introspective beliefs about our current sensations would arise through inference. For example, one might come to believe non-introspectively that one's current stabbing pain non-conceptually represents that some part of one's body is being penetrated by deducing it from two prior beliefs: (i) one's introspective belief that one's current pain is (phenomenally) stabbing, and (ii) one's considered philosophical or psychological opinion that all phenomenally stabbing pains non-conceptually represent that some part of one's body is being penetrated. It is worth noticing that this example is quite consistent with the hypothesis of conceptual encapsulation, even though belief (ii) is a non-introspective belief that includes a phenomenal concept. For though the hypothesis of conceptual encapsulation entails that any predicative concept figuring in an introspective belief is a phenomenal concept, it does not entail that phenomenal concepts figure *only* in introspective beliefs.[24]

The possibility of non-introspective beliefs about our current sensations prompts a natural question. Suppose one believes that one's current stabbing pain non-conceptually represents that one's body is being penetrated somewhere. Can one tell *from the inside* whether or not this belief is introspective? To the extent that one often has a very good idea whether one inferred a belief about a current sensation from other beliefs, or whether, on the other hand, one formed the belief solely as a result of attending to a sensation, one can.

---

[24] Since belief (ii) includes a phenomenal concept to express the property of being phenomenally stabbing, does my thesis (in section 3.9) that it's physically impossible for an introspective belief to be false mean that in believing belief (ii) one must have (or imagine having) a phenomenally stabbing sensation? It doesn't, because my thinking that all phenomenally stabbing pains non-conceptually represent and so on is not a belief of the kind to which my physical infallibility thesis applies: it's not an introspective belief, and it doesn't categorically attribute a phenomenal property to a sensation.

But this way of telling is likely to be fallible, and there is presumably no other way of telling from the inside. This admission, however, casts no doubt on the hypothesis of conceptual encapsulation. The hypothesis certainly claims that the distinction between introspective and non-introspective beliefs turns on what is going on under the hood, so to speak; but it is no objection to an empirical psychological hypothesis that it could only be known to be true by using the experimental and observational techniques of scientific psychology.[25]

5.4 Believing an Identity Claim

As noted above, my novel explanation of the intuition of distinctness assumes a second major hypothesis, namely, that believing that an introspected phenomenal property just is a certain physical or functional property requires that introspection be able to generate (introspective) beliefs that our sensations have the physical or functional property in question, beliefs in which the predicative concept, expressing the physical or functional property, is *not a phenomenal concept*. The second major hypothesis follows, in turn, from (i) the claim that introspection can and does generate beliefs to the effect that one's sensations have certain phenomenal properties and (ii) a certain view about what believing an identity claim amounts to. I begin with the view about the nature of believing an identity claim.

What does believing an identity claim amount to? On one view, believing an identity claim is simply a special case of believing a proposition—whatever believing a proposition turns out to be. So, for example, on Jerry Fodor's (1987) well-known account of believing a proposition, to believe that eggs float is to host a Mentalese sentence, with the propositional content that eggs float, which Mentalese sentence is poised to play the causal and

---

[25] Suppose that introspection is conceptually encapsulated. An important and delicate further question—which I won't investigate here—is whether any other human representational capacities are also conceptually encapsulated. Any other such capacities ought, presumably, to give rise to corresponding kinds of intuition of distinctness. Perhaps the conceptual encapsulation of other representational capacities helps explain why we resist identifying evaluative properties with natural properties, or ourselves with any material object, or so-called secondary properties with uncontroversially physical properties. In this last case, as has often been noticed, we are tempted to divide and conquer: to identify one aspect of, say, redness with an external physical property and another—problematic—aspect with something purely mental, namely, phenomenal redness. Perhaps this is because we are uncomfortable identifying redness *simpliciter* with a certain triplet of reflectance efficiencies, and uncomfortable doing so because ketchup never *looks* to have a certain triplet of reflectance efficiencies.

computational role distinctive of believing. Given this account, to believe that $a = b$ is to host a Mentalese sentence that comprises a Mentalese word for a, the Mentalese identity sign, and a Mentalese word for b, the whole sentence having the content that $a = b$, and poised to play the causal and computational role distinctive of believing.[26] On this view, someone who has adopted the belief that $a = b$ will be able to use it as a premise in deductive inferences to new conclusions, so that, for example, if I already knew that Superman can fly, and then learn that Clark Kent = Superman, I can deduce that Clark Kent can fly.[27]

But there is an alternative view of what believing an identity claim amounts to, and this alternative view is one of the two premises from which the second major hypothesis follows.[28] According to the alternative view, while believing an identity claim requires the explicit representation of the identity claim, it is partly constituted by, and hence requires, something more (see Millikan 2000; 1984, 194–201; 240–4).[29] The idea that believing certain kinds of things requires something more than mentally representing a proposition is hardly unprecedented in philosophy. In ethical theory, for example, motivational judgment internalism holds that to believe that an action is morally wrong is at least in part to be motivated to avoid doing the action. And some philosophers have held that to believe a law-statement is at least in part to be disposed to make certain inferences. The alternative view of believing an identity claim holds that believing an identity claim is partly constituted by, and hence requires, the possession of certain conceptual abilities—abilities to *apply* concepts to things—and hence that *coming* to believe an identity claim requires the *acquisition* of these abilities. What sort of conceptual abilities? I shall begin my answer by developing two elaborate examples, one in which someone comes to believe an object-identity claim, and another in which someone comes to believe a property-identity claim. In each case, I shall first describe the relevant conceptual abilities of the believer

---

[26] "Mentalese" is, of course, Fodor's whimsical name for the representational system (analogous to a language) to which mental representations with syntactic and semantic structure, like sentences of a natural language, belong.

[27] Adopting the belief that $a = b$ may also change the person's *assignments of probabilities* to certain propositions. Even though identity claims are necessarily true, adopting an identity belief might affect the probability assignments of a non-ideal reasoner who does not know every true identity claim.

[28] Perhaps, strictly speaking, the view should not be described as one about *believing* an identity claim. If so, we could, without substantive change, call it a view about *accepting*, or *endorsing*, or *taking on board* an identity claim.

[29] I'm not sure Millikan would agree that believing an identity claim requires the explicit representation of the identity claim.

before the identity claim is adopted, and then describe the relevant conceptual abilities gained by the believer *after* the identity claim is adopted. Then I will formulate the alternative view of believing an identity claim, as it applies to the relevant case of property-identity claims; the formulation generalizes (more or less) from the second example.

I know Jennifer (from Accounting) only through exchanges of cordial but formal business emails. I have learned from these exchanges that Jennifer is efficient and helpful. At the same time, I know Jen (from The Java House, the coffee shop that Jen and I both frequent). I have never spoken to Jen, but I have learned her name, because the barista always calls it out when her order is ready; I have also learned, from seeing Jen, that she is unusually tall. Eventually I discover that Jennifer and Jen are one and the same person; I come to believe that Jennifer = Jen. The identity claim was not at all obvious, of course, because "Jennifer" is a common name, and information about Jennifer reached me through one channel, while information about Jen reached me through an apparently unrelated channel.

Before I learn that Jennifer = Jen, I am able to form new beliefs about Jennifer/Jen[30] that I would express in English by using the name "Jennifer" only because I am able to recognize that someone is her via her emails. For new information about her that I would express in English by using the name "Jennifer" derives solely from certain emails. So I must be able to know which emails are the ones that *she* sent; I must have an ability correctly to apply my subject-concept of her to her—my subject-concept of her being the one I acquired as a result of reading the name "Jennifer" at the end of her first email.[31] And my application of this subject-concept to her as I read her emails in my office is immediate in the sense of arising without conscious inference; I just read an email, note the signature, and automatically think "*Jennifer* sent that" or "*Jennifer* will be away next week." (My application of *predicative concepts* to her may be inferential.) Similarly, before I learn that Jennifer = Jen, I am able to form new beliefs about Jennifer/Jen that I would express in English by using the name "Jen" only because I am able to recognize that someone is her *by her face*—an ability I exercise when I see her in The Java House and immediately think, "Jen looks worried."[32] For new

---

[30] I use the expression "Jennifer/Jen" as a name that refers to the person to whom both the name "Jennifer" and the name "Jen" refer.

[31] As far as I know, of course, I have never set eyes on the woman I call "Jennifer."

[32] My ability to recognize her face does not, of course, have to be infallible. It just has to be *a way I have*, under favorable conditions, of recognizing her face. Similar remarks hold for all the cognitive abilities that I mention in the present discussion.

information about her that I would express in English by using the name "Jen" derives solely from my perception of a woman in The Java House. So I must be able to know that it is *she* who spoke or sneezed; I must be able correctly to apply my subject-concept of her to *her*—my subject-concept of her in The Java House being the one I acquired as a result of learning to recognize her by her face. (Recall that my discovery that her name is "Jen" came only later; so my subject-concept of her is not name-based.) And, as before, my application of this subject-concept to her in The Java House is immediate in the sense of arising without conscious inference; when I hear her speak or see her sneeze I just automatically think "*Jen* said something" or "*Jen* is coming down with a cold"—even if my application of *predicative concepts* to her is inferential.

In coming to believe that Jennifer = Jen, however, I acquire two new conceptual abilities. The first new conceptual ability is the ability to apply to Jennifer/Jen my *name-based* subject-concept of her (acquired from reading the name "Jennifer" at the end of her first email) by exercising my ability to *recognize her face* (rather than by exercising my ability to tell that an email is from her). For example, having come to believe that Jennifer = Jen, I am now able, on *seeing* Jennifer/Jen in The Java House, immediately to apply to her my *name-based* subject-concept of her, and thereby to form a belief that I would naturally express in English by saying, "Jennifer looks cheerful" in just the same way in which I could (and still can) immediately apply to her *my facial-recognition-based* subject-concept of her, thereby forming a belief that I would naturally express in English by saying, "Jen looks cheerful." The second new conceptual ability I acquire is the ability to apply to Jennifer/Jen my *facial-recognition-based* subject-concept (acquired from having learned the look of her face) by exercising my ability to *tell that an email is from her* (rather than by exercising my ability to recognize her face). For example, having come to believe that Jennifer = Jen, I am now able, after reading an *email* from her, immediately to apply to her my *facial-recognition-based* subject-concept, and thereby to form a belief that I would naturally express by saying, "Jen will be on vacation next week" in just the same way in which I could (and still can) apply to her *my name-based* subject-concept of her, thereby forming a belief that I would naturally express in English by saying, "Jennifer will be on vacation next week."

What acquiring these two new conceptual abilities amounts to, then, is this: becoming able, *after* I come to believe that Jennifer = Jen, to apply *either* of my two subject-concepts of her to her immediately by exercising the very same ability by the exercise of which I could immediately apply the *other* concept of her to her *before* I came to believe that Jennifer = Jen, where "immediately" entails that I make no conscious inference from the identity claim that Jennifer = Jen. What I was able (and disposed) to do with the subject-concept I acquired as a result of learning to recognize her face *before* I learned the identity claim I am *now* able (and disposed) to do with the concept I acquired from reading "Jennifer" at the end of her first email; and what I was able (and disposed) to do with the concept I acquired from reading "Jennifer" at the end of her first email *before* I learned the identity claim I am *now* able (and disposed) to do with the concept I acquired as a result of learning to recognize her face.

The story of Jennifer/Jen illustrates the sort of conceptual abilities that, according to the alternative view of believing an identity claim, partially constitute believing an identity claim; but the identity claim in the story is one of object-identity, since Jennifer/Jen is (metaphysically speaking) an object. The intuition of distinctness, however, is concerned with claims of property-identity—to the effect that a certain phenomenal property is identical with a certain physical or functional property. So let me now tell a second story, intended to illustrate the sort of conceptual abilities that, according to the alternative view, partially constitute believing a claim of property-identity.[33]

Consider a nineteenth-century English physician who regularly diagnoses patients with the disease that he calls "consumption," though he does not yet know that having consumption is one and the same property as being infected with *Mycobacterium tuberculosis*. He expresses his diagnostic conclusions in English by using the predicate "has/have consumption" to say such things as "Violetta has consumption." And he reaches these conclusions in direct response to observing in his patients such symptoms as chronic cough with blood in the sputum, fever, chills, night sweats, loss of appetite, weight loss, and fatigue. Now, at some time after 1882 (when the key discovery by Robert Koch was made), our physician learns from his conscientious reading of the latest medical literature that there is such a thing as being infected with *M. tuberculosis*. And, as part and parcel of learning the new English expression "is infected with *M. tuberculosis*," he acquires a new predicative concept, one that expresses the property of being infected with *M. tuberculosis*. He also learns a way of *telling* whether someone is infected with *M. tuberculosis*, by culturing a sample of the patient's sputum and then testing it for the

---

[33] My story is fiction but gains artistic verisimilitude from "Tuberculosis," Wikipedia, https://en.wikipedia.org/wiki/Tuberculosis.

presence of *M. tuberculosis*. Finally, and crucially, he learns that having consumption just *is* being infected with *M. tuberculosis*.

As a result, he becomes able to apply his *new* predicative concept, acquired as a result of exposure to the expression "is infected with *M. tuberculosis*," to a patient in direct response to observing in the patient such long-familiar symptoms as chronic cough with blood in the sputum, fever, and chills—"in direct response to" entailing, at least, that he makes no conscious inference from the identity-claim that having consumption = being infected with *M. tuberculosis*. He also becomes able to apply his *old* predicative concept, acquired decades earlier in medical school as a result of hearing the expression "has consumption" in lectures, to a patient in direct response to observing the results of culturing a sample of the patient's sputum and testing it for *M. tuberculosis*—"in direct response to" again entailing, at least, that he makes no conscious inference from the identity-claim that having consumption = being infected with *M. tuberculosis*. Having come to believe the new claim of property-identity, he can now apply *either* of his two predicative concepts of the same property to a patient in the same way in which he could, and still can, apply the *other* predicative concept to a patient, without relying on a conscious inference from the claim of property-identity.

This two-fold ability involves *predicative concepts* that *express* the same property. It must not be confused with a second two-fold ability also acquired by our physician, which involves *subject-concepts* that *refer* to the same property. The *second* two-fold ability consists, first, of the ability to apply the *subject-concept* acquired from exposure to the *subject-term* "having consumption" to the property of having consumption (= being infected with *M. tuberculosis*) in the same way in which the physician could, before he learned the identity claim, apply the subject-concept acquired from exposure to the referring expression "being infected with *M. tuberculosis*"; it consists, second, of the ability to apply the *subject-concept* acquired from exposure to the *subject-term* "being infected with *M. tuberculosis*" to the property of having consumption (= being infected with *M. tuberculosis*) in the same way in which he could, before he learned the identity claim, apply the subject-concept acquired from exposure to the subject-term "having consumption." This *second* two-fold ability, involving subject-concepts, is analogous to the two-fold ability in the story of Jennifer/Jen; but the *first* two-fold ability, involving predicative concepts, is not.

The alternative view of believing an identity claim, applied to the relevant case of a property-identity claim, is more or less the result of generalizing from the story of the physician. According to the alternative view, then, where P is a property and Q is a property, one's believing that P = Q is partly constituted by, and hence requires, one's having

- at least two predicative concepts that *express* P/Q, that is, two concepts—let us call them "C_P" and "C_Q"—that can be used in thought to attribute P/Q to things;[34]
- the ability, without conscious inference from the premise that P = Q, to apply predicative concept C_P in thought to things in *every* way in which one can apply predicative concept C_Q in thought to things; and
- the ability, without conscious inference from the premise that P = Q, to apply predicative concept C_Q in thought to things in *every* way in which one can apply predicative concept C_P in thought to things.

Of course, if one comes to believe that P = Q but doesn't *already* have two predicative concepts that express P/Q, then, before one can acquire the two abilities, one must first *acquire* a second predicative concept that expresses P/Q.

This formulation of the alternative view of believing a property-identity claim speaks of the ability to apply one predicative concept in every way in which—that is, for every way, in the *same* way in which—one can apply another predicative concept. What is it to be able to apply predicative concept C_P in the *same* way in which one can apply predicative concept C_Q? Suppose that one can apply C_Q to a thing in a certain way. Suppose, that is, that some particular psychological mechanism can operate in one to produce a belief whose predicative concept is C_Q. It doesn't matter whether this psychological mechanism is perceptual or inferential or neither; or whether, if it is inferential, the inference is deductive or inductive, or conscious or non-conscious. The crucial point is that a certain psychological mechanism can operate in one to produce a belief whose predicative concept is C_Q. One can apply distinct predicative concept C_P to a thing in the same way if, and only if, the same psychological mechanism can operate in one to produce, instead of (and not in addition to) a belief whose predicative concept is C_Q, a belief whose predicative concept is C_P. So, for example, if the very same psychological mechanism can operate in one to produce a belief whose predicative concept is C_P, but *only* by *first* producing *also* a belief whose predicative concept is C_Q, then one *cannot* apply predicative concept C_P to a thing in the *same* way in which one can apply C_Q to a thing. Applying two distinct predicative concepts in

---

[34] I use the expression "P/Q" as a name that refers to the property to which both the name "P" and the name "Q" refer.

the *same* way requires that the operation of the same belief-producing psychological mechanism in each case differs only in its final product—either a belief whose predicative concept is one of the two predicative concepts or a belief whose predicative concept is the other of the two predicative concepts. (The subject-concepts of the two beliefs, of course, are irrelevant; they can differ.)

Let us now return to the second major hypothesis assumed by my novel explanation of the intuition of distinctness, according to which believing that an introspected phenomenal property just is a certain physical or functional property requires that introspection be able to generate (introspective) beliefs that our sensations have the physical or functional property, beliefs in which the predicative concept that expresses the physical or functional property is not a phenomenal concept. I said that this hypothesis follows from (i) the claim that introspection can and does generate beliefs to the effect that one's sensations have certain phenomenal properties and (ii) the alternative view of what believing an identity claim amounts to. Let me explain how it follows, now that the alternative view has been laid out.

Suppose the alternative view of believing a property-identity claim is true; obviously it applies to any case of my believing that a phenomenal property just is a certain physical or functional property. So, for me to believe that phenomenal redness just is (say) the property of having such-and-such a functional organization and firing rate,[35] I would have to be able to apply my *non-phenomenal* predicative concept of having such-and-such a functional organization and firing rate to my sensations in every way in which I can apply my *phenomenal* predicative concept of phenomenal redness to my sensations, and do so without conscious inference from the premise that phenomenal redness is having such-and-such a functional organization and firing rate. But obviously I can apply my phenomenal predicative concept of phenomenal redness to my sensations by forming *introspective beliefs* that my sensations have phenomenal redness, beliefs in which the predicative concept that expresses phenomenal redness is my phenomenal concept of phenomenal redness. So, for me to believe that phenomenal redness just is having such-and-such a functional organization and rate of firing, I must also be able to apply my *non-phenomenal* (i.e., physical) predicative concept of having such-and-such a functional organization and firing rate

---

[35] Again, this property is meant to be a property of a particular pattern of neuronal firing in, say, the V4 region of the subject's visual cortex, a particular pattern of firing that either is or realizes the sensation.

to my sensations by forming introspective beliefs that my sensations have such-and-such a functional organization and firing rate, beliefs in which the predicative concept that expresses having such-and-such a functional organization and firing rate is my *non-phenomenal* (i.e., physical) predicative concept of that property; and I must be able to apply this non-phenomenal predicative concept without conscious inference from the premise that phenomenal redness is having such-and-such a functional organization and firing rate.

5.5 The Novel Explanation Elaborated

The two preceding sections have elucidated the two major hypotheses assumed by my novel explanation of how the intuition of distinctness arises. The first hypothesis (of conceptual encapsulation) entails the inability thesis—that we are not able to form introspective beliefs whose predicative concepts are non-phenomenal concepts. The second hypothesis is that believing that a phenomenal property is identical with a physical or functional property requires that we *are* able to form introspective beliefs whose predicative concepts are non-phenomenal concepts. But how exactly, according to the novel explanation, do these hypotheses account for the intuition of distinctness? They do so in accordance with the following narrative (to be elaborated in due course):

> I am attending introspectively to the phenomenal redness of a current visual sensation. At the same time, I consider the identity claim that that very property—phenomenal redness—is literally one and the same thing as a certain neural property, N. Perhaps N is the property, possessed by a certain neural event, of being constituted by neurons firing together at frequencies around 40 Hz. Naturally I try to entertain the identity claim: I try to (sympathetically) imagine believing the identity claim. But really believing the claim that phenomenal redness is N requires being able to form an introspective belief, whose predicative concept is a non-phenomenal concept of N, about the sensation that one is introspecting. So part of my trying to (sympathetically) imagine believing the identity claim is my attempting to (sympathetically) imagine forming just such an introspective belief. But I am unable to (sympathetically) imagine forming such an introspective belief; my attempt fails. I am unable because (sympathetically) imagining believing something requires *simulating* believing it, which in turn

requires the ability *actually* to believe it, which ability I lack: I can't actually believe it, so I can't simulate believing it, so I can't (sympathetically) imagine believing it. But in failing to (sympathetically) imagine forming an introspective belief of the required sort I also fail to (sympathetically) imagine believing the identity claim: I fail even to *entertain* the identity claim when I try to do so. As a result, the identity claim seems to me to be not even possibly true. This seeming is the intuition of distinctness.

Sympathetic imagining, as Thomas Nagel called it, was introduced in section 3.9; but because of its importance to the narrative, it merits a reintroduction. When we imagine something sympathetically, what we imagine is *our being in a mental state*; and we imagine our being in a mental state by "put[ting] ourselves in a conscious state resembling the thing [i.e., the mental state] itself" (Nagel 1974, note 11, 446), where putting oneself in a conscious state resembling a mental state M is best understood as *simulating* being in M, that is, putting oneself in a mental state that has some but not all of the effects that actually being in M would produce, or that has weaker versions of the same effects, or that has some combination of fewer and weaker effects. For example, to sympathetically imagine believing that a close friend has been killed in a plane crash is to simulate believing it; but if we simulate believing it, we won't actually mail a letter of condolence to his mother, though we may think of doing so, and we may put ourselves into a bad mood for the next hour. Presumably simulating being in M is realized by some of the same brain mechanisms that realize our *actually* being in M.[36]

[36] May I digress? To non-sympathetically imagine a flying elephant, I must *represent* a flying elephant, either visually or in thought, in the imagining sort of way. And, plausibly, to *visually* represent a flying elephant in the imagining sort of way is to *simulate seeing* a flying elephant. Plausibly, too, to represent a flying elephant *in thought* in the imagining sort of way—that is, to *conceive of* a flying elephant—is to *simulate believing* that an elephant is flying. If these plausible claims are true, then both sympathetic and non-sympathetic imagining have some connection, direct or indirect, to simulation of a mental state, even though imagining x only requires simulating x *itself* when x is being in a mental state. It follows that the very same mental state—simulating seeing a flying elephant—could be both (i) *sympathetically* imagining one's seeing a flying elephant and (ii) *visually* imagining a flying elephant. (This conclusion follows if the right kind of simulation *suffices* for sympathetic imagination.) Is this a problem? Does it perhaps play right into Bishop Berkeley's idealist hands by making it impossible to imagine a flying elephant without imagining one's *seeing* a flying elephant, and therefore bringing a perceiver into the picture? In fact, it doesn't, though it might explain why Berkeley's inference to idealism is perennially tempting. It doesn't play into Berkeley's hands because what is impossible, if simulating seeing a flying elephant constitutes both (i) and (ii), is *non*-sympathetically imagining a flying elephant without *sympathetically* imagining one's seeing a flying elephant. Two different kinds of imagining are involved. But no doubt is thereby cast on the anti-idealist possibility of *non*-sympathetically (i.e., visually) imagining a flying elephant without *non*-sympathetically (i.e., visually) imagining *one's seeing* a flying elephant. Here only one kind of imagining is involved.

Let me now repeat the narrative in its entirety, but interleaved with commentary; passages from the narrative are italicized.

I am attending introspectively to the phenomenal redness of a current visual sensation. At the same time, I consider the identity claim that that very property—phenomenal redness—is literally one and the same thing as a certain neural property, N. Perhaps N is the property, possessed by a certain neural event, of being constituted by neurons firing together at frequencies around 40 Hz.

This first segment of the narrative describes the state of mind of someone in whom the intuition of distinctness arises. It is a virtue of the proposed explanation that it can explain why the intuition arises when one is in just this state of mind—one in which, it will turn out, one naturally tries to imagine forming an introspective belief, whose predicative concept is a non-phenomenal concept, about the sensation that one is introspecting. Presumably the subject thinks about "that very property" by using a phenomenal subject-concept constructed out of a predicative phenomenal concept (as suggested in section 5.3, note 148).

Naturally I try to entertain the identity claim: I try to (sympathetically) imagine believing the identity claim.

Presumably, other things being equal, one tries to entertain *any* claim that one is considering, because entertaining claims is how one *evaluates* them, for example, by testing them for coherence, broadly understood, with one's prior beliefs: when one entertains the claim, mental mechanisms of assessment automatically operate on the entertained claim.[37] Entertaining a claim is plausibly identified with (sympathetically) imagining believing it. Can we literally *try* to (sympathetically) imagine believing something? We

---

Non-sympathetically imagining *one's seeing* a flying elephant would require *representing oneself as* seeing a flying elephant; but one does not represent oneself as seeing a flying elephant in *sympathetically* imagining one's seeing a flying elephant; one does not represent oneself at all.

[37] Considering a claim, I take it, is not the same thing as, and does not entail, entertaining a claim. One can consider a simple claim, recognize at once that it is free of equivocation and formally contradictory, and for that reason dismiss it; but presumably one cannot *entertain* a simple claim that is free of equivocation and formally contradictory. And perhaps one can consider but not entertain a belief that is intensely repellent psychologically to one (e.g., the belief that one's spouse has always held one in contempt).

can certainly comply with a request to (sympathetically) imagine believing something that we don't actually believe (e.g., that performing an abortion is cold-blooded murder); so we can certainly initiate an act of (sympathetic) imagining. And we are not obliged to think of trying as conscious; what I have called "trying" to entertain the identity claim might simply be the automatic initiation of an unconscious psychological mechanism whose biological purpose is to get one to (sympathetically) imagine believing any claim that one is considering.

But really believing the claim that phenomenal redness is N requires being able to form an introspective belief, whose predicative concept is a non-phenomenal concept of N, about the sensation that one is introspecting. So part of my trying to (sympathetically) imagine believing the identity claim is my attempting to (sympathetically) imagine forming just such an introspective belief.

The first claim here follows from the second major hypothesis assumed by the novel explanation. The second claim here doesn't have to presuppose that the subject *believes* the first claim—or the general hypothesis from which the first claim follows—and then acts so as to conform to the requirement; presumably few if any subjects believe either. It could simply be that the subject, in trying to (sympathetically) imagine believing (hence to simulate believing) the identity claim, thereby *automatically* attempts to (sympathetically) imagine forming (hence to simulate forming) an introspective belief of the requisite sort— simply because *actually* believing the identity claim requires *actually* forming the introspective belief, and simulated mental processes generally mimic actual mental processes as a result of their sharing neural machinery with them.

But I am unable to (sympathetically) imagine forming such an introspective belief; my attempt fails. I am unable because (sympathetically) imagining believing something requires simulating *believing it, which in turn requires the ability to* actually *believe it, which ability I lack: I can't actually believe it, so I can't simulate believing it, so I can't (sympathetically) imagine believing it.*

The first claim here asserts an inability to (sympathetically) imagine forming an introspective belief of the sort required, and the rest of the passage explains it. The inability is explained, ultimately, as a consequence of the inability thesis.[38] But the explanation must proceed via two intermediate

---

[38] The inability thesis is itself, of course, a consequence of the hypothesis of encapsulation.

claims, because the inability thesis implies that I am unable *actually* to form an introspective belief of the sort required, whereas the fact to be explained is that I am unable to (sympathetically) *imagine* forming such a belief. The first intermediate claim is that I cannot (sympathetically) *imagine* forming an introspective belief of the required sort because I cannot *simulate* forming an introspective belief of the required sort. And this claim is true on my working hypothesis that (sympathetically) imagining being in a mental state at least requires simulating being in it. The second intermediate claim is that I cannot *simulate* forming an introspective belief of the required sort because (i) I can't *actually* form an introspective belief of the required sort (as entailed by the inability thesis) and (ii) one can never *simulate* being in a mental state that one can't *actually* be in—because, in turn, simulating being in a certain mental state uses some of the same brain mechanisms as does actually being in the mental state.

> *But in failing to (sympathetically) imagine forming an introspective belief of the required sort I also fail to (sympathetically) imagine believing the identity claim: I fail even to* entertain *the identity claim when I try to do so. As a result, the identity claim seems to me to be not even possibly true. This seeming is the intuition of distinctness.*

Failure to (sympathetically) imagine forming an introspective belief with a non-phenomenal predicative concept entails failure to (sympathetically) imagine believing the identity claim that phenomenal redness is *N* because (by the second major hypothesis assumed by the proposed explanation) *actually* believing the identity claim requires *actually* forming an introspective belief of the relevant kind, and simulated mental processes generally mimic actual mental processes as a result of sharing neural machinery with them. And the failure (when one tries) to (sympathetically) imagine believing the identity claim gives rise to a sense of the impossibility of the identity claim, a sense that the claim *can't* be true; this sense that the claim can't be true, I propose, *is* the intuition of distinctness.[39]

---

[39] Alternatively, perhaps the intuition of distinctness just *is* the psychological condition of being unable to (sympathetically) imagine believing that the introspected phenomenal property is *N*. If this suggestion is correct, the label "intuition of distinctness" isn't really apt, because being unable to (sympathetically) imagine believing that the introspected phenomenal property is *N* is a kind of psychological incapacity, rather than the endorsement of a proposition; a better label than "intuition of distinctness" might in that case be "sense of incredibility," an expression that I actually used in earlier drafts of this material, and that exploits the ambiguity of "incredible" between psychological and normative readings ("incapable of being believed" vs.

This giving rise to—this movement in thought *from* the failed attempt to (sympathetically) imagine believing the identity claim *to* the intuition that the claim can't be true—need not be construed as an inference that is conscious and under the control of the will (even though we do seem to ourselves to have failed in an attempt to do something mental).[40] The movement in thought could instead be construed as an unconscious and automatic transition from one psychological state to another. Such a transition would be akin to the psychological tendency, noted above in sections 3.9 and 3.10, to move from the unimaginability of something to its logical impossibility; and, of course, certain claims that we can't imagine believing (e.g., explicit contradictions and simple arithmetical falsehoods) do strike us as quite impossible. Construing the movement in thought as an unconscious and automatic transition has an important consequence. Reflective physicalists, convinced that the intuition of distinctness is erroneous, could presumably manage to stop themselves from making an inference that is conscious and under the control of the will. But they couldn't block an unconscious and automatic transition from one psychological state to another—not, at any rate, through a sheer effort of will.[41] And if they couldn't block it, that would explain why even they report having the intuition of distinctness.

Finally, let me return to the claim made at the start of this chapter (and elsewhere) that, if my novel explanation is correct, then the intuition of distinctness gives us no reason to think that physicalism is false. The novel explanation describes a psychological mechanism from the operation of which the intuition of distinctness is claimed to arise in us. This mechanism is not the rehearsal of any argument, a fortiori not the rehearsal of a *good* argument. But it is also hard to see how this psychological mechanism could be regarded as reliable (having been produced by a reliable mechanism being the other thing that could make the intuition reason-giving). To be sure, if phenomenal properties happen not to be physical or functional properties, then it generates an intuition that is always correct. But it will generate exactly the same intuition if phenomenal properties *are* physical or

---

"unworthy of being believed"). But the novel explanation of the intuition of distinctness up to this point is not affected, even if the suggestion is correct.

[40] It would in any case be a non-standard inference, because inference is standardly viewed as a movement from one state of belief to another state of belief, whereas the intuition of distinctness is not a belief.
[41] Perhaps they could do so after a suitable program of training; for comments on this possibility, see the very end of section 5.6.1.

functional properties; the mechanism producing the intuition of distinctness is quite independent of, and insensitive to, the physical or functional character of phenomenal properties.[42]

5.6 Some Objections

In the present subsection, I reply to three possible objections to the novel explanation of the intuition of distinctness. My reply to the second (in section 5.6.2) presents a further speculation that, if correct, would deepen the explanation.

5.6.1 Churchland's Suggestion

The novel explanation assumes the hypothesis that our introspection of phenomenal properties is conceptually encapsulated in such a way that we are unable to form introspective beliefs whose predicative concepts are nonphenomenal concepts. Paul Churchland, however, has offered a "positive suggestion," as he called it, that seems to contradict this hypothesis—the suggestion that a certain "enhancement in our introspective vision could approximate a revelation" (1985, 16). He describes the enhancement that he envisages in these terms (1985, 16):

> Consider now the possibility of learning to describe, conceive, and introspectively apprehend the teeming intricacies of our inner lives within the conceptual framework of a matured neuroscience.... Suppose we trained our native mechanisms to make a new and more detailed set of discriminations, a set that corresponded not to the primitive psychological taxonomy of ordinary language, but to some more penetrating taxonomy of states drawn from a completed neuroscience.[43]

---

[42] Might conceptual encapsulation be God's highly indirect way of telling us that physicalism is false? My discussion of appeals to theism in section 3.11 can be adapted to this suggestion.

[43] This passage continues as follows: "And suppose we trained ourselves to respond to that reconfigured discriminative activity with judgments that were framed, as a matter of course, in the appropriate concepts from neuroscience." Given the context, the "discriminative activity" mentioned here must, I think, be that involved in forming introspective beliefs; so "judgments" that respond to this activity must be linguistic reports. Thus the sentence makes a distinct suggestion from the one that I discuss in the text: that, given suitable training, we might *report* what we are introspecting in the *language* of neuroscience.

Churchland clearly means his suggestion to apply to the introspection of sensations and their phenomenal properties. For, regarding Frank Jackson's imaginary Mary, he writes as follows (1985, 25–6):

> Suppose that Mary has learned to conceptualize her inner life, even in introspection, in terms of the completed neuroscience we are to imagine. ... she does not identify her visual sensations crudely as "a sensation-of-black," "a sensation-of-grey," or "a sensation-of-white"; rather she identifies them more revealingly as various spiking frequencies in the nth layer of the occipital cortex (or whatever).

Churchland concludes his paper by speaking of how the "marvelous intricacies" of "our inner life" might be "revealed ... in direct self-conscious introspection" (1985, 28; italics removed). In view of these passages, it is very natural to read Churchland's "positive suggestion" as entailing that we *are* capable, given suitable training, of forming introspective beliefs whose predicative concepts, being neuroscientific, are non-phenomenal (1985, 16).

Obviously Churchland's "positive suggestion" poses no threat to the hypothesis of conceptual encapsulation unless we have some reason to think it true. To the extent that Churchland argues for it, he does so by appealing to an analogy with external perception (1985, 16).[44] He is very impressed by the fact that scientists, as a result of their professional training, can become able to form beliefs, whose predicative concepts are highly theoretical, in the same sort of way in which untrained observers form perceptual beliefs whose predicative concepts are everyday concepts of, say, color or shape.[45] Consider how, upon having our visual systems stimulated by a ripe tomato, you and I immediately and without reflection or conscious inference form the perceptual belief that there sits something red and round. With suitable training, a physicist, upon having her visual system stimulated by a thick, straight track in a cloud chamber, immediately and without reflection or conscious inference forms the belief that there goes an *alpha particle*. Churchland proposes an explanation of such facts. External perception, he thinks, is *theory-laden* in the following very strong sense: all our perceptual beliefs are framed in terms

---

[44] Churchland writes that "the conceptual framework for psychological states that is embedded in *ordinary language* ... shapes our matured introspection profoundly" (my italics); but he gives no argument against the possibility of phenomenal concepts that are acquired language-independently, as I have hypothesized (1985, 15).
[45] By "perceptual beliefs," I mean beliefs formed automatically and without conscious inference as soon as, and because, our sense-organs are suitably stimulated.

of concepts drawn from whatever theories we accept as true of the domains being perceived. For non-scientists, these theories are typically folk theories; the everyday concept of redness, for example, should, he thinks, be viewed as part of a folk theory of macroscopic material objects. In consequence, if we come to accept as true a *new* theory of some domain, perhaps a superior scientific theory, and if we undergo suitable training, then our perceptual beliefs about that domain will change: we will now form genuinely perceptual beliefs that are framed in terms of concepts drawn from the newly accepted theory, rather than in terms of concepts drawn from the abandoned theory. Churchland's next step is to claim that introspection works in the same way in which, according to him, external perception works, so that introspection, too, is theory-laden. And if it is, then, if we come to accept as true a neuroscientific theory of the mental states that introspection is directed on, and if we undergo suitable training, we will form genuinely introspective beliefs whose predicative concepts are neuroscientific concepts, rather than the folk-psychological concepts in terms of which our introspective beliefs are currently framed; neuroscientific concepts will play the role in introspective beliefs formerly played by folk-psychological concepts.

Churchland's "positive suggestion," however, is only weakly supported by his appeal to an analogy with external perception, for we have little reason to take the underlying cognitive and neural architecture of introspection to resemble that of external perception. The etymology of the everyday word "introspection" provides no serious reason to think that introspection is a species of inner perception. Moreover, whereas the five traditional external senses generate sensations and involve obvious specialized sense organs, neither claim is true of introspection.[46] At least equally likely is that the underlying cognitive and neural architecture of introspection resembles that of proprioception, whereby we find ourselves with beliefs about where our limbs are; for, like introspection, proprioception generates no sensations and involves no obvious specialized sense organ.[47] And some evidence for thinking that the underlying cognitive and neural architecture of introspection *doesn't* resemble that of external perception is that I neither see in myself any signs of the introspective transformation that Churchland envisages nor read about such a transformation, even to a limited extent, in other people.

---

[46] On the claim that introspection involves no sensations of sensations, see section 3.8.

[47] True, the representational repertoire of proprioception seems never to expand, whereas, according to the hypothesis of conceptual encapsulation, that of introspection is expanded when we form new phenomenal concepts.

I can't even form the introspective belief that my current sensations have the approximate spatial location of being in my head, even though I am confident that they *are* in my head in the same sense in which a genuine dollar bill is in my wallet (i.e., despite the bill's having properties partly constituted by its relations to objects elsewhere).

Churchland is, however, quite right to be impressed by the fact that scientists, as a result of their professional training, can become able to form beliefs, whose predicative concepts are highly theoretical, in the same sort of way in which untrained observers form perceptual beliefs whose predicative concepts are everyday concepts of, say, color or shape—though I would stress more than Churchland does that scientists whose belief-forming abilities are enhanced by concept-acquisition and scientific training do not in general thereby *lose* their earlier abilities to form perceptual beliefs framed in terms of everyday observational concepts (Kitcher 1993, 219–33); for example, the vision scientist who, upon seeing a red object, can immediately form the belief that the object has so-and-so triplet of reflectance efficiencies remains able, upon seeing a red object, immediately to form the belief that the object is red. In my view, also, the fact that rightly impresses Churchland should be explained, in part, by appeal to the hypothesis that perception (unlike introspection) is *not* conceptually encapsulated—which is why, according to the novel explanation of the intuition of distinctness, we *don't* have an intuition of distinctness when we contemplate such scientific identity-claims as that water = H_2O, alcohol = C_2H_5OH, and temperature = mean molecular kinetic energy.

Finally, even if Churchland's "positive suggestion" regarding "enhancement in our introspective vision" (1985, 16) is correct, it does not entail that we should be able *right now*, just as we are, to form introspective beliefs whose predicative concepts are non-phenomenal. For Churchland insists that, to do so, we must first undergo training in the application of concepts acquired from exposure to a mature neuroscience, and he could claim that our neuroscience is not yet mature or that no one has yet undergone the right training. But what if, in the future, people are exposed to a genuinely mature neuroscience, do undergo the right training, and as a result routinely form introspective beliefs whose predicative concepts are non-phenomenal? We will have to admit that the hypothesis of conceptual encapsulation only holds in the absence of such exposure and training. But the novel explanation of the intuition of distinctness does not itself entail that such exposure and training could not possibly have the effect Churchland envisages. The explanation merely entails that, if people undergo such exposure and training, and if it has the effect Churchland envisages, then they will cease to have the intuition of distinctness; and, for all anyone knows today, maybe they will.

5.6.2 Deepening the Explanation

A second complaint about the hypothesis of conceptual encapsulation is that the larger explanation of which it is a part would be more plausible if the hypothesis could be made to appear less arbitrary through *itself* being given some possible explanation—which it has not received. Let me therefore sketch a possible explanation not, strictly speaking, of conceptual encapsulation itself but of the consequence of it—the inability thesis—that plays the central role in the novel explanation of the intuition of distinctness. The inability thesis, it will be recalled, claims that

> We are unable to form introspective beliefs whose predicative concepts are non-phenomenal concepts, that is, concepts acquired as a result either of learning new words or of perceptual exposure to properties.

The language of encapsulation conjures up images of a functional unit hermetically sealed against contamination by outside influences. But an explanation of the inability thesis does not have to appeal to *barriers*. An explanation might lie instead in the peculiar way in which our introspective beliefs represent sensations' phenomenal properties. I will explore this possibility in the present section.

Let us again assume the unorthodox representationalism introduced in section 3.7. As will no doubt be recalled, unorthodox representationalism takes a sensation to be a distinctive kind of mental representation, like a belief in that its job is to represent how the world actually is, but unlike a belief in its representational format and in the role it plays (or has the function of playing) in the overall economy of the mind. And it takes any phenomenal property of a sensation to be the sensation's property of representing, in the distinctive way in which sensations represent, that so-and-so, where "that so-and-so" expresses some particular thing that the sensation represents. Let us also recall (from Chapter 1) a second assumption—that one's having a sensation, like one's having a car accident, is one's participating in an event (or in a state). The two assumptions together entail that a person's sensation is the event (or state) of a *person's sensorily representing that so-and-so*, so that, for example, my having a phenomenally red sensation is my sensorily representing—it is natural to say my *visually sensing*—that something is red.

Consider now an introspective belief about a current sensation—say, the introspective belief that a current visual sensation of mine is phenomenally red. Given the two assumptions, it is possible (though not obligatory) to model such a belief as consisting of two distinct representational components. The first component is, in effect, a representation-forming operator on complete representations, representations complete in the sense that they represent complete states of affairs: when the first component is combined in the right way with the right kind of complete representation, the combination constitutes a new (complete) representation.[48] This first component itself, however, has an incomplete intentional content—something like the content that *it seems sensorily to me that . . .* or *I am sensing that . . .*, where the ellipsis is replaced by (the content of) the complete representation on which it operates. Presumably, the first component does not represent iconically or pictorially, there being no straightforward way to picture a sensing. Most plausibly, the first component contains no semantic constituents—no constituents that contribute systematically to the intentional content of the whole—that are concepts, and therefore on the present model no concept of *oneself* would be required for introspective beliefs.[49] The second component of the introspective belief, on the present model, is the complete representation on which the first component operates—the complete representation with which the first component is combined in the right way. This complete representation is a *sensation* (which is why sensations have to be representations, on the present model of introspective beliefs). In particular, it is the sensation that the complete introspective belief is *about*, and it has the intentional content (in this case) that *something is red*. The introspective belief as a whole, therefore, has the intentional content that *it seems sensorily to me* (or: *I am sensing*) *that something is red*. We might call this model of introspective belief the "mixed-media model," because it portrays introspective beliefs as combining two different kinds of representational component, rather as if one announced in class, "Next week's guest lecturer will be . . ." and then held up a photo of the guest lecturer.

---

[48] An example of an incomplete (mental) representation would be a concept.
[49] Ruth Millikan would no doubt wish me to note that it does not entirely lack semantic constituents: it has a time of occurrence, its time of occurrence representing the time *at which* it seems sensorily to me that . . .; and it represents different such times by itself occurring at different times.

If the inability thesis turns out to be true—if it turns out that we cannot form introspective beliefs whose predicative concepts are non-phenomenal—then the mixed-media model of introspective beliefs can explain why it is true. For, if we *could* form an introspective belief whose predicative concept is a non-phenomenal concept of phenomenal redness, then the non-phenomenal concept would have to fill a slot, as it were, that is usually, or was formerly, filled by a phenomenal concept. On the mixed-media model, however, the introspective belief that my current sensation is phenomenally red contains no slot for a non-phenomenal concept to fill; as we have seen, neither of the two components of an introspective belief involves a phenomenal concept (on which see below). It follows that, on the mixed-media model, there couldn't be an introspective belief about a phenomenally red sensation whose predicative concept is non-phenomenal. And, if the inability thesis can indeed be explained by the mixed-media model in this way, then, pace Paul Churchland (see section 5.6.1), no amount of training in the introspective application of concepts drawn from a mature neuroscience would enable us to form introspective beliefs whose predicative concepts are non-phenomenal. But although the mixed-media model provides an elegant explanation of the truth of the inability thesis, it faces at least four objections; the first three objections can be met, but meeting the fourth requires significantly modifying the novel explanation of the intuition of distinctness presented in section 5.5.

The first objection is that, on the mixed-media model, introspective beliefs aren't actually *beliefs* at all! For their second components are sensations, and their first components contain no concepts, which philosophers ordinarily take to be the constituents of beliefs. But I don't find these reasons decisive. The *function* of introspective "beliefs," on the mixed-media model, might turn out to be the same as that of beliefs, and introspective "beliefs" may interact causally with beliefs in a belief-like way. At the same time, I think I could live with the result that what I have been *calling* introspective beliefs aren't really beliefs. I could revise my terminology easily enough, substituting "introspective representations" for "introspective beliefs," at no substantive doctrinal cost. And there is no a priori reason to think that the only mental representations that can be true or false, or accurate or inaccurate, are beliefs and sensations. I would have to grant that introspective representations are sui generis; but it would be no great surprise for the human capacity to represent our own sensations to be special.

The second objection is that, because the mixed-media model of introspective beliefs renders phenomenal concepts surplus to theoretical requirements, it appears at first sight to be incompatible with the so-called phenomenal-concept strategy that has often been used (as in Chapter 2 above) to answer standard phenomenal-property-based arguments against physicalism. In fact, however, the phenomenal-concept strategy, despite its popular name, does not require the existence of phenomenal concepts and can still be used in conjunction with the mixed-media model. For what makes it possible to answer standard phenomenal-property-based arguments against physicalism is two *consequences* of the positing of phenomenal concepts; since the mixed-media model also has these consequences, it too can answer the standard arguments.

What it takes to *possess* a phenomenal concept—what it takes to be capable of attributing a phenomenal property to a sensation by using a phenomenal concept in thought—is hypothesized not to require the possessor of the phenomenal concept to associate the concept with *any* definite description (e.g., it's not required that, to possess a phenomenal concept of phenomenal redness, I must think of phenomenal redness *as* the property that is so-and-so). The first consequence of positing phenomenal concepts, then, is that no introspective belief attributing a phenomenal property to a sensation can be inferred a priori from any set of beliefs that use physical or functional concepts to attribute physical or functional properties to the sensation. This consequence is invoked to explain why, for example, zombies are conceivable (i.e., consistent with everything that we know a priori) and why there is an explanatory gap. But the mixed-media model has the very same consequence. For, according to the model, the distinctive part of the representational content of an introspective belief—the part that varies from one introspective belief to another—is the content of the *sensation* that partly constitutes the introspective belief. But it is hard to see how a belief partly constituted by a sensation, which as such belongs (I have been supposing) to a representational system significantly different from that to which beliefs belong, could be inferred a priori from non-introspective beliefs that use only physical or functional concepts. For no one thinks that the representational contents of sensations themselves, or of their constituents, have a priori knowable definitions in terms of physical or functional concepts. Also, if a belief partly constituted by a sensation could be inferred a priori from non-introspective beliefs, then we could presumably infer sensations themselves from beliefs; but nothing in our mental lives seems to count as the inference of a sensation from a belief. The mixed-media model, therefore, can also explain why zombies are conceivable and why there is an explanatory gap.

Phenomenal concepts are also hypothesized to be such that, for some reason or other, one cannot possess a phenomenal concept of a certain phenomenal property unless one has had, or is currently having, an actual sensation with that phenomenal property. The second consequence of positing phenomenal concepts, then, is that we have a way of thinking about the phenomenal properties of our own sensations that is special: the way is such that, if we have never had, or do not currently have, sensations with those phenomenal properties, then we cannot think about those properties in that way. This consequence was invoked (in section 2.4 above) to explain how Frank Jackson's Mary could manage to learn something about visual sensations of color after she is released from her grayscale environment, even if physicalism is true and her knowledge of the physical facts complete. But the mixed-media model has exactly the same consequence. Consider my introspective belief that I am now having a phenomenally red sensation. According to the model, it has the content that *it seems sensorily to me that something is red*. Because what bears the content that *something is red* is a current sensation of mine that is phenomenally red, my introspective belief is (metaphysically) impossible unless I am now having a phenomenally red sensation; and I can't ever have had such an introspective belief in the past if I have never before had a phenomenally red sensation.[50]

The third objection is that, though the mixed-media model can explain the inability thesis, it is inconsistent with the hypothesis of conceptual encapsulation from which the inability thesis follows. For the hypothesis says that (i) introspection is a self-contained, special-purpose capacity whose sole job is to take one's current sensations as inputs and to produce as outputs non-inferential beliefs to the effect that the sensations currently have such-and-such phenomenal properties, and that (ii) these non-inferential beliefs—introspective beliefs—have as predicative concepts only phenomenal concepts. The mixed-media model, in entailing that introspective beliefs don't involve concepts at all, is inconsistent with claim (ii). However, the hypothesis of conceptual encapsulation can easily be reformulated so as to make it consistent with the mixed-media model. It is sufficient to delete claim (ii) and to replace it with the claim that (ii*) these non-inferential beliefs—introspective beliefs—never have non-phenomenal concepts as predicative concepts (which *is* the inability thesis). Claim (ii*) is consistent with the

---

[50] A full development of the mixed-media model would need to include something analogous to an account of how we acquire new phenomenal concepts—some account, that is, of how our capacity to represent phenomenal properties is expanded over time.

mixed-media model. For the mixed-media model entails that introspective beliefs include no predicative concepts *at all*, and a fortiori that introspective beliefs include no predicative concepts *that are non-phenomenal*.[51]

The fourth objection is that, because the mixed-media model doesn't posit (predicative) phenomenal concepts, the novel explanation of the intuition of distinctness can't even get started. For the explanation begins by supposing that people who experience the intuition of distinctness attend introspectively to a current sensation while considering some such identity claim as that that very property—the phenomenal redness of a current sensation— just is a certain physical or functional property, where they think of the phenomenal property by using a phenomenal subject-concept constructed out of a predicative phenomenal concept.[52] I will suggest a response to this objection, though it requires significantly modifying the explanation of the intuition of distinctness proposed in section 5.5.

The response proceeds most smoothly if we treat phenomenal properties as representational properties not of sensations but instead of the people who have sensations; an example of a phenomenal property so treated would be the property of *sensing that something is red*.[53] Let us refer to such phenomenal properties as "phenomenal*" properties. Now suppose that one has a phenomenally red sensation, and that it produces in one an introspective belief, as characterized by the mixed-media model, with the content that *it seems sensorily to me that something is red*. Qua introspecting subject, one has no grasp of the syntactic structure of this introspective belief. But plausibly one can still grasp the semantic fact that it attributes to oneself a certain phenomenal* property. Perhaps one conceives of this phenomenal* property as the property that, necessarily, one has iff one's current introspective belief is true. Conceiving of the phenomenal* property in this way wouldn't mean that one was using a phenomenal concept, or anything like a phenomenal concept, in the sense spelled out above (section 5.3); but one would still be using a concept of a phenomenal* property that was not acquired through exposure to

---

[51] Another worry is whether the mixed-media model is consistent with the objections made against the various lines of anti-physicalist reasoning considered in Chapter 3. My suspicion is that while some of the objections would not work exactly as they stand, since they assume phenomenal concepts, analogs of these objections that assume the mixed-media model instead could be formulated.

[52] As I suggested in section 5.3, phenomenal subject-concepts may be formed from an operator, meaning something like "Being...," that operates on phenomenal (predicative) concepts to yield phenomenal subject-concepts that refer to (rather than express) phenomenal properties.

[53] As noted in Chapter 1, Papineau treats phenomenal properties as properties of the people who have sensations; but he doesn't treat them, as I am suggesting here, as essentially representational properties of the people who have sensations (2021, 1).

the vocabulary of the physical sciences. Suppose now that one considers, and then tries to entertain, the identity claim that this phenomenal* property just *is* having so-and-so activity in the V4 region of one's occipital cortex. What happens next? Alas, we can't continue the explanation as before by appealing to the alternative view of believing an identity claim, and then saying that, in trying to entertain the identity claim, one automatically tries (but fails!) to imagine forming an introspective belief whose predicative concept is a physical concept of the property of having so-and-so activity in the V4 region of one's occipital cortex; for, on the mixed-media model, introspective beliefs don't involve any predicative concepts. The explanation must therefore proceed differently. What I propose instead is that one *mistakenly takes* one's current introspective belief to be a belief consisting of (i) a subject-concept that refers to oneself and (ii) a predicative concept of the relevant phenomenal* property; such a mistake is natural because, although an introspective belief doesn't have this structure on the mixed-media model, it does attribute a phenomenal* property to oneself—that is, it's true iff one has a certain phenomenal* property.[54] So when one tries to entertain the identity claim that the phenomenal* property just is having so-and-so activity in the V4 region of one's occipital cortex, one tries to imagine having an introspective belief whose predicative concept is a physical concept of the property of having so-and-so activity in the V4 region of one's occipital cortex.[55] But one can't *actually* form such an introspective belief, because an introspective belief could only contain such a physical predicative concept if it contained a slot that is usually, or was formerly, filled by some *other* predicative concept, whereas, on the mixed-media model, an introspective belief contains no such slot. There is no such slot in its first component, because, though it has the content that *it seems sensorily to me that* . . . and therefore refers to oneself, it contains no semantic constituent that is a subject-concept of oneself; and it contains no predicative concept of any kind. And there is no such slot in an introspective belief's second component, since it is a sensation. But because one can't *actually* form an introspective belief whose predicative concept is a physical concept of the property of having so-and-so activity in the V4 region

---

[54] The hypothesized mistake is even more tempting if what I'm here calling introspective beliefs really are beliefs, albeit perhaps non-standard ones.
[55] According to the modified explanation, then, unless one mistook a sensation of red for a belief (which seems unlikely), one would *not* expect to be able to imagine something's *seeming visually to have a certain reflectance efficiency property*—even if redness is that reflectance efficiency property. That would explain why we have no intuition of distinctness regarding the claim that redness is that reflectance efficiency property.

of one's occipital cortex, one can't *imagine* forming such an introspective belief either, and therefore one fails in one's attempt to entertain the claim that this phenomenal* property just is having so-and-so activity in the V4 region of one's occipital cortex. As a result, the identity claim seems to one not even to be possibly true; and this seeming is the intuition of distinctness.

I leave readers to decide how plausible this modified explanation of the intuition of distinctness is. It does at least show that there is scope for adapting some of the underlying ideas of the explanation of the intuition of distinctness presented above.

5.6.3 Predicting What Isn't

Pär Sundström (2008) makes an interesting objection to Papineau's account of the intuition of distinctness. According to Papineau, the intuition arises because we have both first-personal and third-personal concepts of experiences. When we use first-personal concepts—phenomenal concepts—to think about an experience, "the experience itself is in a sense being *used* in our thinking, and so is present in us" (Papineau 2002, 170); but the experience is *not* present in us when we use third-personal concepts—for example, scientific concepts—to think about an experience. We notice that our third-personal concepts do not *use* the experiences they supposedly refer to, and then infer that these concepts do not therefore *mention*—that is, refer to—those experiences; the intuition of distinctness therefore arises from "a species of use-mention fallacy" (2002, 171).[56] Sundström objects to this explanation by giving an example of an identity claim that, he says, combines a first-personal way with a third-personal way of thinking of an experience, but that, contrary to what Papineau's account predicts, *doesn't* induce the intuition of distinctness in us:

> the experience of seeing something as red = John's most salient current experience.

Papineau (2011) responds that the objection is not conclusive, because it is not clear what *concepts* we use when we entertain the claim expressed by this English sentence; we might be using first-personal concepts of the

---

[56] This is Sundström's interpretation of Papineau's view. It's a reasonable interpretation, but it doesn't fit everything that Papineau says; see section 4.4 for a full discussion.

experience on *both* sides of the identity sign—which wouldn't induce the intuition of distinctness.

An objection similar to Sundström's objection to Papineau could be made to my proposed explanation of the intuition of distinctness. Imagine (for the last time, I promise) that one is attending introspectively to the phenomenal redness of the visual sensation caused in one by looking at Rothko's *Untitled* (1970). And imagine that at the same time one is asked to comment on the plausibility of the claim that

> *that* phenomenal property [i.e., phenomenal redness] = the (actual) phenomenal property that Paul is now attending to introspectively.[57]

In response, one would surely allow that this claim might very well be true; one would certainly not experience the intuition of distinctness. But one *would* experience the intuition, it seems, if my novel explanation of the intuition of distinctness were correct. For if it were, then one would try to imagine believing the identity claim, and therefore try to imagine forming an introspective belief whose predicative concept expresses the (actual) phenomenal property that Paul is now attending to introspectively. But a predicative concept expressing the (actual) phenomenal property that Paul is now attending to introspectively would have the form "has the (actual) phenomenal property that Paul is now attending to introspectively," and would therefore not be a phenomenal concept. So, given the inability thesis, one would fail to imagine forming the introspective belief, and hence fail to imagine believing the property-identity claim. It would then seem to one that the identity claim couldn't possibly be true, so that one experienced the intuition of distinctness. My explanation of the intuition of distinctness seems, therefore, to predict an intuition of distinctness when none occurs.

But my explanation can easily be modified so that it doesn't make this prediction.[58] When (in section 5.4 above) I introduced the alternative view of believing an identity claim on which my explanation relies, I insisted that believing an identity claim requires hosting an explicit mental representation

---

[57] We should surely construe the definite description rigidly, as "actual" makes explicit. It *is* incredible that *being phenomenally red* should literally be *being the phenomenal property that Paul is now attending to introspectively*—where the embedded definite description is construed non-rigidly, to refer, in each possible world, to whatever in that world happens to be the phenomenal property that Paul is now attending to introspectively.

[58] The reply to follow trades on Papineau's insight that it is not clear what *concepts* we use when we entertain the claim expressed by the English sentence.

expressing the identity claim, that is, a mental representation comprising (i) a subject-concept that refers to a property (e.g., to phenomenal redness), (ii) something expressing identity, and (iii) a distinct subject-concept that also refers to a property (the same property, of course, if the identity claim is true). And insisting on this requirement is not ad hoc, because it's plausible that understanding sentences of a natural language involves "translating" the sentences into equivalent inner mental representations (see, e.g., Millikan 1984, 147–8; Devitt and Sterelny 1999, 187–90). My explanation of the intuition of distinctness can now be modified by the addition of the hypothesis that our psychological propensity to try to imagine believing any property-identity claim that we are considering is triggered *only if* we are hosting an explicit mental representation expressing the property-identity claim.

Let us return to the problematic example. Again suppose that one is asked to comment on the plausibility of the claim that

that phenomenal property [i.e., phenomenal redness] = the (actual) phenomenal property that Paul is now attending to introspectively.

Since the expression on the right-hand side of the identity sign in the displayed sentence is a definite description, the sentence invites the Russellian paraphrase: "There is exactly one thing that is a phenomenal property and that Paul is (actually) now attending introspectively to, and *it* is *that* phenomenal property." In understanding the sentence, one will accordingly "translate" it into a mental representation with the structure of this Russellian paraphrase (or of something equivalent to it, e.g., the sentence "Paul is now attending introspectively to *that* phenomenal property, and there is no *other* phenomenal property that Paul is now attending introspectively to"). But such a mental representation is not an explicit mental representation expressing a property-identity claim, since it doesn't comprise (i) a subject-concept that refers to a property (e.g., to phenomenal redness), (ii) something expressing identity, and (iii) a distinct subject-concept that also refers to a property. So one's propensity to try to imagine believing a property-identity claim is not triggered, and therefore one doesn't try to imagine forming an introspective belief whose predicative concept expresses the property referred to by the second subject-concept in an explicit mental representation of a property-identity claim. Because one doesn't try, one doesn't fail, and so one doesn't experience the intuition of distinctness. And one naturally responds to the request to comment on the plausibility of the claim expressed by the original English sentence by saying that it could well be true, since, for all one knows,

Paul could be attending introspectively now to *that* phenomenal property (i.e., phenomenal redness), and to no other phenomenal property.

5.7 Conclusion

That we experience the intuition of distinctness seems clear, to others as well as to me, from reflection on occasions when one introspects the phenomenal properties of one's current sensations and tries to take seriously the idea that they simply *are* certain physical or physically realized properties; this is the first-person case for believing in the intuition of distinctness. Chapter 2 argued that there is also a third-person case for believing in it, since hypothesizing that people have the intuition of distinctness can account for certain otherwise puzzling attitudes manifested in debates both inside and outside philosophy about whether physicalism can accommodate phenomenal properties. Chapter 3 argued that the natural dualist suggestion to treat the intuition of distinctness as giving us reason to believe that introspected phenomenal properties actually are distinct from whatever physical or physically realized properties we are considering as candidates for identity with the phenomenal properties turns out, when it is subjected to patient scrutiny, not to work. Chapter 4 critically surveyed earlier theories that were intended to explain the intuition of distinctness, or that might plausibly be taken to explain it, in a manner fully consistent with physicalism. Finally, Chapter 5 proposed a novel explanation of this same kind and defended it against objections.

I claim that this novel explanation might be true, in the sense that it is not ruled out by anything we already know, that it has the virtue of predicting the intuition of distinctness as I have characterized it, and that it has some initial plausibility. But I have little confidence that it is *actually* true—not because I can now identify specific flaws in it, but because *no* proposed explanation of the intuition of distinctness merits much confidence in our present state of knowledge. What I hope, nonetheless, is that it makes the project of explaining the intuition of distinctness consistently with physicalism seem worthy of further pursuit; and that it contains ideas that might inspire the development—ideally by empirical scientists—of a better explanatory theory.

I end with a plea to my readers to suppress the urge to conclude that my novel explanation must be defective because they have understood it, and yet their intuition of distinctness abides undiminished. For the explanation itself predicts that the intuition will not go away under these conditions, because it says that the intuition results from features of human psychology that we don't have the power, at least in the short term, and perhaps ever, deliberately to change. And it would be extraordinary if merely *understanding* the explanation caused the effect explained no longer to be produced—as if understanding why one had developed congestive heart failure would necessarily restore one's heart to health. What my novel explanation will do, if true, is give us permission to ignore our abiding intuitions of distinctness in good epistemic conscience. And if I am right to construe the mind-body problem, for sensations, as the problem of reconciling the view of sensations we get as external observers with the conflicting view we get from the inside, such permission would be no small thing; it would dissolve the problem.

References

Arico, Adam, Brian Fiala, Robert F. Goldberg, and Shaun Nichols. 2011. "The Folk Psychology of Consciousness." *Mind and Language* 26 (3): pp. 327–52.
Armstrong, David. 1968. "The Headless Woman Illusion and the Defense of Materialism." *Analysis* 29 (2): pp. 48–9.
Armstrong, David. 1981. *The Nature of Mind and Other Essays*. Ithaca, NY: Cornell University Press.
Armstrong, David. 1999. *The Mind-Body Problem: An Opinionated Introduction*. Boulder, CO: Westview Press.
Bloom, Paul. 2004. *Descartes' Baby: How the Science of Child Development Explains What Makes Us Human*. New York: Basic Books.
Bogardus, Tomas. 2013. "Undefeated Dualism." *Philosophical Studies* 165: pp. 445–66.
Chalmers, David. 1996. *The Conscious Mind: In Search of a Fundamental Theory*. New York: Oxford University Press.
Chalmers, David. 2010. *The Character of Consciousness*. New York: Oxford University Press.
Chalmers, David. 2018. "The Meta-Problem of Consciousness." *Journal of Consciousness Studies* 25 (9–10): pp. 6–61.
Churchland, Paul. 1985. "Reduction, Qualia, and the Direct Introspection of Brain States." *Journal of Philosophy* 82 (1): pp. 8–28.
Churchland, Paul. 1988. *Matter and Consciousness: A Contemporary Introduction to the Philosophy of Mind*. Cambridge: MIT Press.
Clark, Austen. 1989. "The Particulate Instantiation of Homogeneous Pink." *Synthese* 80 (2): pp. 277–304.
Craver, Carl, and James Tabery. 2019. "Mechanisms in Science." *The Stanford Encyclopedia of Philosophy* (Summer 2019 Edition), Edward N. Zalta (ed.), https://plato.stanford.edu/archives/sum2019/entries/science-mechanisms/.
Damnjanovic, Nic. 2012. "Revelation and Physicalism." *Dialectica* 66 (1): pp. 69–91.
Dennett, Daniel. 1987. *The Intentional Stance*. Cambridge: MIT Press.
Devitt, Michael, and Kim Sterelny. 1999. *Language and Reality: An Introduction to the Philosophy of Language*. Cambridge: MIT Press.
Díaz-León, Esa. 2008. "Defending the Phenomenal Concept Strategy." *Australasian Journal of Philosophy* 86 (4): pp. 597–610.
Díaz-León, Esa. 2010. "Can Phenomenal Concepts Explain the Epistemic Gap?" *Mind* 119 (476): pp. 533–51.
Díaz-León, Esa. 2014. "Do a Posteriori Physicalists Get Our Phenomenal Concepts Wrong?" *Ratio* 27 (1): pp. 1–16.
Díaz-León, Esa. 2016. "Phenomenal Concepts: Neither Circular Nor Opaque." *Philosophical Psychology* 29 (8): pp. 1186–99.
Drange, Theodore M. 1998. *Nonbelief and Evil: Two Arguments for the Nonexistence of God*. Amherst: Prometheus Books.
Dretske, Fred. 1995. *Naturalizing the Mind*. Cambridge: MIT Press.
Eccles, John C. 1994. *How the Self Controls Its Brain*. New York: Springer-Verlag.

REFERENCES

Elpidorou, Andreas and Guy Dove. 2018. *Consciousness and Physicalism: A Defense of a Research Program*. New York: Routledge.
Fiala, Brian, Adam Arico, and Shaun Nichols. 2011. "On the Psychological Origins of Dualism: Dual-Process Cognition and the Explanatory Gap." In *Creating Consilience: Integrating the Sciences and Humanities*, edited by Edward Slingerland and Mark Collard, pp. 88–109. New York: Oxford University Press.
Firestone, Chaz, and Brian J. Scholl. 2016. "Cognition Does Not Affect Perception: Evaluating the Evidence for 'Top-Down' Effects." *Behavioral and Brain Sciences* 39: p. e229.
Fodor, Jerry. 1984. "Observation Reconsidered." *Philosophy of Science* 51 (1): pp. 23–43.
Fodor, Jerry. 1987. *Psychosemantics: The Problem of Meaning in the Philosophy of Mind*. Cambridge: MIT Press.
Goff, Philip. 2011. "A Posteriori Physicalists Get Our Phenomenal Concepts Wrong." *Australasian Journal of Philosophy* 89 (2): pp. 191–209.
Goff, Philip, William Seager, and Sean Allen-Hermanson. "Panpsychism." *The Stanford Encyclopedia of Philosophy* (Summer 2022 Edition), Edward N. Zalta (ed.), https://plato.stanford.edu/archives/sum2022/entries/panpsychism/.
Hill, Christopher, and Brian P. McLaughlin. 1999. "There are Fewer Things in Reality Than are Dreamt of in Chalmers's Philosophy." *Philosophy and Phenomenological Research* 59 (2): pp. 445–54.
Hill, Christopher. 2009. *Consciousness*. New York: Cambridge University Press.
Horgan, Terry. 1984. "Jackson on Physical Information and Qualia." *Philosophical Quarterly* 34 (135): pp. 147–52.
Jack, Anthony I. 2014. "A Scientific Case for Conceptual Dualism: The Problem of Consciousness and the Opposing Domains Hypothesis." In *Oxford Studies in Experimental Philosophy (Vol. 1)*, edited by Joshua Knobe, Tania Lombrozo, and Shaun Nichols, pp. 173–207. New York: Oxford University Press.
Jack, Anthony I., and Philip Robbins. 2012. "The Phenomenal Stance Revisited." *Review of Philosophy and Psychology* 3 (3): pp. 383–403.
Jackson, Frank. 1986. "What Mary Didn't Know." *Journal of Philosophy* 83 (5): pp. 291–5.
Kitcher, Philip. 1993. *The Advancement of Science*. New York: Oxford University Press.
Kripke, Saul. 1980. *Naming and Necessity*. Oxford: Blackwell.
Kuhlmann, Meinard. 2020. "Quantum Field Theory." *The Stanford Encyclopedia of Philosophy* (Fall 2020 Edition), Edward N. Zalta (ed.), https://plato.stanford.edu/archives/fall2020/entries/quantum-field-theory/.
Levine, Joseph. 2001. *Purple Haze: The Puzzle of Consciousness*. New York: Oxford University Press.
Levine, Joseph. 2007. "Phenomenal Concepts and the Materialist Constraint." In *Phenomenal Concepts and Phenomenal Knowledge: New Essays on Consciousness and Physicalism*, edited by Torin Alter and Sven Walter, pp. 145–66. Oxford: Oxford University Press.
Loar, Brian. 1997. "Phenomenal States (Second Version)." In *The Nature of Consciousness: Philosophical Debates*, edited by Ned Block, Owen Flanagan, and Güven Güzeldere, pp. 597–616. Cambridge: MIT Press.
Lockwood, Michael. 1993. "The Grain Problem." In *Objections to Physicalism*, edited by Howard Robinson, pp. 271–91. Oxford: Oxford University Press.
Lycan, William G. 1987. *Consciousness*. Cambridge: MIT Press.
Lycan, William G. 1996. *Consciousness and Experience*. Cambridge: MIT Press.
McLaughlin, Brian. 2012. "Phenomenal Concepts and the Defense of Materialism." *Philosophy and Phenomenological Research* 84 (1): pp. 206–14.

Melnyk, Andrew. 2001. "Physicalism Unfalsified: Chalmers' Inconclusive Conceivability Argument." In *Physicalism and Its Discontents*, edited by Carl Gillett and Barry Loewer, pp. 331–49. New York: Cambridge University Press.

Melnyk, Andrew. 2003. *A Physicalist Manifesto: Thoroughly Modern Materialism.* Cambridge: Cambridge University Press.

Melnyk, Andrew. 2015. "The Scientific Evidence for Materialism about Pains." In *The Constitution of Phenomenal Consciousness: Toward a Science and Theory*, edited by Steven M. Miller, pp. 310–29. Amsterdam: John Benjamins Publishing Company.

Melnyk, Andrew. 2018. "In Defense of a Realization Formulation of Physicalism." *Topoi* 37 (3): pp. 483–93.

Millikan, Ruth G. 1984. *Language, Thought, and Other Biological Categories: New Foundations for Realism.* Cambridge: MIT Press.

Millikan, Ruth G. 2000. *On Clear and Confused Ideas: An Essay about Substance Concepts.* Cambridge: Cambridge University Press.

Millikan, Ruth G. 2004. *Varieties of Meaning.* Cambridge: MIT Press.

Molyneux, Bernard. 2011. "On the Infinitely Hard Problem of Consciousness." *Australasian Journal of Philosophy* 89 (2): pp. 211–28.

Molyneux, Bernard. 2015. "The Logic of Mind-Body Identification." *Ergo* 2 (11): pp. 239–65.

Nagel, Thomas. 1974. "What Is It Like to Be a Bat?" *The Philosophical Review* 83 (4): pp. 435–50.

Newton-Smith, W. 1978. "The Underdetermination of Theory by Data." *Proceedings of the Aristotelian Society: Supplementary Volume* 52: pp. 71–91.

Nichols, Shaun. 2012. "The Indeterminist Intuition: Source and Status." *Monist* 95 (2): pp. 290–307.

Nida-Rümelin, Martine. 2007. "Grasping Phenomenal Properties." In *Phenomenal Concepts and Phenomenal Knowledge: New Essays on Consciousness and Physicalism*, edited by Torin Alter and Sven Walter, pp. 307–38. Oxford: Oxford University Press.

Papineau, David. 1993. "Physicalism, consciousness and the antipathetic fallacy." *Australasian Journal of Philosophy* 71 (2): pp. 169–83.

Papineau, David. 2002. *Thinking about Consciousness.* Oxford: Oxford University Press.

Papineau, David. 2007. "Phenomenal Concepts and Perceptual Concepts." In *Phenomenal Concepts and Phenomenal Knowledge: New Essays on Consciousness and Physicalism*, edited by Torin Alter and Sven Walter, pp. 111–44. Oxford: Oxford University Press.

Papineau, David. 2011. "What Exactly Is the Explanatory Gap?" *Philosophia* 39 (1): pp. 5–19.

Papineau, David. 2021. *The Metaphysics of Sensory Experience.* Oxford: Oxford University Press.

Perry, John. 2001. *Knowledge, Possibility, and Consciousness.* Cambridge: MIT Press.

Place, Ullin T. 1956. "Is Consciousness a Brain Process?" *British Journal of Psychology* 47 (1): pp. 44–50..

Place, Ullin T. 1959. "The 'Phenomenological Fallacy'—a Reply to J.R. Smythies." *British Journal of Psychology* 50 (1): pp. 72–3.

Pollock, John. 1974. *Knowledge and Justification.* Princeton, NJ: Princeton University Press.

Robbins, Philip. 2017. "Modularity of Mind." *Stanford Encyclopedia of Philosophy* (Winter 2017 Edition), Edward N. Zalta (ed.), https://plato.stanford.edu/archives/win2017/entries/modularity-mind/.

Robbins, Philip, and Anthony I. Jack. 2006. "The Phenomenal Stance." *Philosophical Studies* 127 (1): pp. 59–85.

Robinson, William S. 2005. "Thoughts without Distinctive Non-imagistic Phenomenology." *Philosophy and Phenomenological Research* 70 (3): pp. 534–61.

Robinson, William S. 2007. "Papineau's Conceptual Dualism and the Distinctness Intuition." *Synthesis Philosophica* 22 (2): pp. 319–33.

Schellenberg, John L. 2015. *The Hiddenness Argument: Philosophy's New Challenge to Belief in God*. New York: Oxford University Press.

Schroer, Robert. 2010. "Where's the Beef? Phenomenal Concepts as Both Demonstrative and Substantial." *Australasian Journal of Philosophy* 88 (3): pp. 505–22.

Schwitzgebel, Eric. "Introspection." *Stanford Encyclopedia of Philosophy* (Winter 2019 Edition), Edward N. Zalta (ed.), https://plato.stanford.edu/archives/win2019/entries/introspection/.

Smart, John JC. 1959. "Sensations and Brain Processes." *Philosophical Review* 68 (2): pp. 14–56.

Sundström, Pär. 2008. "Is the Mystery an Illusion? Papineau on the Problem of Consciousness." *Synthese* 163 (2): pp. 133–43.

Sundström, Pär. 2018. "How Physicalists Can—and Cannot—Explain the Seeming 'Absurdity' of Physicalism." *Philosophy and Phenomenological Research* 97 (3): pp. 681–703.

Thompson, Brad. 2008. "Representationalism and the Argument from Hallucination." *Pacific Philosophical Quarterly* 89 (3): pp. 384–412.

Tye, Michael. 1995a. *Ten Problems of Consciousness: A Representational Theory of the Phenomenal Mind*. Cambridge: MIT Press.

Tye, Michael. 1995b. "A Representation Theory of Pains and Their Phenomenal Character." *Philosophical Perspectives: AI, Connectionism, and Philosophical Psychology* 9: pp. 223–39.

Tye, Michael. 2000. *Consciousness, Color, and Content*. Cambridge: MIT Press.

Tye, Michael. 2003. "A Theory of Phenomenal Concepts." In *Minds and Persons: Royal Institute of Philosophy Supplement*: 53, edited by Anthony O'Hear, pp. 91–105. Cambridge: Cambridge University Press.

Tye, Michael. 2009. *Consciousness Revisited: Materialism without Phenomenal Concepts*. Cambridge: MIT Press.

Wright, Robert. 1996. "Can Machines Think?" *Time*, March 25.

Index

For the benefit of digital users, indexed terms that span two pages (e.g., 52–53) may, on occasion, appear on only one of those pages.

abilities 36, 44–45, 49–50, 150–51, 153, 154–55, 156–57, 159 *see also* belief-forming abilities; cognitive abilities; conceptual abilities
agency 96–97
AGENCY 113, 114, 115–16
agent 109, 113n.16
AGENT 113n.16, 113
analytic-empirical-critical thinking 112
Anselm 137n.4
Anthropological Law 132, 133–34
Anthropological Law Minus 133–34
anti-idealist possibility 157–58n.36
anti-physicalist
 arguments 10, 14n.4, 24, 30n.2, 134–35, 136, 137n.3, 144–45
 intuition 102–3
 reasoning 171n.51
anxiety 49–50, 56–57, 59–60, 78
Arico, Adam 113–16, 113n.16
Armstrong, David 11, 84n.60, 97–101
attention 15n.6, 54n.25, 55–56, 80–81, 84–85, 86, 89, 97, 100, 101n.9, 112, 115–16, 126–27, 146
auditory experiences/sensations 84, 87–88, 118 *see also* hearing/sounds
automatic
 ascriptions 116
 beliefs 146n.23
 initiation 158–59
 mechanism 113
 perceiving 99n.6
 response 98, 99–100
 tendency 20
 transition 161
awareness 1–2, 2n.5, 3–6, 12n.3, 27, 34–35, 68n.42, 84, 98–99, 102–3, 104, 115–16, 117–18, 126–27, 138–39

belief-forming abilities 165
belief-forming mechanism 69, 72, 73

beliefs 1–2n.3, 3–4, 6n.17, 7, 18–19, 20–22, 23, 41–42, 58, 69, 75, 78, 87, 93–94, 108–9, 120–21, 122, 123, 128, 138–40, 146n.23, 149n.27, 150–51, 154–55, 158–59, 161n.40, 163–64 *see also* conscious beliefs; introspective beliefs; non-inferential beliefs; non-introspective beliefs; perceptual beliefs; third-person beliefs
Berkeley, George 157–58n.36
biochemistry 4–5, 18–19, 35, 110–11, 134 *see also* chemistry
biology 4–5, 4n.11, 15–16, 38–39, 60n.32, 102, 134, 158–59
black-and-white environment 18–19, 21–22, 23, 144–45
Bloom, Paul 96n.2
bodily
 movements 49–50
 parts 60n.31
 region 70–71
 sensations 1, 50, 56–57, 58, 59–60, 61, 87–88
 states 42–43
Bogardus, Tomas 25–26, 26n.16, 29
brain 5–6, 12, 34–35, 50, 54–55, 72–74, 79–80, 101–2, 104, 114, 115–16
 activity 34–35, 96–97
 auditory cortex 84
 mechanisms 77n.50, 77n.51, 78, 80–81, 86, 157, 159–60
 occipital cortex 163, 171–73
 processes 6n.18, 47, 96–97, 99, 100–1, 114
 scanning 4–5, 68n.41, 117–18
 somatosensory cortex 49–50
 states 4–5, 12–13, 15–16, 26–27, 64–65, 88–89, 101, 102–3, 105, 107–8, 123–24, 125–27, 131–32
 visual cortex 21–22, 34–35, 46n.16, 48n.18, 49–50, 54n.23, 66n.39, 75n.47, 82n.58, 111–12, 146, 155n.35
 see also mind–brain distinctness

causal
  closure 29n.1
  efficacy 60–61n.33
  interaction 168
  profiles 131–32
  reasoning 112
  role 36–37, 38–39, 58, 63–64, 148–49
Chalmers, David 6nn.18–19, 10, 15, 24, 27n.17, 27–28, 37n.9, 112–13n.15, 136n.1, 138–39
chemical
  constitutions 49–50
  essence 14–15
  expression 41–42
  knowledge 26n.15
  properties 4n.11
chemistry 18–19, 41–43, 134 *see also* biochemistry
Churchland, Paul 77, 144–45, 162–66, 168
cognitive
  abilities 150n.32
  achievement 14, 117–18
  act 38–39
  architecture 114, 164–65
  concepts 44–45
  difficulty 109
  economy 58
  effect 134
  integration 109
  neuroscience 44–45, 66, 67n.40, 138, 143
  pathways 113
  processes 114, 116
  response 90–91
  state 14
  tension 112
color 5n.15, 18–19, 34n.7, 39n.11, 39–40, 44–45, 48, 49–50, 51, 54n.24, 54–58, 61–62, 142–43, 163–64, 165, 170 *see also* black-and-white environment; phenomenal redness; vision
computational
  capacities 140–41
  process 139–40
  properties 124, 125–26, 139–40
  psychology 18–19
  role 38–39, 148–49
  sub-system 139–40
conceivability 24–27, 90–91, 112–13n.15, 130, 144–45, 169
  inconceivability 73
  negative 27–28
  positive 27n.17

conceptual abilities 146–47, 149–50, 151–52
conceptual encapsulation 7, 138–48, 148n.25, 156, 162n.42, 162, 163–64, 164n.47, 165–66, 170–71
conscious
  beliefs 70–71, 97–99
  experience 6n.18, 81–82, 104, 114, 117
  inference 98, 116, 140–41, 150–52, 153, 154–56, 163–64
  mechanisms 31, 33–35, 46, 48, 51, 53–54, 64–65, 74–75, 82, 89, 94–95
  mental representations 69, 72
  mental states 11–13, 24–25, 110–11
  reasoning 64–65, 90–91, 113
  rehearsal 31–32, 34–35, 43, 46, 47, 48, 49–50, 52–54, 62–63, 66–67, 74–75, 81, 82, 88–89, 137
  states 78, 106, 113, 126–27, 157
  see also non-conscious mechanisms; unconscious
consciousness 1–2n.3, 4n.10, 6n.19, 10, 12, 35, 36–37, 96n.1, 110, 114, 116–18, 128, 132, 133, 134–35, 144–45, 161
  see also phenomenal consciousness; unconsciousness
consumption *see* tuberculosis (consumption)

Damnjanovic, Nic 13, 43–44
danger 49–50, 70–71, 92–94, 118–19
default mode network (DMN) 112
defective arguments 136–37
Dennett, Daniel 108–9
Devitt, Michael 174–75
Dove, Guy 116–20
Drange, Theodore M. 92
Dretske, Fred 59
dualism 4–5, 23, 29, 31–32, 40n.12, 54–55, 96–97, 176
dualists 6–7, 29n.1, 92, 99, 134–35, 144n.19

Eccles, John C. 12–13, 144n.19
ectoplasm/ectoplasmic 90n.66, 143–45 *see also* psychons/psychonic
Elpidorou, Andreas 116–20
emotional valence 84, 117–20
emotions 1n.1, 112
environment 8–9, 19–20, 50, 58, 59n.29, 60–61n.33, 69, 96n.1, 139–40, 170 *see also* black-and-white environment
epiphenomenalism 29n.1
epistemic
  conscience 176–77

features 67–68
impossibility 78n.53
possibility 24–28
status 27
essence 13–15, 44–45
events 1, 1–2n.3, 5–6, 20, 53–54, 56–57, 61, 100–1, 117, 119–20, 144n.19, 156–57, 158, 167
explanatory gap 10, 15–18, 18n.10, 27–28, 96–97, 108–11, 112, 113, 114–16, 120, 136, 144–45, 169
external
 color 142–43, 148n.25
 conditions 87–88
 object 141–42
 observers 176–77
 perception 141–42, 163–65
 properties 144–45
 sensation 2–3
 senses 1–2, 42–43, 49–50, 164–65
 surface 17–18, 50

facial
 expression 118–19
 recognition 31n.3
 recognition-based subject-concept 151
fallacy 85n.61, 102, 104, 105, 173
 anti-pathetic 105–8
 phenomenological 96n.1
 stereoptic 101, 102–3
feelings 1, 2n.4, 5–6, 70–71, 101, 102, 106, 107–8, 113
Fiala, Brian 113–16
Firestone, Chaz 140n.11
fluttering 56–57, 59–60
Fodor, Jerry 139–41, 148–49
free will 96–97, 113n.16
functional
 concepts 44–45, 169
 essence 13–14, 15n.6, 44–45
 organization 34–35, 36, 37, 38–39, 40–41, 46, 47, 48, 49–50, 51–53, 54, 62–64, 66, 67–68, 75, 76–77, 82, 88–89, 155–56
 properties 4–6, 7, 13–14, 15n.6, 15–16, 17n.9, 17–18, 22–23, 26–27, 34–35, 36–38, 39–43, 44, 51, 53–54, 54n.25, 63–64, 89–90, 112, 114–15, 132, 133–34, 138, 141, 143–45, 148, 152, 155–56, 161–62, 169, 171
 roles 20–23
functionalist psychology 18–20

God 92, 93–94, 99, 162n.42
Goff, Philip 43–44, 53n.22
grain argument 54n.24

hallucination 2–3, 5n.15, 59, 60–61n.33
Harris. Sidney 136n.2
Headless Woman Illusion 97–98, 99–101
hearing/sounds 41–42, 49–50, 65n.38, 84, 87–88, 99, 118, 150–51, 153 see also auditory experiences/sensations
Hill, Christopher 60, 71n.44
homogeneity 53–54, 63–64
 of phenomenal color 54n.24, 54–55, 57–58, 61–62
 of phenomenal properties 53–64
 of phenomenal redness 55–57, 62–63
Horgan, Terry 19
how-possibly questions 123–24, 127, 128, 129–30, 131–32
Hume, David 99n.6

idealism 157–58n.36
identification 5–6, 51–52, 120–22, 123–24, 127, 128, 129–30, 131–32, 134
identity 4n.12, 6–7, 12–13, 29, 30–31, 32, 33, 35, 36–37, 52–53, 66–67, 68, 81, 89–90, 92–93, 94–95, 99, 116n.19, 173–74, 176
identity claims 7, 14–15, 16–18, 36, 91–92, 97n.3, 104, 114–15, 120–21, 122, 123–26, 127, 128, 129–30, 131–32, 133, 134–35, 148–57, 158–59, 160, 161–62, 165, 171–73, 174–76
identity hypotheses 133–35
imagination/imagining 5–6, 7, 14, 15n.6, 15–16, 23, 30n.2, 44–45, 51, 69, 73–74, 77, 78–81, 85–86, 101–3, 104, 106, 110–11, 115–16, 119–20, 123, 124–25, 143–45, 147n.24, 156–57, 157–58n.36, 158–60, 161, 163, 165–66, 171–73, 174–76
inability thesis 145, 146, 156, 159–60, 166, 168, 170–71, 174
infallibility 65, 74–75, 150n.32
infallibility thesis 83n.59, 147n.24
infallible phenomenal knowledge 74
infinite regress 121–22, 123–24, 128
intentional
 agents 109
 beliefs 146n.23
 content 58–59, 138–39, 167
 domains 109
 mental states 108–9
 mind 109–10

186 INDEX

intentional (*cont.*)
  properties 109–10
  stance 108–12
introspected phenomenal properties 5–6, 7, 8, 13, 15n.6, 27, 29, 31–32, 43, 47, 49–50, 51, 53, 62–63, 81, 86–87, 89–92, 94–95, 99–101, 114–15, 138, 143–45, 148, 155, 160–61n.39, 176
introspective awareness 3–4, 5–6, 68n.42, 98–99, 104
introspective beliefs 15n.6, 19–20, 44–45, 67–68, 69, 77, 80–81, 83–85, 86, 124, 126–27, 132, 140–41, 145, 146–47, 148, 155–57, 158, 159–60, 162n.43, 162, 163–66, 167, 168–69, 170–73, 174, 175–76
introspective knowledge 3–4, 64–65, 68, 71, 72–73, 74–75, 81–82n.57
intuition of revelation 10, 13–15, 27–28, 44, 136

Jack, Anthony I. 108–12, 110n.14, 112–13n.15, 116n.18
Jackson, Frank 15, 18–19, 81–82n.57, 112–13n.15, 144–45, 163, 170

Kitcher, Philip 165
knowing 21–22, 64–65, 66–67, 68, 68n.42, 73–74
knowledge argument 15, 18–23, 27–28, 73–74, 138–39, 144–45
Koch, Robert 152–53
Kuhlmann, Meinard 64

laws of nature 24, 75–76, 77n.51, 79–81, 86, 90–91
Leibniz's Law 52n.21, 54, 67–68, 120–22, 123, 123n.24, 127, 128, 129–30
Levine, Joseph 5–6, 15, 25n.14, 60, 81–82
Lewis, David 11
Loar, Brian 141–42
Lockwood, Michael 11–12
logical impossibility 72–74, 75, 76–77, 78, 78n.53, 79–80, 85, 86, 161
Lycan, William G. 54n.24, 59, 101–3

materialism 101–2
materialists 98, 99, 104, 105–6
McLaughlin, Brian 19n.11, 71n.44
Melnyk, Andrew 4nn.11–12, 5n.13, 17n.9, 21, 25n.14, 28n.18, 31–32, 125, 134

mental
  description 71n.44
  events 144n.19
  features 24
  files 109–10
  images 99, 100–1
  lives 1, 169
  mechanisms 158–59
  phenomena 31–32, 120
  processes 159, 160
  properties 4n.11, 17n.9, 37n.9
  rehearsal 35
  representation 8n.20, 58, 69, 72, 78–79, 85–86, 87, 98–99, 102–3, 149n.26, 166–67, 167n.48, 168, 174–76
  states 2n.4, 3–4, 8–9, 11–13, 24–25, 36–38, 78–81, 85–86, 91n.67, 102–3, 104, 108–9, 110–11, 112, 126–27, 157, 157–58n.36, 159–60, 163–64
Mentalese 148–49
Millikan, Ruth G. 36n.8, 58n.27, 149–50, 167n.49, 174–75
Milosevic, Mirjana K. 97–98
mind 3–4, 31–32, 36, 38–39, 54–55, 58, 73–74, 87, 89–90, 91–92, 93–94, 96n.2, 99n.6, 109–10, 124–25, 137, 144n.19, 144–45, 158, 166–67
mind–body problem 8–9, 12–13, 124, 131, 176–77
mind–brain distinctness 103–4, 105–6, 107–8
mixed-media model 77n.52, 167, 168–69, 170–73
modules 139–40
Molyneux, Bernard 120–32, 122n.23
Monty Hall Problem 106
multimodality 116–20, 118n.21

Nagel, Thomas 78, 102n.10, 112–13n.15, 157
name-based subject-concept 150–51
neural
  activity 5–6
  antagonism 112
  architecture 164–65
  assemblage 63n.36
  causes 73
  circuits 5–6, 52–53, 146
  concepts 117–18, 119
  description 114, 116
  differences 109
  events 100–1, 156–57, 158

INDEX   187

firing 4–5, 34–35, 34n.7, 39n.11, 46n.16, 47, 48n.18, 53–54, 54n.23, 66n.39, 82n.58, 114, 156–57, 158, 159n.38
machinery 159, 160
mechanisms 80–81, 86
network 4–5
organization 79–80, 146–47
properties 100–1, 156–57, 158
stance 109
stimulation 117
systems 116–18
variation 4–5
neurons 53–54, 63–64, 102–3, 106, 107, 111–12
neurophysiological
characteristic 21–22, 80–81, 86
properties 5–6, 20, 24–25, 124, 131
states 68n.41, 110–11, 144–45
neurophysiologists 12–13, 144n.19
neurophysiology 4–5, 15–16, 38–39
neuroscience 18–19, 20, 24–25, 34–35, 44–45, 52–53, 66, 67n.40, 138, 143, 146, 162, 163–64, 165–66, 168
new concept, old property 19–20, 22–23, 27–28
Newton-Smith, William 131–32
Nichols, Shaun 101n.9, 113–16
Nida-Rümelin, Martine 43–44
non-conscious mechanisms 31, 33–34, 33n.5, 89–95
non-inferential beliefs 140–41, 145, 170–71
non-introspective
awareness 3–4
beliefs 146–48, 170
evidence 10
sensations 68n.41
non-phenomenal concepts 67–68, 145, 146, 155–57, 158, 160, 163, 165–66, 168, 170–71
non-phenomenal properties 15–16, 110–11, 145, 146
non-physicality 23, 29n.1, 31–32, 34n.7, 89–93, 116–18
novel explanation 7, 96–97, 136, 138–39, 148, 155, 156–62, 160–61n.39, 165–66, 168, 171, 174, 176–77

ontology 104, 116–17, 137n.4

pain 1, 2–3, 5n.13, 37, 50, 56–57, 58n.27, 59–60, 61, 70–71, 70n.43, 74–75, 87–88, 88n.65, 100, 102–3, 105, 106, 107–8, 116, 118–19, 126–27, 131, 144–45, 146–48
Papineau, David 4n.10, 5–6, 14n.5, 18n.10, 29n.1, 60nn.32–33, 77, 96n.2, 102n.10, 103–8, 171n.53, 173–74, 174n.58
perception 7, 36, 64–65, 66, 72, 138, 141–42, 150–51, 163–65
perceptual
appearance 41–42
beliefs 69, 163–64, 165
capacities 139–40
exposure 141–42, 143–45, 146–47, 166
mechanism 154–55
sensations 1, 50, 58, 59–60, 87–88
Perry, John 5–6
phenomenal character 1–2, 50, 58–60, 61n.34, 73–74, 77, 84, 102–3, 104, 108–9, 111–12, 116–17, 118, 144–45
phenomenal consciousness 1–2, 1–2n.3, 11–13, 24–25, 110–11, 144–45
phenomenal–functional
identity 133
property-identity 132, 134–35
type-identity 97n.3, 104, 114–15
phenomenal knowledge 64–74
phenomenal–physical
identification 123–24, 129–30, 131–32
identity 123–26, 127, 128, 133, 134–35
property-identity 132, 134–35
type-identity 97n.3, 104, 114–15
phenomenal redness 2–3, 5–6, 13–16, 17–19, 21–22, 23, 24–25, 26–27, 34–35, 36, 37, 39–41, 42–45, 46, 47, 48, 50, 51–54, 54n.25, 55–57, 59–60, 60–61n.33, 61–63, 64–65, 66, 67–68, 70–71, 72–73, 75, 82–83, 86–89, 104, 110–12, 118–19, 138n.6, 146, 148n.25, 155–57, 158, 159, 160, 168, 169, 171, 174–76
phenomenal states 10, 107–9, 110, 124
physicalism 4–7, 8–9, 10–12, 13–14, 15, 16, 18–20, 22–23, 24, 27–28, 29, 30, 36–37, 39–40, 43–44, 49–50, 52–53, 76–77, 96–97, 98, 102, 114, 125, 126–27, 132, 134, 135, 136, 141, 142–43, 161–62, 168–69, 170, 176
physicalists 5–7, 23, 24–25, 99, 102–3, 124–25, 131–32, 134–35, 146–47, 161
Place, U. T. 96n.1

Poised Abstract Nonconceptual Intentional
 Content (PANIC) 59
possible worlds 24–25, 63–64, 71n.44, 144–
 45, 174n.57
predicative concepts 19–20, 51–52, 66,
 67–68, 72n.46, 122n.23, 138, 140–42,
 143–45, 146–47, 148, 150–51, 152–53,
 154–57, 158, 159, 160, 162, 163–64, 165–
 66, 168, 170–73, 174, 175–76
psychological
 activity 80
 attitudes 27
 blockage 78–79
 capacities 108–9, 110–11
 concepts 146, 163–64
 connection 41–42
 evidence 108–9, 110n.14
 experiments 4–5
 hypothesis 147–48
 incapacity 160–61n.39
 mechanisms 7, 30–32, 33–34, 33n.5,
  36–39, 85–86, 94–95, 154–55, 158–
  59, 161–62
 modules 139–40
 observation 116–17
 opinion 146–47
 phenomena 16, 103–4
 processes 113, 114
 states 161, 163n.44
 taxonomy 162
 tendency 119–20, 161
psychology 1, 11, 20, 84–85, 140n.11, 147–
 48, 176–77
psychons/psychonic 143–45 see also
 ectoplasm/ectoplasmic

reductionist physicalism 11
reductive explanations 15–18, 90–91, 96–97,
 110–11, 114–15
representationalism 50n.20, 58
 orthodox 59n.28, 59, 61n.34
 unorthodox 1–2n.3, 58–60, 61–62, 70–71,
  87, 166–67
Robbins, Philip 108–12, 110n.14,
 116n.18, 139n.8
Robinson, William 34n.7, 39n.11, 138n.7
Röntgen, Wilhelm 117–18

Rothko, Mark
 Untitled 5–6, 13, 24–25, 34–35, 49–50, 51,
  53–54, 77, 87n.63, 174
Russellian paraphrase 175–76

Schellenberg, John L. 92
Scholl, Brian J. 140n.11
Schroer, Robert 22–23, 138n.6
Sellars, Wilfrid 54n.24
sensory
 appearances 70–71
 environment 59n.29
 experiences 84
 input 139–40
 properties 4n.10
 representations 69, 116–17
 states 71n.44
 stimulus 139–40
 systems 42–43, 140n.11
Smart, J. J. C. 47n.17, 91n.67
spatial location 46–50, 87–88, 99–
 100, 164–65
Sterelny, Kim 174–75
Strawson, Galen 11
subject-concept 19n.12, 51–52, 54, 72n.46,
 140–41, 150–52, 153, 154–55, 158, 171–
 73, 174–76
substance dualism 54–55, 96n.2, 97
Sundström, Pär 132–35, 173, 174

task positive network (TPN) 112
third-person
 appearance 71n.44
 beliefs 124–25, 127, 176
 concepts 173
 point of view 27
 reason 8
 scientific way 68
 way of thinking 104, 173
Thompson, Brad 59n.28, 59n.30
tuberculosis (consumption) 152–53
Tye, Michael 1n.2, 3n.9, 19n.11, 58, 59, 60,
 61n.34, 142–43

unconscious
 inference 143
 mechanisms 31n.3, 158–59

reasoning 31
transition 161
unconsciousness 43

vision 14–15, 18–19, 42–43, 49–50, 65n.38, 87n.63, 99–101, 102–3, 110–12, 139–40, 162, 165–66 *see also* color
visual-phenomenal property 39–40, 42–43, 51–53
visual sensations 1–3, 5–6, 5n.15, 13, 15–16, 18–19, 22, 23, 24–25, 34–35, 39–40, 44–45, 46, 46n.16, 47, 48, 48n.18, 49–50, 51, 53–57, 58, 59–60, 61–63, 64–65, 66, 67–68, 68n.41, 69, 70–71, 72–73, 74, 75, 77n.51, 82–83, 87–89, 101–3, 104, 110–11, 118–19, 125–26, 142–43, 146–47, 156–57, 158, 163, 166–67, 170, 174

Wright, Robert 12

X-rays 117–18, 119–20

zombie argument 15, 24–28, 138–39
zombies 105n.11, 112–13n.15, 169
zombie worlds 24–28, 144–45